G000272911

European History in]
General Editor: Jere

Published

Benjamin Arnold *Medieval Germany*
Ronald Asch *The Thirty Years' War*
Christopher Bartlett *Peace, War and the European Powers, 1814–1914*
Roger Collins *Charlemagne*
Mark Galeotti *Gorbachev and his Revolution*
Brendan Simms *The Struggle for Mastery in Germany, 1779–1850*
David J. Sturdy *Louis XIV*
Peter Waldron *The End of Imperial Russia, 1855–1917*

Forthcoming

Nigel Aston *The French Revolution*
N. J. Atkin *The Fifth French Republic*
Ross Balzaretti *Medieval Italy: A Cultural History*
Robert Bireley *The Counter Reformation*
Donna Bohanan *Crown and Nobility in Early Modern France*
Robin Brown *Warfare in Twentieth Century Europe*
Patricia Clavin *The Great Depression, 1929–39*
Geoff Cubitt *Politics in France, 1914–1876*
John Foot *The Creation of Modern Italy*
Alexander Grab *Napoleon and the Transformation of Europe*
O. P. Grell *The European Reformation*
Nicholas Henshall *The Zenith of Absolute Monarchy, 1650–1750*
Colin Imber *The Ottoman Empire, 1300–1481*
Martin Johnson *The Dreyfus Affair*
Timothy Kirk *Germany and the Third Reich*
Peter Linehan *Medieval Spain, 589–1492*
Marisa Linton *The Causes of the French Revolution*
Simon Lloyd *The Crusading Movement*
William S. Maltby *The Reign of Charles V*
David Moon *Peter the Great's Russia*
Peter Musgrave *The Early Modern European Economy*
Kevin Passmore *The French Third Republic, 1870–1940*
J. L. Price *The Dutch Republic in the Seventeenth Century*
Roger Price *1848: A Year of Revolution*
A. W. Purdue *The Second World War*

(list continues overleaf)

Maria Quine *A Social History of Fascist Italy*
Martyn Rady *The Habsburg Monarchs, 1848–1918*
Francisco J. Romero-Salvado *A History of Contemporary Spain*
Richard Sakwa *Twentieth Century Russia*
Thomas J. Schaeper *The Enlightenment*
Graeme Small *Later Medieval France*
Hunt Tooley *The Western Front*
Peter G. Wallace *The Long European Reformation*
Patrick Williams *Philip II*
Peter Wilson *From Reich to Revolution: Germany, 1600–1806*

European History in Perspective
Series Standing Order
ISBN 0–333–71694–9 hardcover
ISBN 0–333–69336–1 paperback
(outside North America only)

You can receive future titles in this series as they are published by placing a standing order. Please contact your bookseller or, in the case of difficulty, write to us at the address below with your name and address, the title of the series and the ISBN quoted above.

Customer Services Department, Macmillan Distribution Ltd
Houndmills, Basingstoke, Hampshire RG21 6XS, England

LOUIS XIV

David J. Sturdy

Senior Lecturer in History
University of Ulster

MACMILLAN

First published 1998 by
MACMILLAN PRESS LTD
Houndmills, Basingstoke, Hampshire RG21 6XS
and London
Companies and representatives throughout the world

ISBN 0–333–60513–6 hardcover
ISBN 0–333–60514–4 paperback

A catalogue record for this book is available from the British Library.

This book is printed on paper suitable for recycling and made from
fully managed and sustained forest sources.

10 9 8 7 6 5 4 3 2 1
07 06 05 04 03 02 01 00 99 98

Editing and origination by
Aardvark Editorial, Mendham, Suffolk

Printed in Hong Kong

 Published in the United States of America 1998 by
ST. MARTIN'S PRESS, INC.,
Scholarly and Reference Division,
175 Fifth Avenue, New York, N.Y. 10010

ISBN 0–312–21427–8 cloth
ISBN 0–312–21428–6 paperback

*To my mother, Myra Sturdy,
and in memory of my father, George Sturdy*

CONTENTS

SIGNIFICANT DATES

1638 3 September: birth of Louis the Dauphin (the future Louis XIV)

1642 4 December: death of Richelieu

1643 14 May: death of Louis XIII; succession of Louis XIV
18 May: Anne of Austria becomes regent; Mazarin confirmed as chief minister

1644 4 December: beginning of peace negotiations in Westphalia to end Thirty Years War

1648 15–16 January: Parlement of Paris protests against creation of new offices;
beginning of Fronde of the Parlement
13 May: Parlement of Paris invites other sovereign courts to join it in the Chambre Saint-Louis
2 July: Chambre Saint-Louis presents 27 articles of reform
24 October: Treaty of Westphalia signed

1649 5–6 January: royal court leaves Paris
March: negotiations leading to Peace of Rueil

1650 18 January: arrest of the Princes (Condé, Conti, Longueville)

1651 February/March: union of the Fronde of the Princes and the Fronde of the Parlement
6 February: Mazarin goes into exile
7 September: majority of Louis XIV proclaimed

1652 28 January: Mazarin rejoins royal court
4 July: massacre at Hôtel de Ville in Paris
18 August: Mazarin goes into exile again
21–22 October: Louis XIV re-enters Paris

1653 July/August: end of Ormée in Bordeaux

1654 7 June: coronation of Louis XIV in Rheims

1659 7 November: Treaty of the Pyrenees

1660 9 June: marriage of Louis XIV and Maria Teresa

1661   9 March: death of Mazarin; beginning of personal reign of Louis
        XIV
        27 April: alliance between France and Dutch Republic
        5 September: arrest of Fouquet
        27 November: Louis XIV purchases Dunkirk from Charles II of
        England

1664   2 January: Colbert appointed Surintendant des Bâtiments du Roi
        28 May: foundation of French West Indies Company
        August: foundation of French East Indies Company

1665   4 May: beginning of Anglo-Dutch War
        September/January 1666: Grands Jours d'Auvergne
        17 September: death of Philip IV of Spain; beginning of reign of
        Charles II of Spain
        November: Colbert appointed Contrôleur Général des Finances

1666   20 January: death of Anne of Austria
        26 January: France declares war on England

1667   May: beginning of War of Devolution
        31 July: Peace of Breda between France and England

1668   23 January: formation of Triple Alliance against France
        4 May: Treaty of Aix-la-Chapelle ends War of Devolution

1672   6 April: France declares war on Dutch Republic
        3 July: French armies capture Utrecht

1673   1 July: French armies capture Maastricht

1674   February: French armies occupy Franche-Comté

1678   August/February 1679: Peace of Nijmegen

1679–81 Policy of 'Reunions'

1682   19 March: General Assembly of the Clergy adopts the Four Gallican
        Articles
        6 May: Louis XIV, his government and court move permanently into
        Versailles

1683   6 September: death of Colbert

1685   17 October: Edict of Fontainebleau revokes Edict of Nantes

1686   9 September: formation of League of Augsburg

1688   September: beginning of War of League of Augsburg

1689   17 May: England joins war against France

1695   18 January: introduction of *capitation*

1697   September/October: Peace of Ryswick

1698   13 October: first Partition Treaty

1700	March: second Partition Treaty 1 November: death of Charles II of Spain 16 November: Louis XIV accepts will of Charles II of Spain
1701	7 September: formation of Anti-French Grand Alliance at The Hague
1702	15 May: War of the Spanish Succession begins
1705	5 May: death of Emperor Leopold I; succeeded by his son Joseph I
1708	11 July: battle of Oudenaarde
1709	11 September: battle of Malplaquet
1710	14 October: introduction of the *dixième*
1711	8 October: beginning of peace negotiations between France and England
1713	April/March 1714: Treaties of Utrecht and Rastadt 8 September: papal bull *Unigenitus*
1715	1 September: death of Louis XIV

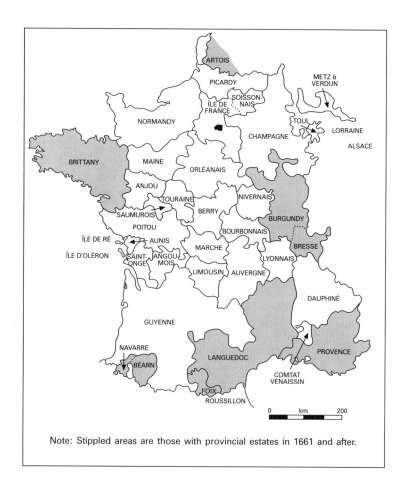

Note: Stippled areas are those with provincial estates in 1661 and after.

Map 1   The provinces of France in the seventeenth century

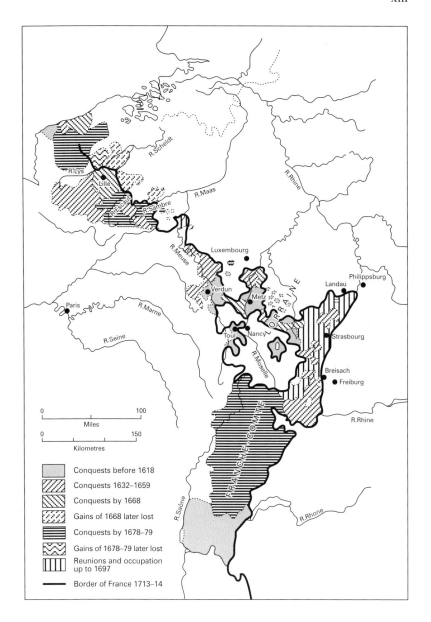

Map 2   The north-eastern frontier of France, 1618–1714

The Bourbon Family Tree

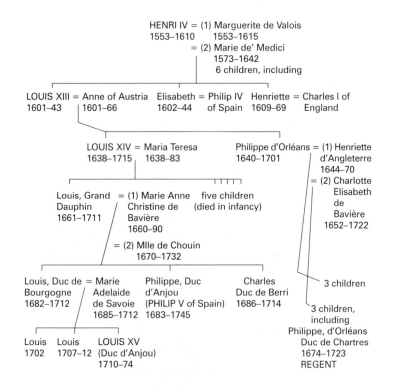

HENRI IV = (1) Marguerite de Valois
1553–1610   1553–1615
= (2) Marie de' Medici
1573–1642
6 children, including

LOUIS XIII = Anne of Austria   Elisabeth = Philip IV   Henriette = Charles I of
1601–43   1601–66   1602–44   of Spain 1609–69   England

LOUIS XIV = Maria Teresa   Philippe d'Orléans = (1) Henriette
1638–1715   1638–83   1640–1701   d'Angleterre
                                                                 1644–70
                                                                 = (2) Charlotte
Louis, Grand = (1) Marie Anne   five children   Elisabeth
Dauphin   Christine de   (died in infancy)   de
1661–1711   Bavière   Bavière
                1660–90   1652–1722

             = (2) Mlle de Chouin
                1670–1732

Louis, Duc de = Marie   Philippe, Duc   Charles   3 children
Bourgogne   Adelaide   d'Anjou   Duc de Berri
1682–1712   de Savoie (PHILIP V of Spain) 1686–1714   3 children,
                1685–1712 1683–1745   including
                                                                 Philippe, d'Orléans
Louis   Louis   LOUIS XV   Duc de Chartres
1702   1707–12   (Duc d'Anjou)   1674–1723
                  1710–74   REGENT

The Legitimated Children of Louis XIV

Louis and Louise de la Vallière (1644–1710)
1. Marie Anne (1666–1739) = Prince de Conti
2. Louis, Comte de Vermandois (1667–1683)

Louis and Mme. de Montespan (1640–1707)
1. Louis-Auguste, Duc du Maine (1670–1736)
2. Louis-César, Comte de Vexin (1672–1683)
3. Louise-Françoise (1673–1743) = Prince de Condé
4. Louise-Marie-Anne (1674–1681)
5. Françoise-Marie (1677–1749) = Philippe d'Orléans, Regent of France
6. Louis-Alexandre, Comte de Toulouse (1678–1737)

The Spanish Succession

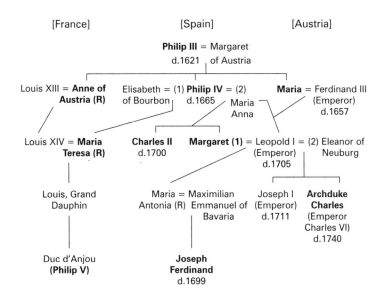

[France]   [Spain]   [Austria]

Philip III = Margaret
d.1621   of Austria

Louis XIII = **Anne of**   Elisabeth = (1) **Philip IV** = (2)   **Maria** = Ferdinand III
Austria (R)   of Bourbon   d.1665   Maria   (Emperor)
Anna   d.1657

Louis XIV = **Maria**   **Charles II**   **Margaret (1)** = Leopold I = (2) Eleanor of
Teresa (R)   d.1700   (Emperor)   Neuburg
d.1705

Louis, Grand   Maria = Maximilian   Joseph I   **Archduke**
Dauphin   Antonia (R) Emmanuel of   (Emperor)   **Charles**
Bavaria   d.1711   (Emperor
Charles VI)
d.1740

Duc d'Anjou   **Joseph**
(Philip V)   **Ferdinand**
d.1699

(Spanish Habsburgs and claimants to the throne in bold)
R = renounced claim to throne

Acknowledgements

A book of the present type owes much not only to the published work of other historians past and present, but to accumulated friendships and conversations which over the years have shaped my ideas on French history. Numerous people directly and indirectly continue to educate me in the history of seventeenth-century France, and although it would not be appropriate to name them all here, I acknowledge the unselfish assistance and cooperation which fellow historians and other scholars have shown over the years. On this occasion, however, I should like to pay special tribute to several friends and colleagues whose observations and comments improved the quality of the text. Professor Jeremy Black invited me to write the book and conveyed pertinent criticisms on a completed draft. Professor Robert Knecht saw an outline of my early ideas on the structure of the book, and indicated other directions which I might follow with profit. Dr Nigel Aston read most of the chapters in early draft; his notes and suggestions invariably were well directed and greatly improved what I had written. Dr Michael Lemon, one of my colleagues at the University of Ulster, discussed questions of absolutism with me, and on one occasion treated me to a lengthy and informative private tutorial on the intricacies and inconsistencies of the thought of Bodin. Finally, I owe more conventional thanks to my wife, whose critical reading of the text removed numerous stylistic slips and ambiguities.

David J. Sturdy
Coleraine, August 1997

INTRODUCTION

No author can aspire to write a history of Louis XIV and his reign which treats every conceivable aspect comprehensively, for even the longest books must be selective. How much more does the writer of a short study have to impose a structure which, by virtue of the themes which it selects, excludes much potential subject-matter. It is appropriate, therefore, to open this discussion by explaining the principles underlying the present study. Because it is aimed at students and others who have had little or at best a modest acquaintance with the history of the reign of Louis XIV, it does not presume extensive prior knowledge. Nevertheless, although it attempts to provide the reader with a framework necessary to an understanding of the reign of Louis XIV, it does seek also to meet the needs of the reader who hopes to work towards a more extensive grasp of the subject by raising wider questions of interpretation which are significant to present-day historians.

The main thesis of the book can be expressed simply: it is that Louis XIV was a man of his times, struggling to resolve problems which he both inherited from the past and encountered during the course of a very long reign, and that he did so by resorting to seventeenth-century methods. Such a statement might appear straightforward, but is less simple than it seems. Much historiography from the eighteenth century down to recent times (especially that emanating from France) has represented Louis XIV tendentiously. He has been depicted variously as a model of the absolute monarch, a progenitor of the Revolution, a founder of the modern centralised state, an agent of class-war, a broker of the rise of capitalism, the mastermind who determined French foreign policy over the next two centuries, and in many other guises. Of course, it is a legitimate exercise to assess Louis's contribution to the long-term movement of French history (and in the expectation that future generations would do so, Louis took pains to create an appropriate 'image' as a guide to posterity), but the historian's primary aim must be to interpret the reign of Louis XIV in terms of seventeenth-century values, problems and expectations. Teleological perspectives inevitably introduce distortion: incidents and episodes which appear highly significant when viewed from the nineteenth or twentieth centuries could seem of relatively little importance to contemporaries, and vice versa. Historians increasingly attempt to approach Louis XIV from the standpoint of the forces and problems which he inherited from the past rather than through the retrospection of the twentieth century, and as they do so they encounter a king who is very different from the figure often presented by writers who sought to incorporate him into a particular version of the history of France. This shift of focus owes much to the recent work of French historians, but credit must also go to non-French scholars, including many from the English-speaking world, whose assumptions and methodologies serve to counterpoise those of French colleagues. As Louis and his regime are reinterpreted in the light of modern scholarship, Louis becomes a more 'rounded' figure than in some nineteenth and early twentieth-century histories; he appears as much a captive as a maker of his times, and less amenable to the simple labels which have been attached to him in the past.

Throughout this discussion the focus will be kept on the person and government of Louis XIV, for this book does not purport to be a general history of France from 1643 to 1715. Aspects of economic and social history, provincial history, religious, cultural and other types of history are treated in so far as they were influenced by the actions and policies of Louis XIV. The book opens with a discussion of Louis and French monarchy. It is essential to know something of the traditions of French kingship and of Louis's personal understanding of what it meant to be king. Every public action and policy which he undertook was influenced by the fact that he was a king (as against some other form of head of state). Kingship was not only a powerful determinant in the nature of his government, but set limits on what he could or could not do. Louis thought of himself in conservative terms, being very conscious that the Bourbons were relatively new to the throne. Adherence to tradition did not imply an absence of innovation; but even the modifications which he introduced into the exercise of French kingship were designed to strengthen tradition, not overturn it. The second chapter looks at the procedures by which Louis governed France, and here the argument is somewhat similar. Louis did not attempt a 'revolution' in government in the sense of creating a 'modern' bureaucracy in central and provincial government; his purpose was to restore patterns of government and administration which he thought had once existed, but had perished in the sixteenth and early seventeenth centuries under the pressures of civil war, rebellion and international conflict. Louis's ambition in this as in so much else was to restore what he took to be former practices, not to pioneer some imagined future which happened to correspond with nineteenth and twentieth-century notions of centralised, bureaucratic government. The third chapter deals with Louis's relationships with his subjects. This is a most complex subject, for Louis was pulled in several directions at once. The harsh realities of governing a modern state forced him to impose heavy exactions on his subjects, especially in the realm of taxation, and to punish rebellion with uncompromising retribution; yet he recognised the demands of Christian paternalism and other traditions which imposed upon him the obligation to serve the best interests of his people. Furthermore, he sensed that history had bequeathed him the immense task of healing the breaches between crown and social elites, and within the elites themselves, which had resulted from the Wars of Religion in the sixteenth century, and from the rebellions of more recent times. Hence he devoted much thought to the question of how to ameliorate relations between crown and social elites. Chapter 4 continues the theme of Louis and his subjects by examining the question of religion. The Catholic Church enjoyed a pre-eminent position both in relationship to the crown and to society at large. Quite apart from its strictly religious functions, it was conspicuous in providing many of the services which in modern times are assumed by the state: education, medical and charitable functions. Louis himself underwent a religious conversion in his middle years, and brought to his religious policies a zeal which at times distorted his judgement. He exhibited an intolerance towards religious deviants which caused adverse comment even by the hard-bitten standards of his day; his Huguenot (Protestant) subjects felt the full weight of his persecution, but he proved to be almost as oppressive in his pursuit of heterodox movements within Catholicism. With regard to the realms of ideas, the literary and visual arts, the sciences and education – which are the subject of Chapter 5 – the regime of Louis XIV made some of its most enduring contributions to the history of France. This was a sphere in which Louis and his ministers showed a willingness to be led as much as to lead. A 'contract' existed between the crown and cultural elites whereby the former patronised many of the latter; they in turn used their talents in the service of the king. This is not to imply that French cultural activity under Louis XIV was a vast propaganda exercise on behalf of Louis XIV; anybody familiar with French literature, painting, architecture, philosophy and science of the period would recognise such a claim as a travesty. However, the regime did have a cultural policy which is as important in 'explaining' the reign of Louis XIV as his domestic and foreign policy. The latter is discussed in Chapter 6. Louis's relations with other European states could not conform neatly to some preconceived master-plan, for the Austrian and Spanish Habsburgs, Dutch, English, Swedes and the German states had their own ambitions to which Louis XIV had to respond. Moreover, in spite of his declarations of pacific intentions, Louis involved his country in over fifty years of warfare. The price which he demanded of his subjects was heavy, yet by 1715 France had replaced Spain as the principal power in western Europe. Whether the same outcome could have been achieved at less cost is a matter for speculation, and whether it was a worthy objective in itself begs many questions. Nevertheless, in 1715 France dominated western Europe in spite of severe reversals in the War of the Spanish Succession, the last war of Louis's reign; Louis bequeathed to his kingdom a largely favourable international position. The final chapter of the book considers some broad questions of interpretation, principally that of 'absolutism'. Was Louis an absolute monarch; if so, in what senses; and can 'absolutism' still command respect as a category of historical explanation, or should it be modified or even abandoned altogether?

1
LOUIS XIV AND FRENCH MONARCHY

Louis XIV was the product of a monarchic tradition which was instilled into him from childhood. His tutors read to him each evening several pages of François Eudes de Mézerai's *Histoire de France* (3 vols, 1643–51)[1] which was intended to inculcate in him a reverential sense of standing in a line of French kings stretching back many centuries. The young king was instructed in the development of French monarchy from earliest times to the present, and was acquainted with the personalities, achievements and failures of his predecessors; his favourite reading in his youth was the biography of his grandfather, Henri IV, written by Louis's tutor Hardouin de Péréfixe, later Archbishop of Paris.[2] Louis's historical studies avoided sentimental or romanticised interpretations of the past. They stressed the immense challenges which monarchy in France had surmounted – the Hundred Years War, the Wars of Religion – and forewarned Louis that he too would encounter difficulties and hardships as he ruled a notoriously volatile kingdom. They encouraged him nevertheless to be positive in the exercise of kingship. Monarchy, he was taught, was the very focus of the nation; in a sense the king was France.[3] French monarchy could draw upon a rich and varied heritage; it had copious resources at its disposal, some divine in origin, others arising from the rights and powers attaching to the crown; and Louis was urged to be confident that, provided he ruled in accordance with the will of God, his reign would be numbered among the more glorious in the history of France. Throughout his reign Louis perceived himself as a monarch ruling and governing within long-standing custom. This should not be taken

1

to mean that he held a static view of kingship; on the contrary, he was committed to a dynamic concept of monarchy through which he sought to manipulate and extend the conventions within which he ruled. But traditional kingship surrounded him with 'fundamental laws' which had accumulated over the centuries and had been formulated by medieval jurists. The 'fundamental laws' defined the nature, functions and obligations of kingship, and Louis XIV no less than his forebears accommodated his rule to their precepts. Two of the laws had particular significance for Louis: the law of succession, and the sacred character of kingship.

The Law of Succession

A king of France was succeeded by his nearest legitimate male heir; a queen regnant was inadmissible, as was the male descendant of a French princess or an illegitimate son of the king. Jurists held that legitimately born kings had followed each other in legal succession since the reign of Hugues Capet (987–96), and perhaps even since Clovis in the fifth century. The pretence was upheld even though the parentage of some kings, notably among the Merovingians in the seventh and eighth centuries, would not bear too close a scrutiny; moving into more recent times, there were doubts as to whether Charles VII (b.1422) really was the son of Charles VI (d.1422) in view of the scandalous behaviour of the queen, Isabeau de Bavière. It is sometimes stated that French succession law was a variation of Salic Law, which precluded females from inheriting land; it would be more accurate to say that it was governed by political necessity, jurists invoking Salic Law to provide retrospective legal principle.[4] Succession law placed Louis XIV in a monarchic lineage stretching back well over a thousand years; that the Bourbons were relative newcomers who had ruled only for some fifty years, paled into insignificance against the magnificence of this allegedly unbroken royal ancestry of more than ten centuries into which Louis XIV entered.

Succession law nevertheless posed potential problems for Louis XIV which caused him to attempt to depart from tradition. The main Bourbon male line had come uncomfortably close to extinction before his birth in 1638 (his parents had been married for twenty-three years before producing a child), and the disturbing fact was that Louis and his wife, Queen Maria Teresa, also experienced difficulty in raising healthy offspring. The family tree shows that of their six children, five died either at birth or within two or three years; only the first-born, Louis the Grand Dauphin, grew to maturity. In the normal course of events he would have succeeded his father as king, but he died in 1711 and so predeceased Louis XIV by four years. The Dauphin's death was followed within a few months by those of his eldest son the Duc de Bourgogne, Bourgogne's wife Marie-Adelaide de Savoie, and their eldest son. The question of guaranteeing the succession drove Louis XIV to exceptional measures: he legitimated eight of his illegitimate children by his mistresses Louise de la Vallière and Madame de Montespan. Even more controversially, he proclaimed the right of two of his legitimated sons – Louis-Auguste, Duc du Maine, and Louis-Alexandre, Comte de Toulouse – to succeed him should the Bourbon male line fail. Louis was not the first king of France to legitimate children born to his mistresses, for Henri IV had done so; but even Henri had not attempted to extend the right of succession in this way. In 1717 the Council of Regency, which governed during the minority of Louis XV, annulled the putative rights of Maine and Toulouse on the ground that the fundamental law of succession debarred sons who were illegitimate by birth, whatever their legal status later in life. The legitimated daughters of Louis XIV were married into other branches of the Bourbon family. Marie-Anne married Louis-Armand de Bourbon, Prince de Conti; Louise-Françoise married Louis III, Prince de Condé; and Françoise-Marie married Philippe d'Orléans, Duc de Chartres and Regent of France after the death of Louis XIV. By these matches Louis XIV grafted newer stock on to the Bourbon stem in the hope that future generations would prove more fruitful than those of the recent past. The measures worked, the Bourbons surviving the short-term dangers and lasting throughout the eighteenth and most of the nineteenth centuries (the direct line died out in 1883). Even so, the rate of mortality within Louis's immediate family during the later years of his reign remained high, and when he died in 1715 he was succeeded not by a son or even a grandson, but by a great-grandson.

In the seventeenth century, succession law also affirmed that the king succeeded at the moment when his predecessor died. It had not always been so. In the early Middle Ages the reign of a king began on the day of his coronation; an interregnum therefore was common. The beginnings of a change can be traced to 1270 when Louis IX died in Tunis while on a crusade. His son and successor, Philippe III, had accompanied him and was recognised as king by the acclamation of French lords also on the crusade. Philippe's coronation in 1271 therefore confirmed the events in Tunis. Thereafter it became customary to date a reign from the death of the preceding king. The concept of interregnum was abandoned, and coronations increasingly confirmed rather than conferred kingship. Medieval theologians and jurists turned this newer tradition into the theory of 'the king's two bodies':[5] the king was deemed to possess a physical body with the physical, mental and moral attributes which any human being might have, but also a mystical 'body' which incorporated kingship and was assumed by his successor at the moment when the physical body expired. If the new king were a minor (under thirteen years of age), a regent headed the government in his name; on the king's thirteenth birthday the regency ended. During the first eight years of Louis XIV's reign his mother, Anne of Austria, served as regent (Louis was four when Louis XIII died on 14 May 1643) until her son's majority in 1651. She relied heavily on the chief minister, Cardinal Mazarin; together they oversaw Louis's education, prepared him to assume kingship, and sought to uphold the rights of monarchy during the turbulent 1640s.

The Sacred Character of Monarchy

French kings had been Christian since the conversion and baptism of Clovis in 496. According to tradition they were held in special regard by God, who afforded two signs of divine approbation. First, at the baptism of Clovis a dove descended from heaven and carried to Remi, the Bishop of Rheims who officiated, an ampulla filled with holy oil. Remi used some of the oil to baptise Clovis, the ampulla with the remaining oil later being kept at the abbey of Saint Remi.[6] The ampulla and oil – preserved at the abbey over the centuries – were used at the coronations of Louis IX (1226) and most of his successors, including Louis XIV. The second sign was the Royal Touch: the power given by God to kings of France to cure sufferers of scrofula – a skin disease which affected especially the face and neck – by touching or stroking their pustules.[7] Some jurists traced the gift to the reign of Philippe I (r.1060–1108), but others to that of his grandfather Robert the Pious (r.997–1031). Kings of France, again including Louis XIV, exercised this divinely conferred power of miraculous healing as further proof that God looked upon them with exceptional favour. They first exercised it after the coronation, thereafter 'touching' periodically for scrofula, with numerous miraculous cures being reported.

Sacred Monarchy Reaffirmed

Well before Louis XIV's reign the question of the sacredness of monarchy was posed anew by the Wars of Religion in the second half of the sixteenth century. The product of aristocratic rivalries, a monarchy weakened by minor kings and an embattled regency, socio-economic tensions, and ideological conflicts arising from the impact upon France of Calvinist Protestantism, the civil wars endangered the kingdom not simply because of widespread violence and destruction, but because they raised ideological questions concerning the nature of monarchy, the state and society.[8] Traditional social thought in France drew parallels between human society and the structure of the universe. Just as God invested the universe with a configuration wherein every planet and star has its fixed location and motion, and the whole of creation – spiritual as well as material – is linked in a continuum rising from the most elemental particles of matter to the very summit of heaven, so human society has a divinely ordained structure within which every group and individual has a fixed position. Should the planets and stars stray from their orbits, or the relationships of the material and spiritual entities of which creation is composed be inverted, chaos would result. Likewise social chaos is threatened when the established social and political order or hierarchy is challenged; and just as an imminent God constantly holds the universal order in place, so the king, in the image of God, works ceaselessly to protect social order and hierarchy. This mode of thought found expression in much medieval and early modern political literature; it is encountered, for example, in the *Catalogus Gloriae Mundi* (1529) of Barthélemy de Chasseneux, wherein the author analyses French society in the context of the structure and composition of the universe. Drawing an analogy with creation, he presents French society as a finely balanced constellation of social groups, corporations and institutions, each with its natural and legitimate place in a hierarchical society. Overseeing all is the king, whose earthly role is analogous to that of God in the universe.

The Wars of Religion presented to the social and political order precisely the fundamental threat which traditional social thought abhorred. Calvinism represented not just a body of Protestant belief and church organisation, but the prospect of the reordering of society along theocratic lines: the socio-economic, as well as the religious, position of the Catholic Church would have been undermined, and the existing social elites could not be assured of their continuing pre-eminence. Calvinist visions found concrete expression in Protestant towns in France, and further afield in parts of Switzerland, Germany, the Netherlands, Scotland and New England colonies, where bold experiments were attempted in new forms of social and political organisation. On his death by assassination in 1589, Henri III, the last Valois King of France, was succeeded by a member of the Bourbon family, Henri IV; but Henri IV was a Huguenot (as Calvinists were known in France). His succession therefore implied much more than a change of dynasty: it raised the possibility that he would impose upon France a socio-political revolution along Calvinist lines, and it posed the question of whether a Protestant king could be regarded as 'sacred' in the traditional sense. To Henri IV's Catholic subjects (about 90 per cent of the population) the creation of a 'Protestant' state and society was an intolerable prospect, and a 'sacred' Huguenot king a contradiction in terms. Faced by widespread opposition to his rule, Henri adopted two measures to transform his position: in 1593 he underwent a public ceremony of conversion to Catholicism,[9] and in 1594 was crowned. The coronation presented problems since Rheims, where it normally took place and where the regalia was stored, was in the hands of his enemies. Henri was crowned instead in Chartres cathedral; and in place of the ampulla and oil from Saint Remi there was used oil said to have been given miraculously to Saint Martin of Tours by the Virgin Mary, and guarded by the monastery of Saint Martin at Marmoutier, not far from Tours.[10] By these public acts – conversion and coronation – Henri IV confirmed that he was embracing not just the Catholic faith, but traditional sacred monarchy and traditional social hierarchy.

The measures were crucial to the collapse of popular opposition to his succession and to the ending of the Wars of Religion in 1598. Even the Edict of Nantes (1598), which afforded religious and politi-cal rights to Huguenots, did not signal any weakening of Henri's commitment to tradition, for the edict in effect marginalised the socio-religious values which Huguenots allegedly espoused. The principle of the sacredness of French monarchy not only committed Henri IV to the defence of the Catholic Church, but to the preservation of a conservative social system. These imperatives bound Louis XIV as much as his grandfather. Louis, in spite of (or perhaps even because of) his Protestant antecedents, was to prove ultra-Catholic in private conviction as well as in public policy; and, as will be seen later in this chapter, he remained committed to conservative attitudes regarding the social hierarchy. Louis was no social radical; it was no part of his purpose to diminish the social status of nobles and aristocrats by espousing the interest of, for example the bourgeoisie (whether that term is understood in either the seventeenth or twentieth-century sense). The implications of the Wars of Religion (to which might be added the Protestant uprisings of the 1620s) continued to weigh upon Louis XIV, who never forgot that he had no option but to preserve traditional social structure, and therefore the social supremacy of the nobility and aristocracy.

Such were some of the principles of traditional and more recent kingship that were instilled into Louis by his teachers, his mother and the chief minister Cardinal Mazarin. Yet how did he himself understand kingship; how did he view himself, and to what extent, if at all, did he modify the traditions which he inherited? These are questions to which simplistic answers are inadequate. Difficulties confront the historian on many sides, not least because of the absence of a comprehensive edition of Louis's correspondence. Nevertheless, we do possess one invaluable source, namely his so-called *Mémoires* which were composed in the 1660s. Although they were written while Louis was in his late twenties and early thirties, they testify to his philosophy of kingship during that important phase of his life and reign.

The *Mémoires* of Louis XIV: Conception and Composition[11]

From at least the beginning of his 'personal reign' in 1661, Louis XIV entertained the idea of preserving for posterity a formal record of his reign. He could look to the comparatively recent examples of the Duc de Sully and Cardinal Richelieu who, in their *Economies Royales* and *Testament Politique*, respectively had left vindicatory accounts of their policies. By the mid-seventeenth century a well-developed theory as to the nature and purpose of memoirs had developed.[12] Memoirs were understood not as a straightforward narrative of events, but as a selective account in which the author demonstrated the principles, purposes and meanings behind those events. Memoirs, in other words, had a didactic purpose: to explain to the reader the political, moral, psychological and other conclusions which followed from the narrative; and the text would be peppered with maxims which encapsulated the lessons which the author sought to convey. The memoirs of a great political figure were expected to fulfil a further purpose: to reveal the 'grand scheme' which he had brought to his policies. Richelieu's political testament, for example, claimed that throughout his period in office he had endeavoured consistently to subdue the aristocracy and the Huguenots, and to curb Spanish power. Political memoirs – as understood in the seventeenth century – were a moralising comment upon public events, a medium for the exposition of the beliefs and commitments to which the author adhered, and proof of his ability to rise above mere circumstance and to impose his own will upon public affairs. In deciding to compose his memoirs, Louis XIV turned to a well-defined literary genre whose purposes were understood by author and reader alike. It was the birth of the Grand Dauphin in 1661 which provided the immediate impulse for the composition of the memoirs; indeed, they are often referred to as *Mémoires pour l'Instruction du Dauphin*. The Dauphin was their intended recipient, and he is addressed directly by his father over a hundred times in the text. When completed, the *Mémoires* covered the years 1661–62, and 1666–68.[13] Modern readers sometimes are surprised at the brevity of the period which they treat; yet although it is true that pressures of government caused Louis XIV to abandon them in the early 1670s, in another sense the memoirs had fulfilled their purpose: the 1660s provided sufficient material for Louis XIV to identify the chief principles and lessons which he aimed to instil into his son. The Dauphin, after all, was still a young boy in the early 1670s; the *Mémoires* were appropriate to his intellectual development over the next few years.

Although it is the content of the *Mémoires* which is mainly at issue here, a few words on their composition are in order.[14] In the early 1660s Louis began amassing notes and other material in collaboration with his minister, Jean-Baptiste Colbert who, because of the heavy demands of his ministerial functions, stood down from these particular duties in 1665 after having produced a draft in note form for the king's comments. In 1666 one of the Dauphin's tutors, Périgny, took up where Colbert had left off; he gathered further material (some of which came from the king, who also had been keeping notes), and in 1668 began to produce a text. Périgny died in 1670, whereupon his services towards the *Mémoires* were assumed by Paul Pellisson, a well-known writer and former secretary of Fouquet; Pellisson had a completed version ready in 1672.

That several people were involved in their composition does not mean that the *Mémoires* were anything other than a reliable expression of the king's thoughts. Nothing in them passed without his consent. From the earliest stages to the finish Louis was consulted, and we know that on occasion he modified what Pellisson had written, or added passages of his own. The *Mémoires* express only Louis's thoughts and convictions, and are very much his work. A modern reader could not fail to observe the extent to which they revolve around Louis himself. They stress *his* analysis of the problems he faced at the beginning of the 1660s, *his* struggles against domestic and foreign adversity, *his* achievements and triumphs against heavy odds, and *his* contribution to the glory of French monarchy; by contrast, other figures such as his father, mother and Cardinal Mazarin, are afforded but infrequent and passing references (although he does devote a passage to the memory of his mother in the memoirs for 1666, and those for 1661 include brief assessments of some ministers). It is as if he owed little that was positive to his parents, the chief minister and his team; indeed, at one point he summarises the domestic situation which he inherited in a famous phrase: 'le désordre régnait partout'. To present-day scholars this statement is a gross exaggeration, but it does permit Louis then to present himself in the *Mémoires* as the heroic monarch who overcomes resistance at home, imposes order upon the kingdom, dispenses justice to his suffering subjects, exacts obedience from ministers, assumes personal responsibility for government, smites his foreign enemies, and through the vigour and insight with which he rules, earns the respect of friend and foe alike. It should perhaps be added in passing that this glowing self-image is one which most monarchs of the period had of themselves.

Louis, then, is the focus of the *Mémoires*; but it is a Louis who exhibits a range of qualities which constitute the highest ideals of monarchy. In accordance with the requirements of traditional monarchy, the religious theme is emphasised. Louis views public affairs 'with the eyes of a master', much as God oversees the working of creation. It is God who places kings on their thrones, and it is to

God alone that kings are answerable; and just as the will of God is absolute – that is, made by God alone – and may not be resisted by the true Christian, so the will of the king is absolute, and is worthy of the same unquestioning obedience. In a famous passage, written perhaps with the Frondes in mind, Louis states that, 'no matter how unworthy the king, a revolt by his subjects is always infinitely criminal. He who gave kings to men wants kings to be respected as His lieutenants, reserving to Himself alone the right to examine their conduct. It is His will that, whoever is born a subject, must obey without question.'[15] The suppression of civil disorder by Louis is therefore an expression of his love for God, whose will it is that mankind should live in a condition of harmony and respect for social hierarchy. The preservation of social order is an obligation which God has placed on Louis. Louis stands in a paternal relationship to his subjects, as does God to mankind, and it is Louis's duty to ameliorate the condition of his people (he uses the phrase, 'soulager le peuple') just as God seeks to preserve His people from danger. And to assist Louis in the fulfilment of these great purposes, God confers upon him – as upon all legitimate kings – powers of wisdom, insight and instinct which are denied to all others. The *Mémoires* contain numerous references to Louis's symbiotic relationship to God; but it is a relationship which imposes awesome responsibilities and duties upon Louis, who is conscious of the temptations and pitfalls awaiting him. He will be surrounded by flatterers whose blandishments he must learn to resist (echoes of the temptation of Jesus by the Devil); and love affairs may well entice him to allow women to exert political influence over him (in a self-critical passage for the year 1667, he reflects on his susceptibility to Louise de la Vallière, and warns his son against the dangers represented by pretty women). The king's unique position will expose him to allurements from every side; the wise king recognises his vulnerability, and in the exercise of his duties calls upon 'le secours du ciel'.

To the succour which comes directly from God, Louis adds gifts of the mind as a resource of which the wise ruler avails himself. The monarch must learn to think rationally and sagely; the *Mémoires* make numerous references to the need for good sense, wisdom and reason in the management of government. 'The function of kingship', he insists, 'consists mainly of allowing good sense to operate.'[16] He complains that the Comte de Brienne, Secretary of State for Foreign Affairs, had the fatal weakness of 'not thinking things through...

according to reason'.[17] The comment on Brienne is illuminating, for it illustrates the importance which Louis attached to the quality of reason in his ministers. In a passage in which he urges his son to seek advice before deciding great matters of policy, he writes: 'The most important decisions should never be taken without consulting, if possible, the most enlightened, rational and wise of our subjects.'[18] Of course, all European monarchs from at least the Middle Ages onwards had sought advice, usually from members of the extended royal family, great aristocrats and prelates. In pressing his son to seek advice, Louis was uttering a truism; but it is the qualities he sought in his advisers which marked him out. There are sections of the *Mémoires* which could have been written by an 'Enlightened Despot' of the 1760s or 1770s. Louis's appeal to 'reason' as a basis of paternal and benevolent government has a late-eighteenth century ring to it. For Louis XIV, 'un grand choix de personnes'[19] was crucial to the creation of a ministerial team which was trustworthy, assiduous and successful; and it is notable that in passages in which he presents the Dauphin with maxims concerning the selection of ministers, Louis picks on rational mental qualities rather than factors related to birth or aristocratic titles as the guiding principle. We should not jump to conclusions here: Louis was not necessarily urging his son to a ministerial revolution; he was not suggesting that high birth was incompatible with a capacity to reason. But he was contending that meritocracy rather than aristocracy was the desideratum.

Another prominent theme of the *Mémoires* is a 'Renaissance' commitment to the concept of the glorious prince which is encapsulated in the phrase, '*la gloire*', a term which could mean glory or reputation, depending on the context. It appears frequently in the *Mémoires* and has come to epitomise one of the defining principles of the personal reign of Louis XIV; indeed, we shall shortly be considering *la gloire* as it was manifested through the arts, state rituals and the life of the court of Louis XIV. The Renaissance had bequeathed to the seventeenth century an ideal of the prince which still commanded widespread respect. To Louis XIV *la gloire* was a priority, not so much because he felt it necessary to impress his subjects or anybody else, but because he viewed it as an inherent quality of kingship. When they are truly kings, he asserts, monarchs are governed by 'a dominating passion ... namely their interest, grandeur and gloire'.[20] Here are the commanding values to which Louis was attached. Indeed, they may be read almost as synonyms: interest,

grandeur and glory for Louis XIV were three interlocking imperatives to which all others must be subordinated. Louis describes himself
as being motivated by 'a single desire: la gloire'.[21] *La gloire* was insep-
arable from great monarchy; but – and Louis was frank in his admission – it was immensely difficult to achieve and notoriously easy to
forfeit. *La gloire* was not to be bought, nor was it to be won by military conquest alone; it came through unremitting hard work, attention to the minutiae of government, and through a personal conduct
conducive to a glorious reputation.

One other feature of the *Mémoires* is important for the present
discussion: Louis is emphatic that he must be an absolute monarch.
Modern ideas on what constituted 'absolute monarchy' will be considered in the concluding discussion to this book, but it is a phrase which
Louis himself employed. From the moment when he records that, on
the death of Mazarin, he cast round his kingdom 'with the eyes of a
master',[22] he writes as one conscious of being, or seeking to become,
an absolute monarch. Having surveyed the condition of the kingdom
in 1661 he concluded that widespread reforms were crucial, but a
necessary precondition was 'to make my will truly absolute'.[23]
Certainly, kings should take advice from their ministers, but decisions
belong to kings alone. All policy must be conducted in the name of
the king, and in total obedience to his will. The king is 'above all other
men';[24] he sees things more clearly than they do; he experiences
depths of understanding beyond the comprehension of his subjects,
and therefore must require their total acquiescence in his will.

Louis is insistent that in drawing the attention of the Dauphin to
absolute monarchy he is calling for the restoration of a monarchy in
which there is no place for a Richelieu or a Mazarin. He does not
suggest that his concept of monarchy is innovative; on the contrary,
he perceives his task as being to restore a form of monarchy whose
powers had been diminished by the combined effects of civil war,
rebellion, chief ministers (faithful though they had been), and the
depredations wrought by foreign enemies. Louis devotes lengthy
passages of the *Mémoires* to his dealings with the *parlements*, various
provincial assemblies and other quasi-political institutions which, in
his judgement, had greatly exceeded their legitimate authority. He is
insistent that his aim was not to abolish or persecute them; it was to
deny them any claims to a share in sovereignty which they might have
developed in the recent past, and to oblige them to return to their
'traditional' relationship to the crown. Louis understood 'absolutism'

to mean that sovereignty was vested in the king alone; it was not shared, either with another person or with any institution or court of law. There did exist 'sovereign courts' – the *parlements*, the Grand Conseil, the Chambres des Comptes, the Cours des Aides and the Cour des Monnaies – but in Louis's *Mémoires* they were 'sovereign' only in the sense that they fulfilled their judicial and other functions on behalf of the crown; they were agencies through which the crown exercised its sovereignty, and were invested by the crown with aspects of sovereignty. Most emphatically, however, they were not 'sovereign' in the sense of sharing sovereignty with the king; they administered the crown's justice, but had no part in creating that justice.

Louis XIV and the Ritual of Monarchy[25]

All regimes use ritualistic and symbolic expressions to affirm their legitimacy, define their powers and attributes, and justify their actions, and Louis XIV was to devote extraordinary attention to ritual as a medium through which to expound his views on monarchy. Moreover, rituals can be more than symbols, and in the reign of Louis XIV much of the ceremonial with which he was surrounded embodied the essence as distinct from the mere trappings of power.[26] It was this – the substantive in ritual – which influenced Louis's attitude to two ceremonies through which he was inaugurated as king. The first was the *lit de justice* (a ceremony which he came to associate with episodes of royal weakness) held at the Parlement of Paris,18 May 1643, just four days after his father's death. The *lit de justice*, whose origins went back to the 1300s, was a ceremony whereby the king made a personal and formal appearance at the Parlement of Paris, or occasionally a provincial *parlement*, to exercise justice or enact legislation. By the sixteenth century it had also acquired royal inaugural significance. Thus, on 15 May 1610, the day after the death of Henri IV by assassination, Louis XIII held a *lit de justice* at the Parlement of Paris. His aim was to ease the political tension resulting from the murder of his father by providing a public demonstration that his succession had proceeded unhindered; this *lit de justice* also declared his mother, Marie de' Medici, to be Regent of France. Louis XIV's *lit de justice* of 18 May 1643 likewise acknowledged his mother, Anne of Austria, as regent. The adoption of inaugural functions by the *lit de justice* was a response to the succession of minors at times of political uncertainty.

This was one of the factors behind the antipathy which Louis XIV later showed towards the *lit de justice*. After 1643 he held few *lits de justice*, the last two being in 1667 and 1673; and even their purpose was to impose limitations upon the legislative procedures of the Parlement of Paris.

The second inaugural ceremony was the coronation. Even though it no longer conferred kingship, it was indispensable as a public affirmation of the rights and powers attaching to French kingship. Louis XIV conformed to custom by being crowned in Rheims cathedral, but not until 7 June 1654, eleven years into his reign. The delay is to be explained by the combined pressures of international war and the Fronde rebellions (1648–53). There was an element of political calculation in the timing of Louis's coronation, which was a highly effective means of celebrating his authority in the aftermath of the Frondes; and the fact that aristocrats who had participated in the rebellions were in attendance, provided public attestation of their submission to the king. Similar motives were behind Louis's decision to omit one traditional feature of the post-coronation ceremonial. It was usual for the newly crowned king to proceed in triumph to Paris. The royal entry into the capital city took place amidst highly organised public celebrations. Tens of thousands of people crowded the streets; there was music, fairs and entertainments; the royal route was decorated with triumphal arches, flags and bunting; the city fathers joined the royal procession, as did the guilds, religious confraternities, members of the university, representatives of the law courts and a host of other Parisian notabilities and institutions. To the city of Paris, the post-coronation royal entry was as much a part of the king's inauguration as the coronation itself. Yet after his coronation Louis XIV deliberately snubbed Paris, the centre of Frondeur resistance. He dispensed with the royal entry as a mark of royal displeasure at the conduct of the city during the Frondes. Paris stood shamed and humiliated; and it was not until 1660 that Louis 'forgave' the city by honouring it with a formal entry, when he was accompanied by his Spanish bride, Maria Teresa.

These episodes occurred when Louis was young. We may presume that it was his mother and Cardinal Mazarin who persuaded Louis of the potential uses of ritual. Throughout his adult life, Louis proved to be an unrivalled master of the art of ceremonial and self-presentation. He authorised a vast outpouring of statues, paintings, engravings, medallions and other representations of himself, not as 'mere propaganda', but as a means of communicating with his subjects and instructing them in the nature of his regime. Louis employed every conceivable device to represent the principles and purposes of his reign through the literary and visual arts, architecture, tapestries, medals, music and court ritual. In recent years, historians have paid renewed attention to these features; they no longer dismiss them, as did many nineteenth-century scholars, as elaborate charades unworthy of serious scholarly attention. Responding to the promptings of social scientists who have developed a sophisticated understanding of the social and political functions of ritual, historians have recognised that here is a sphere which they have hitherto neglected. Indeed, some historians have belatedly arrived at a conclusion which Louis XIV regarded as self-evident: that public representations of the king, and the ritual with which he was surrounded, were central to the functioning of seventeenth-century kingship.

Public Representations of Louis XIV

The Bourbons, mindful that their succession to the throne was recent, had no option but to give high priority to 'propaganda'. From Henri IV, whose succession was controversial and whose life constantly was in danger, they devoted considerable resources to the cultivation of their public image. Among the measures which Henri adopted, two were of enduring importance. First, in 1602 he created the post of Surintendant des Bâtiments. The Surintendant was placed in charge of the royal palaces in and near to Paris, and was responsible for their management and purchase of all the goods and accoutrements which they needed. The Surintendant thereby exercised considerable powers of patronage, since he decided which architects, artists, sculptors, tapestry weavers, furniture makers and others should receive royal commissions. In 1664 Louis XIV appointed Jean-Baptiste Colbert to this influential position. Second, in 1608 Henri IV created a royal training-school for painters, sculptors, goldsmiths, engravers and architects. It was named after accommodation placed at its disposal in the Louvre: the Grande Galerie du Louvre. There were workshops and lodgings for the students, and over the next two centuries many of France's finest painters and architects were produced by this institution. Both Simon Vouet and Nicolas Poussin, for example, studied there; so did André le Nôtre, who designed the gardens at Versailles.

As well as looking elsewhere for artists, the French crown generated
its own talent which was put to work on embellishing the royal palaces
and glorifying the king.

As part of their strategy of inculcating respect among their subjects
and among foreign governments, the Bourbons devoted considerable
energy to the transformation of Paris from a chaotic medieval city into
a modern metropolis comparable with the finest European cities.[27] The
Bourbons strove to make Paris a modern capital; that is to say, not
just the centre of royal government and justice, but a city through
which they could exemplify their aspirations for the whole of the
kingdom. Paris, under the Bourbons, entered upon one of its most
brilliant phases as a centre of intellectual and artistic achievement. The
metamorphosis of Paris by the Bourbons aimed to cultivate a civic
pride which would translate into a reverential esteem for this modern,
reforming monarchy. Under Henri IV and Louis XIII magnificent
squares were laid out (the Place Dauphine, the Place Royale – now the
Place des Vosges), new bridges across the Seine were built (notably the
Pont Neuf), large promenades were constructed (the Cours de la Reine
to the west of the city, and the Mail de l'Arsenal to the east), and the
Jardin Royal des Plantes was designed as a leisure garden as well as
a centre of scientific research. Again, additions to the Louvre were
made by Henri IV; but it was his widow, Marie de' Medici, who worked
on the most ambitious scale: just to the south of the city she built a
new palace with magnificent gardens, the Luxembourg. Other examples of Bourbon munificence could be given, such as the church of
Val-de-Grâce, built by Louis XIV's mother as a thank-offering for his
birth; they too would testify to the commitment of the Bourbons to
Paris as the focus of much of their image-building.

Louis XIV continued this tradition, providing Paris with yet more
expressions of royal beneficence. To the existing squares of Paris he
added the Place des Victoires (1686) and the Place Louis le Grand –
now the Place Vendôme – (1699). Triumphal arches were built at the
Porte Saint Antoine (1671), the Porte Saint Denis (1673) and the Porte
Saint Martin (1674). Two great Parisian buildings of scientific and military importance were commissioned by Louis XIV: the Observatory
(1667–72) and Les Invalides, which combined a great church and
military hospital (1692–1704). To these should be added the extensions to the Louvre undertaken in the 1660s: the famous colonnade
was built, a development which took the palace to its point of
maximum easterly development (any further extensions eastwards

would have entailed the unthinkable demolition of churches and urban property). This list of royal commissions no doubt could be lengthened, but it would simply confirm what has already appeared: that Louis XIV was truly 'Bourbon' in continuing to cultivate his image of a royal benefactor of his capital city.

A Bourbon innovation which Louis XIV also preserved was that of public statues of the king.[28] Before the reign of Louis XIII there were no public statues of kings in France (the only statues were on royal tombs, or on the portals of churches or palaces). It was Marie de' Medici who introduced this 'Roman' tradition by arranging for the erection of a large equestrian statue of Henri IV on the Pont Neuf. An equestrian statue of Louis XIII was located in the Place Royale in 1639, and in 1647 a group depicting a young Louis XIV and his parents was completed on the Pont-au-Change in Paris. Three more statues of Louis XIV were erected in Paris during his reign. First, in 1686 an equestrian statue was unveiled at the Place des Victoires after an elaborate parade and public ceremony; second, in 1689 a pedestrian statue of Louis in Roman dress was erected in front of the Hôtel de Ville; and third, in 1699 an equestrian statue was erected in the Place Louis le Grand (Vendôme). The background to the statue of 1689 is of particular significance. It commemorated a decision taken in 1680 by the city fathers of Paris to confer on the king the title of 'Louis le Grand'. Henceforth, all public monuments and official documents in which the king was named referred to him by this nomenclature. This particular decision is of importance on several counts: it reinforces the proposition that relations between Louis and Paris remained good; but it represents almost a reversal of roles, for here was the city conferring a 'title' on the king. Paris was by no means the only city in which statues of Louis XIV were erected. During the course of his reign, others appeared in most of the major towns and cities of France; while most of his subjects never saw him, a large proportion were reminded of the grandeur of their king by the presence of imposing statues as well as by coins and medals.

Versailles and Court Ritual[29]

From his predecessors Louis inherited a string of palaces and châteaux which stretched from Paris and its surrounding area (the Louvre and Tuileries, Saint Germain, Marly and other royal residences) south through Fontainebleau to Chambord. Yet it was upon the relatively modest residence which his father had built at Versailles that Louis conferred his favour. The new building programme began in 1669 and continued throughout most of the rest of the reign. Louis moved the court and government to Versailles in 1682. The decision to develop the domain was Louis's own; Colbert, for example, urged him to make the Louvre his principal palace. Versailles offered several attractions to the king in the early 1660s: it was close enough to Paris for easy communication, yet distant enough to create the illusion of a bucolic retreat far from the pressures of the city; it was surrounded by forests which afforded excellent opportunities for that most 'noble' of occupations, hunting; and the Louvre, even after its extensions in the 1660s, did not correspond to Louis's ideas on how a royal palace should be designed. The decision committed him to the most ambitious building programme of the century; but when Versailles was completed, it provided a model imitated by monarchs and princes throughout Europe. Whereas his father and grandfather had seen in the development of Paris the possibility of turning that city into a microcosm of France which the rest of the kingdom would imitate, Louis, especially in the light of the Parisian Fronde, regarded that experiment as a relative failure and opted to build a palace which would represent his ideal of monarchy, of the king's relationship to his subjects, and of the functioning of the kingdom as a whole. The principal architects were Louis le Vau and Jules Hardouin Mansart; Charles Lebrun was responsible for most of the artistic decoration; and the gardens were designed by André le Nôtre. Louis created a palace whose financial cost was heavy, but not as excessive as later critics sometimes alleged. During the 1670s and early 1680s the annual expenditure on Versailles was about 2 million livres, and from the mid-1680s to early 1690s, about 4 millions per annum. With one or two exceptions (notably 1685 when there was extra outlay on the diversion of the river Eure towards Versailles), these sums consumed about 3 or 4 per cent of the state budget.[30]

The symbolism employed by Lebrun and other artists and sculptors who decorated Versailles often derived from classicism. Sometimes Louis himself was represented mythologically, sometimes classical figures were used to depict the attributes of Louis XIV. Certain figures provided much of the iconography: Jupiter, most powerful of all the gods of antiquity and conqueror of the Titans; Apollo, son of Jupiter, often associated with the sun, and god of the fine arts, medicine, music, poetry and eloquence (and, incidentally, Louis's personal favourite among the gods of antiquity); Mars, also son of Jupiter, and god of war; Mercury, messenger of the gods; Hercules, whose heroic deeds earned him admission to the ranks of the gods after his death; and Neptune, god of the sea, rivers, lakes and fountains, and given to inflicting earthquakes on those who earned his displeasure. These and other deities festooned the walls, ceilings, stairways, halls and gardens of Versailles; and the qualities which classical antiquity attributed to them were conferred upon Louis XIV by simple analogy. In other scenes, great figures of Roman and Greek history (Augustus, Julius Caesar, Alexander the Great) figured prominently; and, of course, Louis himself was the subject of much of the decoration, notably in the Hall of Mirrors, whose ceiling was devoted to a cycle of paintings representing his assumption of personal power in 1661, and his victorious wars; and the Salon of War was dominated by a great plaster relief showing a triumphant Louis XIV on horseback. Of all the symbols at Versailles with which contemporaries and posterity associate Louis XIV, that of the sun has been paramount. Yet in adopting the sun as his emblem, 'le roi soleil' acknowledged, not that he was a 'new' type of king, but a traditional monarch, for the sun had often been used as a symbol by medieval kings. Charles VII of France employed it in the fifteenth century, while in England, Richard II, Edward IV, Henry VII and Henry VIII all included the sun among their cognizances.[31]

Court Ritual

It was in the pattern of court life that Louis XIV made his most individual contribution to royal ritual. The royal court was truly like a mini-state in which various groups and individuals struggled to establish and preserve their interest. Courtiers learned to conduct themselves according to an elaborate etiquette – deriving in part from native French traditions, but also from ducal palaces of Renaissance Italy and from the royal court of the Spanish monarchy – which defined their status and governed their relations with each other. The principal function of court etiquette, however, was to confirm the relationship of courtiers to the king. It was one of unequivocal submission to Louis's authority. Louis conferred or withheld favour, not just through grants of titles, land or money to favoured recipients, but through the equally effective ceremonial of the court. A word of compliment from the king, a gesture of recognition, a mark of respect could raise a courtier in the hierarchy of Versailles; conversely, a cold dismissal or, worst of all, the exile of a recalcitrant nobleman from the court, could be disastrous for the individual concerned.[32] The royal court at Versailles was a highly regulated society focused upon the king, a finely tuned vehicle for the execution of his will. Louis subjected himself to a similarly regulated lifestyle. His daily routine rarely changed. He woke at 8.00; at 8.15 there began his ceremonial rising with the 'petit lever', followed at 8.30 by the 'grand lever'. From 9.30 he received individual ministers or others in private audience until Mass at 10.00. At 11.00 he met ministers in council until lunch at 13.00. The afternoon was spent hunting, walking in the gardens, or on some other outdoor pursuit. At 17.00 he again received individual courtiers, ministers or others granted a private audience. The evening was usually devoted to leisure: a ball, a play, or – three times a week – receptions hosted by the king. A royal reception – known simply as 'l'Appartement', since it was held in the king's chambers – was a splendid occasion: the courtiers dressed sumptuously, food and drink were offered, games of cards and billiards were enjoyed, while background music was provided by royal musicians. It was on these occasions above all that Louis manipulated his courtiers as he passed among them, flattering some with his attention and subtly, but effectively, conveying his displeasure to others. Louis dined at 22.00, and retired to bed at 23.00 after the ceremonies of the 'grand coucher' and 'petit coucher'.

Versailles and the royal court were extraordinary affirmations of monarchy as understood by Louis XIV. By the early 1680s, between 4000 and 5000 nobles were attached to the court; and if servants, workmen, gardeners and the host of others employed there are included, then over 10,000 people were attached to the palace. What had been the village of Versailles was a major beneficiary. It too grew in size as houses and apartments were built for the nobles and others who did not have rooms in the palace. Versailles was Louis's outstanding physical bequest to France. Its court was an idealised representation of the kingdom. The modern student who wishes to gain a sense of the atmosphere of this remarkable creation still can find no better guides than the letters and memoirs of those who experienced it at first hand. Figures such as Madame de Sévigné, the Marquis de Dangeau and the Duc de Saint Simon left accounts which, even allowing for their partisan attitudes, describe the mechanisms, ceremonies, intrigues and dynamism of the court in unsurpassed detail. It is clear, however, that the social structure and values which the court epitomised were emphatically traditional. Great prelates were received and honoured in accordance with the dignity due to the First Estate, but otherwise it was the aristocracy and nobility, within which there were gradations of rank and status, who constituted the bulk of the courtiers. Versailles, in short, testified to a king whose social values were rooted in conservatism and tradition, as were his views on monarchy.

2

LOUIS XIV AND THE GOVERNMENT OF FRANCE

The governmental history of Louis XIV's reign is customarily divided into two parts: 1643 to 1661 when Mazarin was chief minister, and 1661 to 1715 when Louis XIV ruled personally. This demarcation possesses a certain logic, but we should perceive the 'personal reign' as an extension or development of the first period, not as a reaction against it.

The Period 1643 to 1661

The essential context to these years is one of warfare. In 1635, when Cardinal Richelieu was chief minister, France formally entered the Thirty Years War (1618–48) by opening hostilities with Spain.[1] The financial cost of war placed intense pressure on the French government, which responded by creating more and heavier taxes and by a proliferation of extraordinary measures to raise money (notably the creation and sale of offices, forced loans and manipulation of the currency). These multiplying fiscal demands, especially when they were imposed at times of socio-economic distress, were responsible for much of the unrest of the 1630s and 1640s. In 1635 widespread revolt broke out in Guyenne, in 1636 and 1637 there were risings around Saintonge and Périgord, and in 1639 began the most serious revolt of the decade, that of the 'nu-pieds' of Normandy. The government responded by a mixture of coercion and concession, but social protest and conflict remained endemic throughout the 1640s, reaching another climax between 1648 and 1653 when the 'Fronde' rebellions all but brought the regime to its knees.

From 1643 until 1651, when Louis XIV's majority was reached, the government was headed by his mother Anne of Austria as Regent of France, with Cardinal Mazarin as chief minister.[2] In view of the importance of Mazarin in the lives both of the regent and of Louis XIV (to whom the cardinal was godfather), a brief glance at his origins and earlier career will be of help.

Cardinal Jules Mazarin (1602–61)

By birth, upbringing and temperament he was a Roman. He was born near that city in 1602 (he was baptised Giulio Mazzarini, but later gallicised his name as Jules Mazarin), son of a father of Sicilian origins who served in the household of a prominent Roman noble family: the Colonnas. Giulio had a fine education at the Jesuit college in Rome and at the University of Alcalá in Spain. He excelled as a student, but in 1624, after his university studies, was appointed captain in the papal army (thanks to the patronage of the Colonna family). Within a few years he had moved into the diplomatic service of the papacy, his first posting being to Milan in 1628. The move which proved pivotal in the history of his career came, however, in 1630 when he was sent on mission to France.

At this time the governments of France, Spain and the Holy Roman Empire were locked in dispute over who should succeed to the strategically important north Italian duchy of Mantua, whose territories included the great fortress at Casale. The former duke had died in December 1627; the French Duc de Nevers had the best claim to succeed him, but in view of the military significance of Mantua the Austrian and Spanish Habsburgs presented their own candidate. Although no formal war was declared, between 1628 and 1631 fierce fighting took place between the forces of the French and the Habsburg powers for control of the territory. The papacy was attempting to mediate a settlement, and Mazarin was sent to France both to seek clarification of the French position, and to encourage a peace settlement. Mazarin met and negotiated with Louis XIII's chief minister, Cardinal Richelieu. Each was profoundly impressed by the other: Mazarin judged Richelieu – seventeen years his senior – much the most gifted statesman he had ever encountered, while the Frenchman saw in the young papal diplomat an extraordinary talent. After much diplomatic and military manœuvring, in which Mazarin was prominent, the Mantuan Succession was settled in France's favour by the Treaty of Cherasco (1631).

In 1632 Mazarin was back in Rome where he cultivated the patronage of another great family, the Barberinis; he acquired the protection of Cardinal Antonio Barberini, nephew of Pope Urban VIII. It was through Antonio's good offices that in 1634 Mazarin secured the posting which he most coveted: that of papal nuncio (ambassador) to the court of France. Once in Paris he renewed his contacts with Richelieu; and although he failed to prevent the French declaration of war on Spain in 1635, the mutual admiration between the two men grew apace. He was recalled to Rome in 1636, where he sought to represent the French interest against powerful pro-Spanish factions. In appreciation of his efforts, Louis XIII in 1638 proposed that he be made a cardinal (Mazarin had prepared for the priesthood, although he was never ordained), and in 1639 granted him letters of naturalisation by which he became legally French. Mazarin could do little against the pro-Habsburg circle which surrounded the pope; in 1640 he left Rome for the last time and entered the service of Cardinal Richelieu.

Richelieu regarded his recruitment as a major coup, so highly did he prize Mazarin's abilities. His own health was failing, and he was having to give thought to the future. Mazarin became his right-hand man both with respect to his private affairs and to the government of the kingdom. Richelieu persuaded Louis XIII to allow Mazarin into his immediate circle of advisers, and secured the cardinal's hat for his new protégé in 1641. Mazarin's meteoric political rise continued. As Richelieu lay dying in 1642 he recommended to Louis XIII that Mazarin be next chief minister, and when Louis XIII died the following year, Mazarin retained his position and joined the Council of Regency headed by Anne of Austria. His relations with the queen mother, whom he had met on his earlier visits to France, were extremely close, and gave rise to malicious gossip; and the paternal affections which he displayed towards the young Louis XIV further caused tongues to wag. Anne relied on Mazarin heavily, and took no important decisions without consulting him first.

Powerful dynasties related to the Bourbons through kinship – the Orléans, Condé and Vendôme families – objected to Mazarin's status, and pressed for a form of government wherein the crown would turn

to them and their peers for its advisers. In 1643 the Duc de Beau-
fort (a Vendôme) attempted to overthrow Mazarin. Anne of Austria
had him arrested and imprisoned, but in the face of such manifest
hostility grasped the fact that she and Mazarin must stand together
if their authority were to be secured. The Council of Regency which
governed on behalf of Louis XIV was small. In addition to Anne of
Austria and Mazarin it included the king's uncle Gaston, Duc d'Orléans (his inclusion was a political necessity), the Chancellor Pierre
Séguier, and Léon Bouthillier, Comte de Chavigny. Two interlocking
imperatives faced the council: to pursue war to a successful conclusion, and to raise the necessary money while at the same time grap-
pling with social unrest. As regards war, diplomatic moves for peace
were afoot in 1643, although formal negotiations did not begin until
December 1644; they were held in Westphalia, and were long and
arduous. The French representatives led by Claude de Mesmes,
Comte d'Avaux, and Abel Servien, followed Mazarin's instructions
from Paris. His chief priority was to continue Richelieu's policy:
undermine the power of the Habsburgs, especially the Spanish
branch. When the Peace of Westphalia was signed in 1648,[3] one
welcome outcome from the French point of view was its confirmation
of the autonomy of the states of the Holy Roman Empire, the constitutional position of the Habsburg emperor remaining weak. It also
included territorial gains for France, which acquired most of Alsace
and bridgeheads across the Rhine at Breisach and Phillipsburg. On
the other hand, although no settlement was reached between France
and Spain, the latter did make peace with its other principal enemy,
the Dutch Republic, and could now concentrate on the war with
France. The Franco-Spanish conflict was to last another eleven years,
until the Peace of the Pyrenees (1659).

The Frondes

The imminence of peace at Westphalia did not prevent that widespread
violence and resistance to the regency known as the Frondes.[4] These,
the most serious uprisings in France between the sixteenth-century
Wars of Religion and the Revolution, formed part of a much wider
process of rebellion, civil war and – in the case of England – revolution, which swept across much of Europe in the 1640s and 1650s.
Britain and Ireland, Spain, Portugal, Germany, Italy, the Ukraine and

other parts of Europe were caught up, like France, in a deluge of civil
conflict which, to many historians, constituted the 'general crisis' of the
seventeenth century.[5] The Frondes lasted five years and involved all
sections of society: *parlementaires*, *officiers*, nobles, Princes of the Blood,
clergy, urban and rural masses. The risings may be organised into three
classes: the Fronde of the *parlements* (led by the Parlement of Paris)
from 1648 to 1649, the Fronde of the princes from 1649 to 1652, and
the Fronde of the provinces which lasted until 1653.

The Frondes arose from a compound of popular hostility to fiscal
exploitation by the government, opposition by the *parlements* to fiscal
and other bodies of legislation which they deemed 'unconstitutional',
resistance by the *parlements* to the crown's attempts to impose
constraints on their powers, the use made by the government of extraordinary commissioners and intendants[6] to override the authority of
legal and financial bodies in the provinces, and the 'tyrannical' powers
ostensibly wielded by Mazarin in the name of the king. To many Frondeurs all the problems were encapsulated in Mazarin himself.[7] From
1648 onwards he was vilified from Parisian pulpits, lampooned in the
streets, and censured by the Parlement of Paris. Thousands of
pamphlets were published – 'Mazarinades' – denouncing him as a
Machiavellian Italian adventurer who had enriched himself at the
expense of the French state. They reviled his character, his 'sinister'
influence over the queen mother and the young king, and accused
him of monstrous 'crimes' including that of tyranny.[8] So hazardous
did his position become that in February 1651 Mazarin had to flee
the country; and although the king recalled him in December, the
Parlement declared Mazarin an outlaw and put a price on his head.
He rejoined the safety of the royal court in January 1652, but in
August felt it prudent once more to go into self-imposed exile. It was
only when the Parisian Fronde had abated by the end of the year
that Mazarin felt able to return.

The outbreak of the Parisian Fronde may be taken up in the early
weeks of 1648 when there occurred a dispute between the Parlement
of Paris and the crown over the *paulette*. This was an annual sum
which *officiers* paid to the government in order to retain their offices
as private property. In theory the crown could cancel the *paulette*,
whereupon all offices would revert to the king. In practice, French
governments were so dependent on the money raised by the *paulette*
that they regarded it as a form of taxation; periodically the government formally renewed the *paulette*, but also revised the rates at which

it was paid. In April 1648 the regency announced that *officiers* would continue to pay *paulette* (and thus retain *de facto* ownership of their offices), but that, in view of the grave financial situation, the government intended withholding four years' salary from the majority of *officiers*. Since this added to a long list of recent financial artifices by the government, delegates from the Parlement of Paris and other sovereign courts gathered in Paris at the Chambre Saint Louis in June 1648 to draft a formal list of grievances. The text of twenty-seven articles which they issued called for the suppression of the intendants and all special commissioners, a prohibition on the creation of new offices, and a cessation of royal intervention in the normal proceedings of law courts. Shortly afterwards the Parlement of Paris demanded that the crown cancel all of its contracts with tax farmers, and reduce the *taille* – the principal direct tax – by a quarter. The *parlementaires* and their allies were seeking a restoration of what they considered time-honoured procedures in legislation, administration, law and taxation. However, in the precarious financial and international circumstances of 1648 the regent dared not concede reform. She and Mazarin feared that they would not be able to keep a process of financial, legal and constitutional change under control; it would expose them to further constitutional demands which could seriously weaken the crown. The regency did make tactical concessions in the summer of 1648: it dismissed the Surintendant des Finances, Particelli d'Emery, agreed to recall most commissioners and intendants, and reduced the *taille* by 12 per cent. When the Parlement of Paris continued to press its demands, Anne of Austria ordered the arrest of several of its leading members on 26 August 1648. This heavy-handed action provoked riots in Paris which rapidly spread to other parts of France. Throughout the autumn and winter Paris suffered chronic unrest even though Anne ordered the release of the imprisoned *parlementaires*. In January 1649 the royal family left Paris and ordered royal troops to reduce the city to obedience. Paris was placed under siege. The Parlement, reluctant to be implicated in open rebellion, especially after news arrived of the execution of Charles I of England, entered into negotiations with the regency. In March 1649 the Peace of Rueil was signed by which the crown promised to abide by many of the demands of the Chambre Saint Louis and the Parlement agreed to end opposition.

The parlementary Fronde had won the support of many aristocrats, including Princes of the Blood. To them, Mazarin was a particular

object of loathing. Figures such as Gaston d'Orléans (who in 1651
withdrew from the Council of Regency), the Duc de Longueville and
the Prince de Conti openly sympathised with the Fronde. One of the
leading lights in aristocratic resistance to the regency was Jean-
François-Paul de Gondi, later Cardinal de Retz (1652). This master-
intriguer in January 1649 drew prominent aristocrats into an oath of
union against Mazarin. When Gondi heard of the Peace of Rueil he
angrily denounced the 'cowardice' of the Parlement of Paris and
continued marshalling the 'Fronde of the princes'. His major coup
was to persuade the Duc de Condé to join. Hitherto Condé had
remained loyal to the crown (it was he who besieged Paris early in
1649), and his transfer into the Frondeur camp was a heavy blow
against the regency. Meanwhile, the troubles had spread to the
provinces: in 1649 there were revolts in Normandy, Anjou, Poitou,
Bordeaux and Aix. In January 1650 Anne of Austria decided on
resolute action: she ordered the arrest of three leading princes,
Condé, Conti and Longueville. Paris once again rose up, and there
were further revolts in Burgundy and Normandy where Condé and
Longueville respectively were governors. In August a royal army,
accompanied by Anne of Austria and Louis XIV, besieged Bordeaux,
which surrendered to the royal forces; but this was a rare success for
the regency in a year which also saw Spanish incursions across the
northern frontier.

The early weeks of 1651 proved exceedingly dangerous to the
crown. In January, Gondi and other aristocrats formed an alliance
with representatives from the Parlement of Paris. This powerful 'union
of the Frondes' had the potential to impose its will on the crown and
extract political and constitutional reform from the regency. The
union's immediate objectives were the release of the imprisoned
princes and the overthrow of Mazarin. On the night of 6–7 February
Mazarin, aware of the precariousness of his position, fled Paris and
went to Germany, releasing Condé, Conti and Longueville *en route*;
the three princes returned to Paris in triumphant procession. From
this stage onwards, however, the 'union of the Frondes' began to disin-
tegrate. The princes and other aristocrats displayed little natural unity.
They were prone to personality conflicts, disputes over arcane questions of precedence, they quarrelled over the central and provincial
political offices which they intended distributing among themselves
once the regency was brought to heel, but were far from unanimous
in their views on the future of monarchy and government in France.

Likewise their relations with the Parlement of Paris were fractious, for most *parlementaires* were as suspicious of the political ambitions of great aristocrats as they were hostile to Mazarin. The presence of the detested Mazarin had been the necessary magnetic force keeping the union of the Frondes intact. His departure from the country released centrifugal forces within the union of the two Frondes, and within the Fronde of the princes. The declaration of Louis XIV's majority on 7 September 1651 placed further pressure on the Frondeurs: the regency had ended, and the pretence that resistance to royal policy did not imply rebellion against the king was now untenable.

Condé and Gaston d'Orléans nevertheless opted to continue fighting against the crown. Condé mustered forces in southern France and sought help from the Spanish. The crown might have isolated him had it not been for the return of Mazarin in December 1651. His presence once more drove aristocratic and parlementary Frondeurs into alliance. In 1652 a savage war broke out around Paris as crown and Frondeurs fought for control of the city and region. This was a particularly brutal phase of fighting. Condé had returned north with his army; both he and the royal forces hired German mercenaries demobilised after the Peace of Westphalia. These tough, battle-hardened troops wreaked havoc indiscriminately. Farms and villages were looted and destroyed, crops and livestock were stolen, atrocities against the civilian population were committed, and as people fled into Paris for safety they placed further strains on the dwindling resources of the overcrowded city. Meanwhile the Parlement admitted the troops of Condé and Orléans into the suburbs and agreed to hold discussions with the princes as to the possibility of some form of 'provisional government'. On 4 July an assembly of *parlementaires* and representatives of the different 'quarters' of Paris met in the Hôtel de Ville to discuss plans. Seeking to intimidate them, Condé brought troops into the city. Discipline broke down; shooting began; a mob, in which Condé's troops were heavily implicated, attacked and set fire to the Hôtel de Ville where over thirty of the assembly were killed; some two hundred rioters also perished in the violence. The affair ruined the reputation of Condé and of the Fronde of the princes; within Paris he and his co-Frondeurs were now seen as self-seekers, ruthlessly pursuing their own ambitions. When Mazarin left France for the second time in August 1652, the way was open for the Parlement of Paris to seek reconciliation with the king. Condé's army began to desert in droves; he too left the country and offered his services to the Spanish. In October 1652 Louis XIV made a formal entry into his capital; the Fronde in Paris was finished. Several *parlementaires* were banished, Louis forbade the Parlement from meddling in affairs of state, and Condé's property was declared forfeit. Mazarin returned in 1653. Frondeur movements continued in the provinces, but with the ending of violence in Paris they petered out in 1653, the last being that in Bordeaux.

The Significance of the Frondes

Modern historians of these turbulent years are generally agreed that, however dangerous they appeared at the time, there was no real prospect that the Frondes would turn into an 'English Revolution'. Although it is possible to identify common factors in their origins, the English civil war and Frondes developed along very different lines. There was no 'Cromwell' or 'Fairfax' in France, no 'alternative' ideology comparable to Puritanism (the French Protestants remained overwhelmingly royalist during the Frondes), no 'Scotland' or 'Ireland' to complicate matters, and no desire to overturn monarchy.[9] The Frondeurs were riven by divisions. The Parlement of Paris contained radical and conservative minorities whose extremism forced the majority to seek a middle way which would hold the Parlement together. The political and constitutional demands which the Parlement presented to the government during the Frondes, were formulated with an eye to the unity of the Parlement of Paris as much as to the 'reform' of the state.[10] The Chambre Saint Louis, which appeared to presage a united front of sovereign courts, proved short-lived. The Parlement of Paris failed to create a community of interest with the other courts or provincial *parlements*, which were left to fight their own battles with the crown. Between the Parlement of Paris and the city council there were mutual suspicions; and 'middle class' elements in the city feared the social breakdown which mass violence threatened. The aristocracy was notoriously fragmentary. The Condéan faction had little time for Gondi and his associates; relations between Orléans and Gondi blew hot and cold; and the conduct of many aristocratic Frondeurs appeared to be governed by little other than self-interest. Many aristocrats moved between factions, or even changed between royalist and Frondeur camps as circumstances required; the Vicomte de Turenne, for example, changed sides several times during the Frondes. The provincial Frondes were equally particularist. Many parts of the country stood apart from the Frondes. Brittany, Gascony, Languedoc, Dauphiné and central parts of France remained either neutral or loyal to the crown, as did numerous provincial cities, including Marseille and Lyon. The Frondes in Provence, Normandy, Alsace and Burgundy were certainly influenced by events in Paris (questions of the 'rights' of provincial assemblies and law courts, and of the fiscal demands of the crown played their part; also, princes such as Condé and Longueville could raise rebellion in the provinces of which they were governors), but owed even more to local struggles for power.[11] The one provincial Fronde which appeared to display novel features was that of Bordeaux, where the 'Ormée' populist rising of 1650 (led in the main by artisans) took control of the city, and eventually ousted the Parlement of Bordeaux. It set up a new governing council of 500 with an executive committee of thirty. The targets of the Ormistes were not the crown and central government, but local nobles, wealthy merchants and *parlementaires* whom they considered their exploiters. The Spanish sent money and troops to support the Ormée, and in 1653 emissaries came from England to discuss aid. By this time, however, the government was reimposing its authority throughout the country and the Bordeaux Fronde collapsed.

On all sides, therefore, the Frondes were marked by factionalism, division, disunity of purpose, and to this extent we may conclude that the crown was bound to 'win' and the Frondes 'fail'. But is such a straightforward conclusion justified? There is no question that Frondeurs did have genuine grievances which could not be obscured by the violence and confusion of these years; warfare indubitably had driven the regency to policies, especially fiscal, which, to put it mildly, were questionable. This the government tacitly acknowledged and, as later passages of this book will show, took steps to address the problem. Mazarin, for example, was not replaced as chief minister when he died in 1661, and later in the 1660s Louis's government undertook to reform the taxation system, reduce governmental expenditure, regularise procedures for creating and implementing policy, clarify relations between crown, *parlements*, provincial estates and other legal bodies. The intendants were reintroduced, but were subjected to close scrutiny by the government to ensure that they cooperated with, rather than antagonised, provincial social and political elites. No 'white terror' was launched by the government against former Frondeurs. Condé and other aristocratic Frondeurs eventually were reconciled to the king, who during his personal reign regarded the restoration of harmonious relations between crown and aristocracy as one of his highest priorities. The Frondes, then, may have collapsed in 1653, but they were not ignored by the government; in both positive and negative respects they influenced the personal reign of Louis XIV.

From the End of the Frondes to the Death of Mazarin

In the short run, the government still faced a formidable range of problems in the immediate aftermath of the Frondes. Financial difficulties remained acute, and when in 1655 the Parlement of Paris sought to delay the registration of financial edicts which Mazarin had prepared, Louis XIV went in person to the Parlement on 13 April, and in a trenchant display of royal authority instructed that body to proceed immediately to registration. It was on this somewhat histrionic occasion that Louis is reputed to have proclaimed that 'l'Etat, c'est moi!' In his approach to government, especially that of the financial management of the affairs of the kingdom, Mazarin followed Richelieu's example of working through favoured families and their 'clients' or 'creatures'. The most important of these auxiliaries was the Fouquet family. In 1653 Nicolas Fouquet was appointed Surintendant des Finances, but Mazarin also used his influence to advance Nicolas's brothers: in 1659 François was appointed Archbishop of Narbonne and Louis was made Bishop of Agde; Gilles and Yves Fouquet went on respectively to careers in the army and diplomacy, while the Abbé Basile Fouquet served Mazarin as an administrative assistant. One of the features of Richelieu's ministry which most frustrated the great aristocracy was his use of 'creature' families; it was a tradition which Mazarin preserved. However, as will shortly be seen, it was one with which Louis dispensed in 1661, and Nicolas Fouquet was to be the first prominent victim of the illusion that the king was not serious in his intent.

Meanwhile Louis's coronation in 1654 affirmed his monarchic powers, and throughout the remainder of the decade Mazarin concentrated on preparing him to govern personally. The cardinal met the king almost every day to discuss politics and government. Mazarin took him into council meetings, explained their functions and, in brief,

taught him how to govern a modern state. Louis's instruction from
Mazarin gave him to understand that in order to rule a kingdom which
was large and diverse in geography, languages, religion, legal customs,
economic potential and regional loyalties, it would be necessary to
employ not just formal instruments of law and administration, but skills
of manipulation, negotiation and compromise with provincial elites and
institutions; and he would have to exercise political patronage judi-
ciously. On a personal level Louis came to appreciate that in addition
to acquiring a comportment befitting a king, he would have to develop
the qualities of a good administrator: vigour, command of detail, a
readiness to receive advice, but then a willingness to take a decision
clearly and unhesitatingly. His political education under the guidance
of Mazarin persuaded him that whatever his theoretical powers as king
of France, the exercise of those powers would be conditioned by a host
of factors over which he might have little control. He must adopt an
approach to government which, however consistent in its underlying
principles, was flexible in their execution.

To Louis's training in government Mazarin added experience of
war. On several occasions the king accompanied Mazarin and the
Maréchal de Turenne on campaigns against the Spanish. In 1653
Mazarin persuaded Anne of Austria to consent to Louis observing the
capture of Mouzon and Sainte-Menehould; in 1657 Louis was present
at the fall of Montmédy, and in 1658 he and Mazarin joined the army
after it took Dunkirk (on this occasion Louis fell gravely ill, and came
close to death). By the time he was in his early twenties, Louis XIV
knew a great deal about warfare as well as government and the
management of people. The war against Spain – fought mainly in
Flanders, the Franco-Spanish border, and Italy – was turning in favour
of France, whose forces were strengthened in 1657 when Mazarin
secured an alliance with England and in 1658 with several German
states (France joined the League of the Rhine to curb the influence
of the new Holy Roman Emperor, Leopold I). Nevertheless, serious
social unrest broke out again in Normandy (1658), and in Languedoc
and Provence (from 1656 to 1659). Spain too was riven with socio-
political conflict, and both governments were anxious for peace. After
laborious negotiations the Peace of the Pyrenees was signed in
November 1659. France secured yet more territorial gains in the
north (Artois, Flanders, Hainaut and Luxembourg) and in the south,
where Roussillon and Cerdagne were annexed; a marriage was agreed
between Louis XIV and Maria Teresa, daughter of Philip IV of Spain

(the marriage took place in 1660). For the first time in twenty-five years France was at peace; the government now had an opportunity to undertake the urgent task of economic reconstruction and the restoration of social stability.

For his services to the crown Mazarin was made a peer of the realm, but by early 1661 his health was failing. He nevertheless continued to give political counsel to the king, including suggestions as to future ministers whom Louis might employ; but it was clear that his life was approaching its end. He died 9 March 1661. His career had been truly remarkable. An Italian by birth, he had reached the height of political power in France. During his eighteen years as chief minister he had, in all essentials, continued the policies of Cardinal Richelieu, and had done so against sustained and sometimes violent opposition. In retrospect, he appears an outstanding if controversial servant of the French crown. He also exploited his situation so as to enrich himself and his family: it is thought that, by the time he died, he had amassed the largest private fortune in the history of pre-Revolutionary France. He understood and pursued the interests of the crown, but also became convinced of the need for personal government by the king. He was often accused of 'Machiavellianism' by his critics, but he needed no instruction from the writings of his fellow-countryman as to the necessity of a monarch who personally governed. Hard experience taught him that French aristocrats and bodies such as the *parlements*, venerable though they were, offered no positive alternatives to personal monarchic rule. When, on 10 March 1661, there occurred the famous encounter between Louis XIV and the Archbishop of Rouen, who asked to whom he and others should now go for instructions, and Louis replied, 'A moi, Monsieur l'archevêque!', the king acted entirely in accordance with Mazarin's wishes.

The Personal Reign, 1661 to 1715

a) *Central Government*

How did Louis govern and what instruments did he have at his disposal? The body through which he formed policy was known usually as the Conseil d'en Haut, a compact body whose members attended at the king's invitation, not as of right. Louis usually presided over its meetings, which were held at least twice a week. This council discussed policy on every aspect of government; but when it had investigated a matter and advised the king, Louis alone decided policy. In March 1661 it included only three in addition to the king. Hugues de Lionne was an expert on international relations, and in 1663 was made Secretary of State for Foreign Affairs. Michel le Tellier, a long-time supporter of the crown, had stood by Mazarin during the Frondes and was Secretary of State for War. Nicolas Fouquet was Surintendant des Finances. He had been appointed to this position jointly with Abel Servien in 1653, but when the latter died in 1659 Fouquet remained sole Surintendant. Having admitted him to the Conseil d'en Haut, Louis quickly came to suspect him of aspiring to become the next 'Richelieu' or 'Mazarin'. This was utterly at variance with Louis's resolve to govern personally. He concluded that it was not sufficient simply to dismiss Fouquet; it was necessary to provide a public and unambiguous statement that the era of chief ministers was over by utterly destroying the Surintendant. One of Fouquet's chief assistants, Jean-Baptiste Colbert, a former protégé of Mazarin, was instructed by Louis to prepare grounds for charges against Fouquet. Colbert, who also had ambitions to rise in royal service, did so, and in September 1661 Fouquet was arrested and accused of treason. After a lengthy and dramatic trial he was imprisoned for life.[12] Colbert replaced Fouquet in the Conseil d'en Haut. Throughout the rest of Louis's reign the council remained small, normally numbering only the king plus four members. Louis preferred continuity and stability in this, the most important of his councils. Its membership rarely changed and came from a small number of families, especially those of Le Tellier, Colbert and Phélypeaux. By contrast, Louis excluded from the Conseil d'en Haut members of the royal family, great aristocrats, prelates, and the Chancellor of France. Louis's closest advisers had no political power bases beyond service to himself. Their fidelity was rewarded with wealth and noble titles, but, with the example of Fouquet in mind, they carefully avoided any suggestion that their ambitions ran beyond conformity to the royal will.

Louis personally presided over two more councils: the Conseil des Dépêches and the Conseil des Finances. The former had emerged in the early seventeenth century and was an administrative not advisory council dealing with internal affairs. Louis used it to put into effect the domestic policies upon which he had decided in the Conseil d'en Haut. Its membership usually comprised the chancellor, the four secretaries of state (each responsible for administering one-quarter of the kingdom), and any others whom the king invited when necessary. A

Conseil des Finances had existed in the 1560s, and had been reintroduced in 1615 and again in 1630. On the fall of Fouquet, Louis
suppressed the Surintendance des Finances and revived the council
under his own chairmanship. It assessed the amount of taxation to be
raised each year, oversaw its collection, kept accounts of income and
expenditure, and even acted as a court of justice on financial matters.
The membership of the Conseil des Finances was again usually only
four or five in addition to the king. The key figure until his death in
1683 was Colbert, who was appointed Contrôleur Général des Finances
in 1665. When we bear in mind that the Conseil d'en Haut met at
least twice a week (and often three or four times), the Conseil des
Dépêches once a week, and the Conseil des Finances twice a week, it
is evident that Louis devoted much time to committee work. To these
councils should be added the numerous private meetings between
Louis and his ministers, and the time which he devoted to studying
governmental papers (Colbert in particular was an inveterate writer of
long and detailed reports and proposals). Louis was a diligent and
hard-working monarch who, as the years went by, developed into an
extremely well-informed and experienced head of state. Among his
contemporaries, no monarch excelled him in the intimacy with which
he came to know the problems and techniques of government. The
so-called 'absolutism' of Louis XIV doubtless owed much to profound
historical forces, but it was also a product of his personal commitment
to the routine and detail of government and administration.

Alongside the councils over which the king presided were others
which he did not attend, but whose work was crucial to central government. They included the Conseil de Commerce, which had first existed
in 1602 but was disbanded in 1604. Colbert revived it in 1664 as the
instrument through which he sought to execute much of the king's
economic policy. It was disbanded in the mid-1670s, to be restored
again in 1700. Another was the Conseil des Parties, a judicial body
which had emerged in the sixteenth century and was staffed by lawyers,
chief of whom were the *conseillers d'état*; the more junior figures were
maîtres des requêtes. If any council displayed features of a modern
bureaucracy it was this. It helped to draft much legislation, acted as a
court of appeal, prepared briefs for cases involving the crown, and its
personnel were used by the crown when it selected commissioners to
go on missions into the provinces. Later the question of the intendants
will be discussed; many of these, too, were chosen from the Conseil
des Parties. To be a *conseiller d'état* was a pinnacle of the legal profes-

sion; their number had varied in the sixteenth and seventeenth centuries, but was fixed at thirty-three in 1673.

Here, in brief, was the structure of central government during the personal reign; but how should we interpret it? Does it constitute a 'royal revolution',[13] a monarchy committed to 'modernisation', 'absolutism', and 'bureaucratisation'?[14] There is a problem of terminology here, for in twentieth-century historiography the word 'revolution' implies fundamental political and constitutional change. In the seventeenth century, however, 'revolution' was not understood in that sense. It was an astronomical term – as in 'the revolutions of the planets' – which, as a political metaphor, could imply a return to earlier conditions (as a planet revolves through its orbit and resumes its former position). Nevertheless, 'revolution' was also being used as a synonym for 'sedition', and thereby carried an implication of violent change.[15] Many modern French historians have upheld the 'revolution' thesis in the twentieth-century sense of the term. It was advanced by Lavisse in his classic work on Louis XIV and has been reaffirmed by more recent French scholarship.[16] Non-French historians have often been less convinced. The British historian Roger Mettam, and others, have preferred to interpret Louis's personal government in terms of 'reorganisation' rather than 'revolution'.[17] This question will be examined at greater length in the concluding discussion to this book, but at this juncture the point can be made that the tenor of Louis XIV's education, his formation as king, and the values expressed in his *Mémoires* suggest that, far from possessing progressive ideas on monarchy and government, and far from aspiring to lay the foundations of a 'bureaucratic' state which would mature in the distant future, Louis perceived himself to be restoring a monarchic government which was no longer forced by circumstance to have recourse to a chief minister. This kind of notion made sense in a society which was reverential towards the past and tended to judge the present in the light of the past. Louis saw himself fulfilling the logic of the Regency and of the reign of his father by reverting to personal government; we might therefore say that he instigated a 'royal revolution' in a seventeenth-century sense, but not that of the twentieth century. The central councils were inherited by Louis, he did not create them; and even the exclusion of the royal family, great aristocrats and prelates from these councils does not necessarily imply radical 'modernisation'. Such figures still had regular access to the king at court, where they also met ministers and secretaries of state. It was in the nature of court life that the king, ministers and courtiers mingled and conversed. It is not necessary to conclude that under no circumstances did the king discuss political matters with, or receive political advice from, people other than those in the Conseil d'en Haut. Moreover, great aristocrats continued to exercise other functions, such as governorships of the provinces and ambassadorships (not to mention their monopoly of command of the royal armies), which Louis himself continued to recognise as appropriate only to the social elites.[18]

The twentieth-century 'revolution' thesis also rests upon the proposition that Louis XIV consciously appointed ministers and secretaries of state from relatively humble backgrounds. Whatever its merit, this argument should be advanced only with qualifications. The point can be made by taking the three principal families upon which Louis XIV drew for his advisers and ministers: the Le Telliers, Colberts and Phélypeaux. The Le Telliers had been members of the *noblesse de robe* (that is, nobility exercising mainly legal and administrative functions in great law courts and governmental councils) since the late sixteenth century. Michel le Tellier (1603–85), who served Louis XIV as Secretary of State for War from 1643 to 1677, as a young man had been a lawyer in the Cour des Aides, then a *conseiller d'état*, and later an intendant attached to the army. He was made a marquis in 1656 (a marquis was surpassed only by duke and prince in the noble hierarchy), and both his son François-Michel le Tellier, Marquis de Louvois (1641–91), and his grandson Louis-François-Marie le Tellier de Barbézieux (1668–1701), followed him at the department of war.

The Colberts were distantly related by marriage to the Le Telliers, and indeed Jean-Baptiste Colbert was indebted to Michel le Tellier for the progress of his early career. The Colberts were wealthy merchants and bankers from Rheims who also had financial and political connections in Paris. Colbert's cousin, Jean-Baptiste Colbert de Saint-Pouange, married Michel le Tellier's sister in 1628, and later served in the war office under Le Tellier. It was Saint-Pouange who used his influence to find Jean-Baptiste Colbert a post, first in the war office, then as secretary to Le Tellier. From there Colbert moved into the service of Mazarin, who later recommended him to Louis XIV. Colbert was appointed to several important charges by the king, most notably those of Surintendant des Bâtiments (1664), Contrôleur Général des Finances (1665), and Secretary of State for the Navy (1669). In this last post he was succeeded by his son, the Marquis de Seignelay. Meanwhile Colbert's brother, the Marquis de

Croissy and Croissy's son, the Marquis de Torcy, were Secretaries of State for Foreign Affairs. In 1708 another of Colbert's nephews, Nicolas Desmarets, joined the Conseil d'en Haut. The Colberts were wealthy, ambitious commoners when they entered royal service, but were ennobled by the king, again with the title of 'marquis'.

Two branches of the Phélypeaux family were prominent in royal service. The senior line was represented by Louis Phélypeaux de la Vrillière (1599–1681), his son, the Marquis de Châteauneuf and grandson, the Marquis de la Vrillière, all of whom were Secretaries of State for Protestant Affairs and the Pays d'Etats. The junior line was represented by Louis Phélypeaux, Comte de Pontchartrain (1643–1727) and his son, the Comte de Maurepas, both of whom were Secretaries of State for the Navy. The Phélypeaux had been noble since the sixteenth century, and although their title of 'comte' came below that of marquis in the noble hierarchy, they were a family of considerable social distinction.

This brief glance at the three families indicates that, while Louis did not invite princes and dukes into his innermost councils, he confirmed the 'noble' character of government either by choosing his closest advisers from the nobility, or by conferring appropriate titles upon them. The Colberts, Le Telliers and Phélypeaux became exceedingly wealthy, and as they married into aristocratic dynasties (three of Colbert's daughters married dukes) they gradually added social distinction to their titles and prosperity. Louis ensured that those who helped him to govern were raised into the upper ranks of the nobility, and thereby affirmed that government was an aristocratic activity. Nevertheless, critics of the king (among whom the Duc de Saint Simon is the best-known; his memoirs amount to a sustained, if partisan, criticism of the latter part of the reign), objected that in spite of their noble titles, Louis's ministers still came from unsuitable backgrounds: they might have been noble in law, but they were not 'gentilshommes'. In seventeenth-century France, social prestige was governed not only by the possession of a noble title, but by the length of time the title had been held. 'Gentilshommes' were nobles of long lineage who often claimed that their titles originally came from acts of military valour. Titles acquired more recently, including those received through political service to the crown, did not confer this quality of 'gentilhommerie'. Even this argument, however, is of limited validity in sustaining the charge that Louis's ministers came from inferior stock. By custom a family acquired the status of 'gentilhomme' after three generations of nobility; with the passage of time in what proved to be the longest reign in European history, these three families naturally entered the ranks of the 'gentilshommes'.

b) Provincial Government

It was one thing for Louis XIV to rearrange central government, but the provinces posed intricate problems for they displayed wide variety in their patterns of government and administration. We may visualise a series of transparent maps of France superimposed upon each other: first a map of the provinces, on to which might go a fiscal map showing the main areas upon which taxation was based (*généralités* subdivided into *élections*), then a map of the principal judicial divisions of the *parlements* and lesser courts, and perhaps an ecclesiastical map showing the dioceses. To modern eyes, the result of this process of superimposition would appear confusing in the extreme; and it can be added in passing that the revolutionaries of 1789 also found the situation intolerable, one of their chief priorities being to simplify the map and harmonise the areas of administration, justice, taxation and the Catholic dioceses. In the seventeenth century, however, it was accepted that, in a kingdom which had grown piecemeal, different aspects of government and administration should correspond to different geographical areas. Colbert's attempts to correct some of the more extreme anomalies will be discussed in a later chapter; but Louis XIV's government adhered to the *ancien régime* tradition of working within and manipulating the various strata of provincial government which it inherited. There was no question of Louis attempting as it were to anticipate '1789' by imposing wholesale change, for the overlapping functions and administrations of provincial government satisfied too many vested interests. The France of the 1660s contained a plethora of 'intermediate bodies': provincial assemblies, municipalities, law courts and a host of other institutions which had emerged in the Middle Ages and continued to exercise a variety of administrative, judicial and fiscal functions. Much royal policy and legislation had to be transmitted through these bodies, since the crown did not have a separate civil service at its disposal. The crown had to come to terms with provincial institutions, for without their cooperation effective government would have been impossible.

Before we examine some of these bodies, the question of their personnel should be considered. The phrase 'civil service' is out of place, for it carries modern connotations of salaried persons working for the state, and performing duties according to prescribed rules. Many of the people who held senior positions in provincial bodies dealing with law and finance were *officiers*; that is, they had bought the posts – offices – whose functions they fulfilled. Venality of office – the sale by the crown of offices in law and finance – went back to the fourteenth century, but became common in the sixteenth. It was formalised in 1522 when a special governmental bureau, the Recette des Parties Casuelles, was created to administer the sale of offices. In 1604, Henri IV introduced the *paulette* (named after Paulet, the financier who devised the plan): by this device, the holder of an office could pay an annual sum to the government and thereby retain the office as a hereditary possession, passing it from one generation to the next. The implications of venality of office were considerable. Because the profits of offices were high (large sums were made by *officiers* in the form of charges to the public through the exercise of legal and financial duties), they attracted intelligent, gifted people; *officiers* had to provide evidence of their competence before exercising their offices (by possessing, for example, a degree in law), or alternatively were empowered to appoint a qualified person to exercise it on their behalf. Because they effectively owned their offices, *officiers* also enjoyed a certain independence from the crown; and as the Frondes showed, this spirit could lead them into resistance against the government. Yet venality of office ultimately bound *officiers* to the crown. Families invested large amounts of money in offices, not only because of their financial returns, but because they were a means of social climbing. A family might begin by buying a relatively humble office, then over the next two or three generations acquire more senior offices, leading up to those in the great law courts which carried noble titles. The *noblesse de robe*, whose titles came through legal service to the crown, enjoyed the privileges of nobility and the social distinction which accompanied a noble title. The crown had the power to abolish offices if it wished and thereby could threaten *officiers* with social demotion as well as financial penalties; *officiers* might therefore be involved in social protest, but there were limits beyond which they would not go. They would never present to the crown a challenge which would place venality of office in jeopardy. From the crown's point of view venality was a financial necessity, but it also had drawbacks: financial pressure caused the crown to create too many *officiers* at the expense of efficiency (many *officiers* fulfilled their functions only for six or even three

months in the year, then handed over to another); venality greatly
complicated the crown's finances (redemption of offices was very
costly), it meant that the crown's direct control over *officiers* was only
partial, and it helped to underpin the mosaic-like character of provincial government. In the 1660s, Colbert attempted to reduce the
number of *officiers*, who by then numbered some 46,250: in 1664 he
addressed a memoir to the king calling for a diminution in their
numbers, and royal edicts of 1665 and 1669 used Colbert's ideas as
the basis for the redemption of offices by the crown. Nevertheless, the
system was integral to French government and administration, and
renewed warfare in and after the 1670s forced Louis XIV once again
to create and sell offices to bolster state finance.

Among the 'intermediate bodies' which conditioned the practice of
government, two categories deserve attention. First there were the
parlements which had the potential to assimilate and integrate the
provinces into the kingdom. The *parlements* were primarily law courts,
but they also possessed legislative functions. By far the most important body was the Parlement of Paris[19] whose jurisdiction extended
over about one-third of the country; it claimed to be the final court
of appeal. As the kingdom expanded during the fifteenth and
sixteenth centuries, other *parlements* were created by the crown at
Toulouse (1443), Grenoble (1453), Bordeaux (1462), Dijon (1477),
Rouen (1499), Aix (1501) and Rennes (1554). More were created in
the seventeenth century at Pau (1620), Metz (1633), Besançon (1676)
and Tournai (1686) in the interests of extending royal law. In theory,
these smaller, provincial *parlements* formed one body with the
Parlement of Paris which, in effect, acted as spokesman for all. Relations between the Parlement of Paris and the crown had long been
ambivalent, for the Parlement was the point at which royal and local
authority and interests intersected. Most of the activities of the
Parlement were purely judicial and of limited direct concern to the
crown, but there were two areas of dispute. One concerned the extent
to which the Parlement of Paris was indeed the final court of appeal.
The Parlement thereby considered itself guardian of the 'fundamental
laws' of the state, and within its rights in resisting actions from any
quarter, including the crown, which undermined those laws.[20] The
Parlement of Paris reinforced this argument by an appeal to history:
in its view there had been occasions during the French Wars of Religion when it, not a weakened monarchy, had saved France from disin-
tegration. Moreover, the Bourbons should not forget that at a critical

moment it was the Parlement's recognition of Henri IV's claim to the throne which saved the day for him. The Parlement also contended that during the Fronde it had been attempting to drive the crown back towards 'legitimate' policies from which the ministries of Riche-lieu and Mazarin had diverted it; that in no sense had it aspired to undermine legitimate royal authority, but had engaged in 'legitimate' resistance to the 'illegal' policies wished on the crown by the two cardinal-ministers. The second area of dispute arose from the Parlement's legislative functions. When the king created law, it was then drafted by the Chancery and sent to the Parlement of Paris (and any other *parlement* as necessary) for registration. Only when the law was registered by the Parlement did it come into force. Most legisla-tion was registered as a matter of course, but should the Parlement be faced with laws which, in its opinion, were of dubious validity, it was empowered to 'remonstrate': that is, refuse to register the laws, and send them back to the king with a request that he modify or even suspend them. The point at issue was this: was the power of remonstrance a right which the Parlement possessed and which the crown therefore must respect, or was it a privilege which the crown allowed it to exercise, but which the king could suspend whenever he wished? By tradition the Parlement of Paris defended the first interpretation, and the crown the second.

In his approach to the Parlement Louis again trod warily, for he recognised that the relationship of *parlement* to crown was, in some respects, ambiguous, and he had no desire to disable the Parlement in the exercise of its legitimate functions. The point about the Parlement's having assisted his grandfather's accession was not lost on Louis, and at several junctures during his personal reign he too looked to the Parlement of Paris for legal corroboration of his poli-cies, most notably during his disputes with the papacy.[21] Both prin-ciple and pragmatism caused Louis to refrain from a vengeful assault upon the Parlement. It is true that as early as 1653, at Mazarin's behest, he commanded the Parlement of Paris to desist from discussing royal policy, and to limit itself to judicial and legislative functions; but this was in the immediate aftermath of the Fronde when Mazarin felt it necessary to confirm the independence of royal policy against the intrusion of the Parlement. There was no suggestion that the king would never again ask the Parlement for an opinion on policy. As regards remonstrance, in 1667 Louis instructed the Parlement that acts of remonstrance must be executed quickly and on one occasion only; if the king returned disputed legislation unaltered, it must be registered by the Parlement without delay. In 1673 Louis gave a further twist to remonstrance by informing the Parlement that, henceforth, it must first register legislation and only remonstrate later if it wished. This, of course, nullified the point of remonstrance, which was to have legislation revised by the king. However, one historian has argued that even the regulation of 1673 should not be misinterpreted: it was perceived by Louis as a temporary wartime measure to hasten the passage of fiscal legislation which might otherwise be delayed. The rule remained in force until the end of Louis's reign because war itself also lasted until 1713; when the Duc d'Orléans became regent in 1715 he reverted to the older pattern of remonstrance before registration.[22]

The second set of institutions to be considered is the provincial estates. During the Middle Ages they had emerged as representative assemblies in the medieval, although not modern, sense. They were composed of members of the three 'Orders' or 'Estates' which made up medieval society: the clergy (First Estate), nobility (Second Estate), and commoners (Third Estate). In practice, the Third Estate members usually represented towns or *communautés* (collections of villages). The provincial estates exercised considerable responsibilities within their territory: they raised local taxes, collected royal taxation on behalf of the crown, supervised public works, stimulated commerce and manufactures, and upheld the many rights and privileges which they and other bodies in the provinces possessed. They met at royal command, some annually, others biennially or triennially, and were attended by royal commissioners whose purpose was to represent the king's interest and authority, receive statements of grievances from the estates to the king, and negotiate the amount of taxation which the provinces would pay in the form of a *don gratuit* (literally a 'free gift', but in reality the taxation which the crown sought). Although several estates disappeared during the fifteenth and sixteenth centuries, there were still over twenty in the early seventeenth century. The kings of France had gradually diminished the number of provincial estates, not by abolishing them (this would have raised the question of whether the king possessed such power), but simply by not convening them. Louis XIV continued this process of attrition, ceasing to call the estates of Normandy (last met 1655), Basse-Auvergne (1672), Quercy and Rouergue (1673), Alsace (1683), and Franche-Comté (1704). Nevertheless, for reasons of military strategy if no other, there were four provincial estates which were too important to be ignored, and which the crown had to manage with care: Brittany, Burgundy, Provence and Languedoc.

All were very large and on the extremities of the kingdom, hence their military significance: Brittany for naval reasons, Burgundy on the troublesome eastern frontier, Provence with its access to and from Italy, and Languedoc which bordered on Spain. Other factors caused the crown to treat them with respect. In Brittany, Provence and Languedoc, French was a minority language. Each of the four provinces possessed an array of legal and fiscal traditions towards which the estates were extremely protective. Languedoc had a size-able Huguenot minority. The inhabitants of these provinces had a strong sense of regional identity; the people of Provence, while acknowledging that they were subjects of the king, considered that they were Provençaux first, and French second.[23] Again, within these provinces were prosperous cities and ports which helped to 'define' them, and acted as centres of regional economic activity or as entre-pôts of international commerce. These provinces had a vigorous politi-cal life, separate from policy-making at Paris or Versailles. The local social elites forged chains of alliance through intermarriage, exercised political patronage by placing their kinsmen and other followers in municipal and provincial offices, and effectively dominated the politi-cal and administrative affairs of the region.[24] Of course, there were rivalries too, for provincial elites were as prone to factions, hostilities and conflicts of interest as anybody else. Much of the social unrest of the 1630s, 1640s and 1650s arose from local rather than national tensions and problems. Recognising the strength of these 'network' systems in the provinces, but also the potentiality for exploiting them, Louis wisely concluded that the most profitable approach to the estates was through an expedient blend of negotiation, machination, division and coercion. Recent studies of the crown's relations with provincial estates[25] explain in remarkable and illuminating detail the shifting balance of forces in the estates, the tortuous negotiations between the estates and royal commissioners on the question of a *don gratuit*, the financial 'gifts' which commissioners bestowed upon deputies whom they thought might vote as the crown wished, and the threats which commissioners issued, hinting that the king might curtail the privileges of a provincial estate which withheld a sufficiently generous *don gratuit*. In short, Louis XIV, like his predecessors, used a variety of tactics in his handling of the provincial estates.

Languedoc provides an instructive example. Louis XIV appreciated that it was in his interest to cultivate the cooperation of the estates
rather than drive them into resistance. The central government therefore invested in large-scale capital projects in the province, notably
from the late 1660s when it began the construction of the Canal des
Deux Mers linking the Mediterranean and the Atlantic, and expanded
the port of Sète. While commercial considerations were important in
these enterprises, the government was also mindful that extensive
public works would stimulate the economy of Languedoc and
encourage in the provincial estates a mood of collaboration with a
benevolent crown. Moreover, the crown appealed to the self-interest
of the social elites of Languedoc. In the 1660s and 1670s, only about
40 per cent of money raised to pay the *don gratuit* actually left the
province for the government coffers in Paris; some 60 per cent was
spent within the province itself (and much went into the pockets of
financiers, *officiers* and other provincial notabilities). The *don gratuit*
did not constitute money 'lost' by Languedoc to the government; over
half remained in the province and thereby eased the path to agreement between the estates and the royal commissioners.[26] Louis's desire
for harmony between king and provincial estates arose also out of his
social thought. The great task of the restoration of royal authority to
which he had devoted himself involved a commitment to a traditional
social hierarchy. Provincial estates were institutions within which the
social elites had legitimate functions to perform; Louis was predisposed to confirm those functions, provided they were compatible with
his own authority. His ministers Colbert and Louvois, who thought
in terms of efficiency and achievement, would have liked him to have
abolished the provincial estates; to them, they were medieval accre-
tions with limited relevance to a 'modern' society. Louis, however,
thought as a king: he would countenance a reduction in their number,
but not their suppression as a matter of policy.

The Intendants

If it was the case that Louis XIV broadly remained within traditional
limits with regard to provincial government and his relations with the
parlements, what of the intendants, the so-called 'new men' sent from
Paris to impose royal will? They have often been represented as
evidence of a forward-looking, bureaucratising monarchy[27] which was

seeking to circumvent traditional provincial administration by imposing its own agents and authorising them to appropriate the functions of provincial *officiers*. Here again, we should be wary of straining the evidence too far, for other scholarship has produced a more nuanced interpretation.[28] The origins of the intendants went back to the fifteenth century when the crown occasionally sent commissioners into the provinces to conduct specific investigations. By the 1620s these commissioners were being referred to as *intendants de justice*, police [that is, administration] *et finances*, although these three functions did not exhaust their responsibilities. By then, they were being sent into the provinces with increasing frequency to report on particular problems (municipal debt, social unrest, economic difficulties) and to oversee the execution of government policy. They were also being attached to the army to ensure that such matters as the provision of artillery and ammunition, and the recruitment and movement of troops were pursued efficiently by the military authorities. France's entry into the Thirty Years War gave further impulse to the use of intendants by the government, so much so that *officiers* came to regard them as a menace. One of the main demands of the parlementary Fronde was for the suppression of the intendants; for a time the government yielded, but after the Fronde had ended it gradually reintroduced them until they had become a permanent feature of provincial administration by the late 1660s.

If we are to understand their significance to government, we should be clear as to certain facts. First, they were not very numerous: at any one time there was a maximum of only thirty-two intendants to cover the whole country. It is true that they could appoint local assistants (*subdélégués*) and had secretaries to help them, but it would be unrealistic to suppose that thirty-two officials alone could turn a country as large as France into a centralised state. The intendants were appointed from the ranks of the *maîtres des requêtes* and *conseillers d'état* in the Conseil des Parties. They were, therefore, chiefly lawyers with experience of central administration. They were chosen by the Contrôleur Général des Finances[29] and approved by the king. By the 1670s the practice was established whereby an intendant was attached to each *généralité* or *pays d'état*. In principle, intendants were moved every three years, but in practice the average time which they spent in a *généralité* between 1661 and 1715 was five years. In a few cases they stayed for much longer periods: Claude Bouchu was intendant in Burgundy from 1656 to 1683, and Nicolas Lamoignon, Marquis de

Basville, served in Languedoc from 1685 to 1718.[30] Some figures spent almost the whole of their careers as intendants; for example, Louis de Machault (1623–95) was son of an intendant, but served first as a *maître des requêtes* before being an intendant for twenty-seven years successively in Montauban, Champagne, Picardy, Orléans and Soissons; Thomas de Miromesnil (d.1702) likewise was a *maître des requêtes* who then spent twenty-two years as an intendant in Poitou, Champagne and Tours. The intendants received annual instructions from the government, which usually emphasised the need to make an annual tour of the *généralité*, to be well informed on the state of the rural and urban economies, to visit towns to ensure the equitable distribution and collection of taxes, to work towards good relations between the military and civilians, to root out financial and administrative corruption, and oversee the processes of local justice. Their real strength was that they had direct access to government ministers and, through them, to the king himself; all of their actions, be they investigative, executive, supervisory, advisory or disciplinary, were carried out in the name of the king. This certainly conferred upon the intendants an authority which in some respects made up for their lack of numbers, but it also imposed heavy responsibilities. Louis XIV was at pains to present himself as a king who did not exceed his rightful powers, and the correspondence between the *contrôleurs généraux* and the intendants[31] contains frequent warnings from the former to the latter that the intendants likewise must exercise their powers with tact and sensibility, refraining from actions which could be interpreted as despotic; they must cooperate with local judicial and financial officers, not exercise a gratuitous authority over them. It was in this spirit that Colbert wrote letters of reprimand to the intendant at Rouen in 1672 and 1673, warning him that, 'you must take care to contain yourself within the limits of your powers as granted to you by the council in its decrees…'.[32] The intendants were not free agents, but were subject to constant scrutiny by the government. Correspondence between government and intendants often creates the impression of the former often having to rein in the latter, an impression that ministers feared that if the intendants imposed their authority upon local institutions and officers without due sensibility, they might provoke the kind of social protest which had been such a feature of the 1640s and early 1650s. The intendants provided the government with information and enforced the execution of its policies, but were expected to do so within the limits which Louis XIV acknowledged in the exercise of his own duties. Important as intendants were to the imposition of royal authority upon the provinces, the crown was anxious that it should not be achieved at the price of serious social breakdown. The intendants were carefully chosen, often from within one of the great ministerial clans which could impose its own restraints and discipline. From the wider entourage of the Colberts, for example, came Michel Colbert (intendant at Alençon), Louis Béchameil de Nointel (Tours), Claude Pellot (Dauphiné), Claude Méliand (Alençon, Caen, Rouen), and others.[33] They and their colleagues were expected to bring social and psychological skills to their duties, as well as legal and administrative abilities. They had a marked impact upon provincial government and administration, but were under constant pressure from the government to conform as far as possible to the values and norms of the provinces wherein they served.

By present-day standards, the France of Louis XIV was under-governed and under-administered; it bore little resemblance to a modern state with sophisticated decision-making procedures, a large civil service, and immediate contact with its citizens through the elaborate communications systems which now exist. Nor should we necessarily perceive direct lines of continuity between the techniques of government developed by Louis XIV and the present-day bureaucratic state. One of the central premises of the Revolution was that in 1789 France had at last broken free from the *ancien régime*, including its system of government, and was devising new patterns and structures. Leaving aside the thorny question of how far this revolutionary claim was justified, it does caution against any tendentious interpretation which assesses Louis XIV's significance in proportion to his relevance to present-day notions and practices of the state. Louis and his ministers were seeking seventeenth-century solutions to seventeenth-century problems. Although they generated much debate as they did so, they deserve to be assessed by the criteria of their own age, not those of the late twentieth century.

3

LOUIS XIV AND HIS SUBJECTS

In 1966 the distinguished French historian Pierre Goubert published *Louis XIV et Vingt Millions de Français.*[1] Conceived in the *Annaliste* tradition,[2] this work focused as much on the king's subjects as on Louis himself. Goubert assessed the reign not just according to criteria of state-building or the long-term aggrandisement of France, but also in the light of the effects of the reign upon Louis's subjects. Goubert's verdict was mixed. Louis, he concluded, undoubtedly strove to advance the interests of the state and to secure France's pre-eminence in Europe, but at heavy cost to his subjects: the king's mishandling of the economy and his engagement in decades of warfare had ruinous social consequences. Moreover, in the face of natural disasters, especially the great famine of 1693–94 which led to the death of about 10 per cent of the population, and the infamous winter of 1709 which accounted for the death of about 4 per cent, the government could do little to alleviate even the worst of the misery. To Goubert, Louis's personal reign could be deemed 'glorious' only by disregarding the distress endured by the mass of his subjects. Since Goubert published his book, historians have had to come to terms with issues which it raised, and especially the paradox that Louis made frequent and genuine expressions of commitment to 'le peuple', but pursued policies, especially in the international sphere, which were bound to increase social distress.

The King's Subjects

How many subjects did Louis XIV have? Goubert referred to 20 million, but this was an eye-catching figure in the title of his book rather than an accurate estimate. Much work has been undertaken by historians on the subject, but even up-to-date statistics must be regarded as provisional.[3] In the seventeenth century, records of births, marriages and deaths were either not preserved with any high degree of consistency (although the Catholic and Huguenot churches did endeavour to keep such information) or have survived in only a piece-meal fashion; and the frontiers of France changed during the reign of Louis XIV, so adding to the population through conquest. Demographic historians have developed ingenious methods for calculating national statistics on the basis of regional studies, and have estimated that France, as its frontiers changed, had a population of about 21,900,000 in 1675 rising to about 22,400,000 in 1705. A comprehensive demographic study would break down these figures by region, age, sex, status, occupation, religion, and any other category in which the historian was interested. For present purposes, we can note that the population was most dense in the area running from the Loire northwards to Paris and thence north-west to the coast; it was relatively sparse in the war zones of the north-east and south-east, and in the mountainous centre of France. About 75 to 80 per cent of the population were peasants, although this term too requires qualification since it ranges from landless labourers to wealthy farmers. That such a large percentage of the population was attached to the land meant that towns were not heavily populated, even though they had grown in size during the century. In 1700 the largest city was Paris with about 510,000 inhabitants or 540,000 if Versailles is included; then came Lyon (97,000), Marseille (75,000), Rouen (64,000), Lille (57,000) and Orléans (50,000); all other towns had populations under 50,000.[4] In this respect France bears comparison with England which, in London, possessed one very large city, with all other towns being significantly smaller. Although the population increased modestly during the reign of Louis XIV, there were fluctuations as elsewhere in Europe. Temporary regional contractions occurred in the face of local natural disasters (usually food shortages and disease), but there were occasional national calamities when successive harvest failures coincided with adverse weather conditions and the spread of epidemics: such was the case from 1661 to 1663, 1691 to 1694, and

the notorious winter of 1709. During these periods, the population
of the whole country underwent short-term decrease.

Louis XIV himself assumed that he had fewer subjects than modern
historians believe, and for a time that he ruled a larger country than
was the case. From 1697 to 1700 his government attempted what it
termed an 'estimation' of the population (it lacked techniques for an
accurate calculation), and arrived at a figure of about 19 million. It
planned taxation, recruitment to the army and other policies on this
figure; and while it is impossible to define precisely the effects of the
error upon policy, it is evident that rates of taxation, for example,
would have been different had the government known that it had
more taxpayers at its disposal than it believed. As regards the size of
the country, the French Académie des Sciences published a new atlas
of France in 1684 using the newest methods of survey and observa-
tion, and showed that earlier maps had exaggerated the size of the
kingdom. During the ceremony at which the Academy formally
presented the atlas to the king, Louis wryly observed that his cartog-
raphers had succeeded in doing what his enemies had not: they had
reduced the size of his kingdom! Such miscalculations did not alter
the fact that France was the largest and most populous state in western
Europe. In 1700, Britain and Ireland had a combined population of
about 9 million, Spain about 6 or 7 million, Portugal about 3 million,
and the Dutch Republic about 2.5 million.[5] By comparison France
was a giant, and Louis had at his disposal immense human assets
which in turn could be translated into financial resources.

Governmental Finance under Louis XIV

All European governments had regular sources of revenue based on
direct and indirect taxation, but all resorted to borrowing and to
extraordinary measures in the search for cash and credit. Warfare was
by far the most serious drain on French governmental finance. The
percentage of total expenditure devoted to warfare was as follows:

1630–49	35%
1650–56	20%
1662–69	42%
1670–79	66%
1680–89	54%
1690–95	78%[6]

It is extremely difficult to assess the weight of the fiscal burden which Louis's subjects bore during the personal reign, for when statistics on taxation and borrowing are available, their interpretation often has to be impressionistic.[7] The French government was not obliged to produce a budget in the modern sense, and even though the king and his closest advisers possessed extensive information on the financial situation, they acknowledged that their information was far from comprehensive. Modern historians reconstruct tables of income and expenditure as the basis on which to analyse French governmental finances, but such figures must be handled with care: they can conceal regional variations, they might conflate cash actually raised by the government with credit on which it drew, and so on. The burden which taxation represented to French taxpayers depended not only on the amounts demanded, but on their ability to pay; this in turn could be determined by the nature of the local economy, the movement of inflation, climatic conditions which affected agriculture, the number and level of local taxes which had to be paid, and a host of other factors. Bearing such cautionary remarks in mind, we can present recent estimates of total government expenditure as follows:

1616	68 million livres
1670	77 million
1680	96 million
1685	198 million
1690	144 million
1700	182 million
1711	264 million
1714	200 million[8]

Two features of these figures stand out: the extent to which warfare drove up costs (the steepest rises coincided with periods of war and reached peaks in the 1680s and 1700s), and the size of the increase in expenditure: by the mid-1680s fiscal pressures on the government were almost three times higher than in 1661, and by 1711 about one-third higher again. To confront this increasingly complex situation the government had to have recourse to ever more extraordinary measures as well as to increased taxation and borrowing.[9]

The principal direct tax was the *taille*, which down to the 1660s accounted for some 60 per cent of government revenue, but thereafter was steadily reduced to about 40 per cent. It took two forms: *taille personnelle* (assessed on an individual, and common throughout northern France) or *taille réelle* (assessed on land, and widespread in southern France). Numerous groups of people were exempt from the *taille personnelle*: clergy, nobility, the inhabitants of privileged towns including Paris, many *officiers*, university students, officers in the army and navy, and others; in practice, *taille personnelle* fell chiefly on the peasantry. The *taille réelle* was raised on land except that attached to a noble or ecclesiastical title; nobles, prelates or monasteries paid tax on that portion of an estate which was not integral to their titles or ecclesiastical 'dignities'. There was much evasion of the *taille réelle*: landowners concealed ownership of property from tax collectors (especially property distant from the owner's residence), and since collectors had no right to examine legal records showing how much land an individual owned, avoidance was relatively easy.

There was no uniformity in the methods whereby *taille* was collected. The chief distinction was between the *pays d'élections*, which covered almost three-quarters of France, and the *pays d'états* where there were provincial estates. In the former, the main financial areas were the *généralités*, which were large areas comprising several *élections*. At the beginning of Louis's reign there were seventeen *généralités* (an eighteenth, La Rochelle, was created in 1694); each was headed by treasurers who ran a financial bureau staffed by financial *officiers*. During the personal reign of Louis XIV, the intendant in each *généralité* also shared the supervision of the assessment and collection of *taille*. Every year the government informed the treasurers and intendants as to how much was to be raised in *taille*; the financial bureau in each *généralité* then divided the sum among the *élections* where other officers, *élus*, subdivided the sum among the parishes; at the parish level, collectors distributed and gathered the tax. The money then was transferred to the government through this financial structure. The *pays d'états* technically did not pay *taille*, but voted and raised *dons gratuits*, which in effect constituted *taille* under another name. The provincial estates protected their peasants as much as they could: although the *pays d'états* covered about a quarter of the territory of France, they usually contributed only about one-sixth of the *taille*.[10] When provincial estates met to discuss the *don gratuit*, there was much haggling with the intendant, the sum eventually agreed being less than the crown wanted but more than the estates at first proposed.[11]

The *taille* had long been a source of social grievance. Abuses were common in its assessment and collection as financial *officiers* diverted money into their own pockets, parish collectors favoured their friends and relations, and powerful aristocrats used their influence to have the *taille* on their tenants assessed as lightly as possible at the expense of parishes which lacked protectors; and the large number of wealthy people absolved from all or part of the *taille* reinforced its reputation as a tax on the poor. Colbert was fully aware of these corrupt practices, and frequently enjoined the intendants to stamp them out. In a general circular sent to all the intendants in April 1679 he urged them to take all necessary steps to ensure the equitable distribution of the *taille*:

> The first and most important [point] is the imposition of the taille...; although I am persuaded that the diligence which you show prevents many abuses, nevertheless it is certain that in the drafting of the [tax] rolls, in the raising and collecting of taxes, in the receipts which the receveurs take from the collectors, or in the constraints which are used and the charges which are imposed on the taxpayers, there is still much dishonesty which escapes your notice...; the king requires you to investigate these points with great care... and apply the necessary remedies.[12]

A few weeks later Colbert wrote again to the intendants, ordering them to attack 'the abuses which are committed, the discharges and under-assessments which are given to the rich..., the oppression of the poor... and generally everything that can be prejudicial to the people'.[13] Since the early seventeenth century, ministers of the crown had aspired to reform the *taille*, but were frustrated by the demands of war and the vested interests which resisted change. Colbert too sought to alleviate the burden of *taille* by reducing the number of financial *officiers* and using the intendants to expose and punish corruption. His chief strategy, however, was to attempt to diminish the amount of *taille* which the government required, partly by controlling expenditure (although, as the figures above show, this proved beyond his capacity), but also by increasing indirect taxes on consumable goods. By definition, indirect taxes were paid by people who could afford the commodities on which they were imposed; the contribution of wealthier people to government finances thereby would grow. Whereas the *taille* had stood at 53 million livres in 1657, it was reduced to 42 million in 1661, and to about 34 million during the rest of the 1660s. The wars of the 1670s, 1680s and 1690s forced it up again,[14] obliging the government to search for radical alternatives which would spread taxation through as many sections of society as possible and so ease the burden on the poor, if only in a relative rather than an absolute sense. Two were attempted. In 1695 Louis sought to avoid a further addition to the *taille* by introducing along-side of it a new type of tax, the *capitation*,[15] which included two new principles: everybody would pay (the clergy theoretically were immune, but paid the equivalent as a *don gratuit*), and would do so according to their status and estimated income. A government commission divided the population into twenty-two classes which paid at rates ranging from 2000 livres a year for the elites in class 1 (including Princes of the Blood and ministers of the crown), down to 1 livre a year for the poorest in class 22. The tax was suppressed in 1698 having raised about 21 million livres a year (the figure for the *taille* in the *pays d'élections* from 1695 to 1698 was about 31 million per annum),[16] but was reintroduced in 1701 when war again broke out. The second tax, the *dixième*, was also a wartime measure designed to ease pressure on the *taille*. Introduced in 1710, it extended the principle of taxing wealth. Once again everybody was subjected (although the clergy again bought technical exemption through the *don gratuit*), but whereas the *capitation* was based upon status and its presumed wealth, the *dixième* imposed a 10 per cent tax upon real wealth and income which had to be declared by each taxpayer. Before its suppression in 1717 the tax raised between 22 and 28 million livres a year;[17] it was revived on several occasions in the eighteenth century.

The principles that the tax burden of the peasantry should be eased relative to other sections of the community, and that the fiscal immunities which many of the wealthier sections of society enjoyed should be circumvented, underpinned the measures taken by Louis XIV's finance ministers to increase indirect taxes. The major taxes were *aides* (duties mainly on wine, but also on commodities such as paper and cloth) and *traites* (customs duties on goods coming into the country, or moving within France itself). In this latter case, provinces and towns charged duties on goods passing through their territory; there were even internal customs unions in France, of which the largest was the Cinq Grosses Fermes, which covered much of northern and eastern France. The government drove up indirect taxes, especially from the early 1690s onwards when Pontchartrain (1689–99), Chamillart (1699–1708) and Desmarets (1708–15) were Controllers General. They raised the duties on many goods, often to the point where the duty accounted for as much as 50 per cent of the sale value; they also imposed taxes on such items as playing cards (1702), the sale of ice (1704), on wigs (1706), oil (1708) and oysters (1709).[18] There was, however, one other indirect tax which had been the cause of much social protest earlier in the century, and whose manifest injustices remained unchecked by the government: the *gabelle*. *Gabelle* was a tax on salt assessed in three principal ways. Most of northern France was classified as *pays de grande gabelle*: each year every household had to buy a minimum amount of salt as fixed by the government, and at a price (including tax) also decreed by the government. Second, most of the south-east was *pays de petite gabelle*: tax on salt was paid, but there was no obligation to purchase a certain amount each year. Thirdly, the rest of the kingdom enjoyed varying degrees of exemption from the *gabelle*, and sales of salt followed laws of supply and demand. In the *pays de grande gabelle*, the tax continued to provoke discontent which expressed itself through the extensive smuggling of cheaper salt from other parts of the country. In spite of its inconsistencies and illogicalities, *gabelle* remained an important source of revenue: whereas in the mid-1640s the *gabelle* was raising about 13 million livres a year, by the mid-1680s the figure stood at about 23,700,000 livres.[19]

The mechanisms whereby taxes were collected were a further problem. The government itself gathered direct taxes (apart from in the *pays d'états*), but it 'farmed' all of its indirect taxes, including the *gabelle*. It did so by negotiating contracts with groups of financiers (known as *fermiers*, *partisans* or *traitants*), who advanced sums directly to the government and then raised the tax themselves, retaining excess sums as profit. Naturally there was much hard bargaining between the government and tax farmers as to how much the latter should pay, and in the course of the seventeenth century the government had attempted to simplify the system either by negotiating contracts for all indirect taxes within a given region, or by farming a specific tax over the whole country. This was a process which Colbert continued. In 1663 he established a general farm of taxes on wine; in 1664 he negotiated a single contract on the *grandes gabelles* and *traites* outside of the Cinq Grosses Fermes; and in 1681, after many years of working to amalgamate smaller into larger farms, he compressed all the major indirect taxes into a single farm.[20] The structure arrived at in 1681 – the *ferme générale* – remained in force for the next hundred years, and on average brought in one-half of the French government's revenue.[21] Tax farmers and their agents some-

times amassed immense riches from their activities, but there were
risks involved. During the seventeenth century many 'farmers' over-
reached themselves and ended in bankruptcy; it would be a mistake
to imagine that tax farmers invariably prospered, and that by
purchasing the right to collect duties on particular products or in
particular areas, they were guaranteed to prosper. It was this element
of risk which caused them to instruct their agents to collect taxes rigor-
ously, resorting if necessary to the expropriation of livestock and other
possessions of defaulters. Tax farmers proved harder taskmasters in
the collection of taxation than the government, and because of their
reputation as fiscal predators, it was towards them rather than towards
the crown that much popular hostility over taxation was directed.

In the face of inexorably rising expenditure, Louis and his ministers resorted to borrowing and extraordinary measures on an
unprecedented scale. Direct taxes in effect were used by the government to service debt which, like expenditure, escalated from the 1690s
onwards: in 1661 debt stood at about 700 million livres, but was
reduced to 250 million by 1683; in 1699 it had risen again to 410
million, but during the War of the Spanish Succession almost tripled
to 1200 million livres by 1708.[22] Direct taxes were mortgaged by the
government which borrowed from financiers on the promise of repay-
ments from future revenues. Thereby the tax farmers and other
financiers who loaned money were indispensable to the crown. The
greater the expenditure and debt of the government, the more it
relied on *traitants* and *partisans* to provide the necessary credit. It had
to calculate rates of direct and indirect taxation with their interests
in mind, leaving the financiers with a *de facto* veto on the government's fiscal policies. In a fascinating study of financiers, Daniel
Dessert examined over five hundred families which were involved in
negotiating loans to the king.[23] He showed that the majority did not
themselves dispose of considerable wealth; the famous and fabulously
rich banker, Samuel Bernard, who was by far the biggest creditor of
the government, was the exception, not the rule. In addition to using
their own resources, many *traitants* acted as agents for aristocrats and
great landowners who loaned money to the state at one remove. In
short, the government was indebted to large numbers of people, not
simply those with whom it arranged loans or contracts for the farming
of taxes. That the debts of the state were distributed far and wide
among the king's subjects was reinforced by another and widespread
practice: the sale of government bonds (*rentes*). Bonds carried an

annual interest usually of about 5 per cent, although rates fluctuated during wartime. Even people of modest means invested in bonds, and so acquired a stake in servicing the state's debt. Meanwhile the government by the 1690s was once again employing extraordinary fiscal devices reminiscent of the days of Richelieu and Mazarin. Noble titles and offices were being created and sold (in 1692, municipal *officiers* had to repurchase the offices which they already held), in 1700 a national lottery was established, forced loans from *officiers* were contrived, and the currency was manipulated and devalued almost forty times between 1686 and 1709.[24]

The implications of the government's fiscal needs for the relationship between Louis and his subjects were both positive and negative. While taxation, governmental expenditure and indebtedness were all rising, those among the king's subjects who loaned money to the crown profited financially. As ever, it was the peasants who continued to bear the brunt of direct taxation, but the capitation and *dixième* did impose direct taxes on all of the king's subjects for a time. There were outbursts of popular resistance to fiscal policy, although not on the scale of the 1630s and 1640s. There were two main phases: one ran from the early 1660s to the mid-1670s in Boulogne, Gascony, the Vivarais, Guyenne, and most seriously of all, Brittany in 1675, and the second through the first decade of the eighteenth century, the most notable being the risings in Quercy in 1707. Of all the rebellions, that of the 1675 rebellion in Brittany – the so-called 'révolte du papier-timbré' ('the stamped-paper rebellion') which lasted from April to September – was most dangerous to the regime. This was because, although it began as a protest against the government's imposition of stamp duty on legal contracts and on tobacco and pewter, it soon turned into a complex *mélange* of other conflicts and problems: popular resistance to seigneurial justice, peasant repudiation of feudal obligations to the lords, disputes concerning the rights of the Estates of Brittany in relation to the crown, and violence resulting from rumours that the province was to be deprived of its exemption from *gabelle* (the salt tax). The risings began in Rennes and spread to Saint-Malo and Nantes; there were 'copy-cat' troubles further south in Bordeaux. There was no intendant in Brittany, but the governor, the Duc de Chaulnes, gradually restored order through harsh military measures, and the revolts ended in the autumn.[25] By comparison with the 1630s and 1640s, however, even the 1675 troubles were on a smaller scale. This is not to suggest that tax rebellions were of little consequence: at the beginning of the personal reign Louis had to despatch thirty-eight companies of troops to suppress the risings around Boulogne. The soldiers accomplished their mission amidst much bloodshed, many executions, and after consigning four hundred unfortunates to the galleys.[26]

Government and the Economy

National economies scarcely existed in the seventeenth century, for most economic life was local or regional in extent. The influence which the government could exert on the totality of economic activity in France was limited. Colbert and his successors therefore concentrated on those aspects which in their view were directly beneficial to the state. Some economic historians of early modern France have adopted the interpretative model developed by Ernest Labrousse, and taken up by others such as Braudel, Goubert and Le Roy Ladurie. According to this model, there was a fundamental division in French economic life between static rural sectors wherein agricultural production was stagnant (although vulnerable to sudden scarcity because of harvest failures), its methods custom-ridden, and its social context governed by archaic 'feudal' relations which inhibited improvement; and on the other hand, urban economies which in varying degrees were dynamic, flexible and responsive to the changing needs of the population.[27] Other scholars, among whom Jean Meuvret was prominent, expressed doubts about this simple dichotomy. Meuvret studied the production, distribution and sale of corn in France in the seventeenth and early eighteenth centuries, and concluded that the rural economic sectors were not invariably inert, nor were the urban sectors inherently dynamic.[28] He contended that inertia and dynamism were evident at every level of economic activity in France, and that the relative strength of one as against the other depended on factors such as the quality of communications, methods of payment (cash or in kind), the availability of credit and of mechanisms for handling credit, and the efficiency of 'news networks' whereby information about supply and demand was disseminated among consumers and producers. The determinants of economic activity in France, argued Meuvret, had less to do with means of production, 'feudal' relations or urbanisation, than with the sophistication of available market mechanisms; and since those mechanisms in most parts of the country were developing only slowly, the rate of economic change likewise was sluggish.[29] It is not the aim of the present exercise to assess the merits of the 'Labrousse' and 'Meuvret' interpretations, both of which have inspired regional studies which investigate the extent to which agricultural activity was 'static' or 'dynamic';[30] but this much may be said: they both imply that the rapidly escalating fiscal demands of the government of Louis XIV could not be met by existing economic activity, hence the financial contortions discussed earlier. What strikes modern scholars is, in the words of Meuvret, 'The increasingly flagrant contradiction between the needs of the state and the resources that the economic activity of the nation had to offer it... It was not the grand design of a given minister... that mattered. The contradictions manifested themselves year after year on the occasion of the difficulties they [the ministers] faced, and so the solutions they found could never be more than expedients.'[31] The economic policies of Colbert and his successors did not constitute some long-term master plan to reform the whole of economic life in France; they were short-term responses to the fiscal exigencies of the state.

The economic principles which guided Colbert are often termed 'mercantilism',[32] a noun coined by economists of the late eighteenth century. Some modern economic historians have avoided the term as overloaded with spurious meaning,[33] but it is still of value provided that we recognise that mercantilism was less a coherent economic theory than a code of economic behaviour; it is in this limited sense that the word is employed here. Mercantilism was not unique to the seventeenth century, for its origins can be traced at least to the fifteenth century. As the word suggests, it stressed the importance of mercantile activity to the state, the argument being that commerce attracted silver and gold coinage into the realm, helped to circulate money within the country, and thereby made the population richer and more able to meet the fiscal demands of the government. The more commercial activity there was, the greater the amount of coinage in circulation and, by extension, the greater the wealth and power of the state. This was the reasoning behind the shift of taxation under Louis XIV from direct to indirect; as money circulated through the distribution and sale of manufactured and primary goods, the government could extract its portion through duties. The proposition that commerce augmented the power of the state was valid only if the balance of commerce was favourable, with exports exceeding imports and the surplus being paid by foreigners in coinage. If the contrary were the case, coinage was lost to the country and the power of the state was correspondingly diminished. It was essential, therefore, to devise means to create and protect a favourable balance of payments. Mercantilism rested on another precept: that the volume of commercial activity and coinage in Europe at any one time was limited. If one state improved its commercial performance, it must be at the expense of others. Mercantilism was a belligerent doctrine whose objective was to create maximum profits in the form of coinage; it ran contrary to medieval notions of 'fair price', 'fair exchange' and 'fair' profits. Mercantilism spurned the moral and religious dimensions of medieval economic thought, and, in a famous phrase of Colbert, led to 'une guerre d'argent' which could easily turn into a war of weapons. Mercantilism did not ascribe great importance to agriculture which allegedly generated only modest cash profits, since most products were consumed within the country and were often paid for in kind rather than cash. In mercantilist thought, commerce and industry were the mechanisms whereby the volume of cash within the country was augmented. Leading seventeenth-century writers on economic affairs advocated mercantilist principles – in France they included Barthélemy de Laffemas, *Les Trésors et Richesses de la France* (1597), and Antoine de Montchrestien, *Traité de l'Economie Politique* (1615) – but mercantilism was essentially a pragmatic response to the needs of the state at a time when economic stagnation and depression affected much of Europe.

As Colbert devised his economic plans, he was careful to cultivate the mind of the king. He wrote numerous papers and memoirs for Louis on commerce, industry and finance. Probably the most famous is his memoir of 1670.[34] It pointed out that 'The increase of Your Majesty's revenues consists of increasing by every means the amount of silver coinage in circulation in the kingdom... .' This could be done by three means:

> increase the money in public commerce by drawing it from countries in which it originated, keep it within the kingdom..., and devise means whereby people can profit from it. [It] is in these three points that grandeur, the power of the state and the magnificence of the king are to be found... [It] can be shown that if there are only 150 million livres of coinage in circulation among the public, this can be increased by 10, 30 or 50 millions only by taking that amount from neighbouring states... I beg Your Majesty to allow

me to say that, since he took charge of his finances, he has conducted a war of money ['une guerre d'argent'] against all the states of Europe...

Colbert's ideas were drawn from the common stock of contemporary economic thought. Modern historians have discarded the thesis, proposed by Ernest Lavisse, that Colbert was a visionary, a proto-capitalist ahead of his times, who offered Louis XIV a concept of the state based on peace abroad, the modernisation of society and economy through commerce, industry and 'liberal' social reform. Colbert was a man of his time who regarded his economic policies as weapons with which to advance the interests of the state. He was selective as to where he would concentrate his attention: he left agriculture largely to its own devices, and never attempted to bring the whole of French commerce and industry under regulation. He accepted that it was neither desirable nor possible to control the whole of economic activity in France; he targeted only those commercial and industrial spheres which he adjudged directly relevant to state power.[35]

The chief instrument through which he acted was the Conseil de Commerce of which the king himself was a member and to which leading businessmen were invited. Founded in 1664 and active, in its first phase, down to the late 1670s, its recommendations led to almost 200 laws and regulations on industry and commerce; they included the famous law of 1669 which standardised throughout France the measurements to be used in the cloth industry, and laid down minimum standards of quality. In the provinces, the intendants and a corps of industrial and commercial inspectors were recruited to enforce the laws. To stimulate industries capable of generating high cash profits, Colbert created *manufactures royales*: state-sponsored companies which produced mainly luxury items. The first was the Gobelins, founded by Colbert just outside Paris in 1662. Under its director, Charles Lebrun, its output was mainly tapestries, paintings, furniture, statues and other ornamental works; many went to the royal palaces, but a high proportion was also sold in France and abroad. In 1663 Colbert reorganised the Savonnerie, also near Paris. So-called because it occupied the site of a former soap-works, it had been founded in 1626 for the manufacture of carpets. Lebrun again was put in charge; it produced high-quality goods aimed at domestic and foreign markets. Finally, in 1664 Colbert established in the northern town of Beauvais another royal company for the manufacture of tapestries. The northern provinces traditionally dominated the French cloth industry, with Beauvais being among the most important centres. However, French producers continued mainly to weave heavy-duty cloths at a time when popular taste in France and abroad was changing in favour of lighter materials. Dutch, Flemish and English manufacturers were exporting fine cloths to France, earning considerable profits and outselling native producers. Colbert intended the Beauvais venture both to produce high-quality tapestries that would reduce foreign imports, and to provide a challenging example to conservative French cloth manufacturers to adjust their practices to modern markets.[36] Colbert employed other devices: monopolies and privileges for successful manufacturers such as the famous Van Robais cloth company in Abbeville; subsidies to selected industries including metallurgy in Champagne and Burgundy, the glass industry in various parts of the country, and the production of silk at Lyon; and the reaffirmation of the rights of many guilds. Although it was consistent with mercantilism, the wisdom of this last tactic is open to question, since guilds were medieval organisations which existed to protect the interests of their members; but Colbert deemed them to be conveni-ent instruments through which to influence commerce and industry. To give added protection to French industry and keep coinage within the country, Colbert devised tariff barriers against foreign imports. Two major measures were adopted. In 1664, the government issued an edict imposing punitive duties on goods brought to France mainly by Dutch, but to a lesser extent English, ships: certain cloths, oil, soap and other commodities were affected. In 1667 a second edict extended the list, and doubled or tripled existing tariffs.

To expand French commercial activity abroad, trading companies were founded with a mixture of state and private investment: the West Indies Company (1662), the East Indies Company (1664), the Northern Company (1669) and the Levant Company (1670). In accordance with mercantilist principles, Colbert encouraged the growth of colonies in Canada, Louisiana, the West Indies and the Indian Ocean; they supplied France with primary products and markets for manufactured goods (by 1682, some 200 ships were involved in trade between the French West Indies and the ports of Bordeaux, La Rochelle, Nantes and Rouen).[37] A major problem in the 1660s was the lack of French merchant shipping; most French overseas commerce was conducted by Dutch ships. Accordingly, Colbert encouraged the expansion of the mercantile marine by stimulating shipbuilding. Whereas only about eleven ships were trading out of Bordeaux in 1660, there were over thirty by 1683; and the La Rochelle fleet rose from 32 to 92 in the same period.[38] Internal communications likewise were regarded by Colbert as crucial to his plans. The most efficient way of moving goods around France was by water, for in the Seine, Loire, Rhône and Garonne the country was fortunate in possessing major rivers capable of binding the different economic regions together. Much work was undertaken to improve the rivers, but Colbert also continued building canals to provide links between these and other river systems. In 1692 the Orléans canal was opened to complete the Seine–Loire link, but the most ambitious was the Canal des Deux Mers (completed 1681) which provided access between the Mediterranean and the Atlantic. The proposal which led to this latter project came from the great civil engineer Pierre-Paul Riquet. In 1662 he put to Colbert a plan for linking Toulouse, on the river Garonne, with the Mediterranean by making some of the smaller intermediary rivers navigable and by completing the chain via a short canal between Villefranche and Castelnaudary. A royal commission, which sat from 1664 to 1665, examined the idea; it approved the principle, but suggested instead a canal all the way from Toulouse to the Mediterranean, and the development of the port of Sète at the point of egress. Riquet was charged with overseeing what was the largest French engineering project of the century. He drove the scheme through triumphantly, but died a few months before it was opened in May 1681. When completed, the canal was 150 miles long and included 100 locks. Goods henceforth could be carried from Sète to Toulouse via the canal, and thence down the Garonne to the Atlantic.

Colbert died in 1683, and as the fiscal, commercial and agricultural crises of the late 1680s, 1690s and early 1700s unfolded, they generated bodies of economic thought which began to challenge some of the premises of mercantilism.[39] Warfare, problems of public finance, and above all the famine of 1692 to 1694 which was followed by further harvest failures between 1698 and 1700, forced members of the government, the business community and social commentators to reassess economic policy. The fact that the trading companies which Colbert had founded were struggling, and that the tariff barriers had been reduced in the face of English and Dutch retaliation, further stimulated critical evaluation. It is most important to stress that critics did not argue that Colbert's policies had been 'wrong', or that there had been alternatives which he ought to have adopted; but times had changed and the policies of the 1660s and 1670s were increasingly inappropriate. One source of criticism came from the Conseil de Commerce which Colbert had founded in 1664. It had fallen into disuse in the late 1670s, but in 1700 Chamillart, the Contrôleur Général, persuaded Louis XIV to revive it. The new body consisted of six government representatives and twelve merchants from Paris and the main ports. The merchants had a prominent voice in the council, and urged the king to modify and simplify commercial and industrial regulations in favour of private enterprise. The merchants were not 'free traders' (they favoured restricting French colonial trade to French merchants and shipping), but they did advocate an economic ethos of less state intervention and greater individual initiative. Private initiative, especially in the ports, was already flourishing as, for example, new overseas markets were found in South America and elsewhere. The new Conseil de Commerce urged the further development of these trends through private enterprise rather than governmental direction.[40]

The comparative neglect of agriculture by the government was another theme taken up by contemporary commentators, some of whom sought to reintroduce into economic thought the moral dimensions which mercantilism had disclaimed. An early and influential figure of this type was the theologian, the Abbé Claude Fleury, whose *Pensées Politiques* (1670–75) called for the alleviation of socio-economic distress through agricultural improvement which would drive up prices and profits to the benefit of peasants.[41] The capacity of agriculture to inculcate uplifting moral qualities as well as to create wealth, was advocated by influential figures around Archbishop Fénelon. This theory of 'Christian Agrarianism'[42] envisaged the regeneration of agriculture as a necessary precondition of general economic recovery; it also foreshadowed Rousseau by arguing that the obsession with coinage had encouraged the sins of pride, envy and avarice, and to that extent had contributed to social disharmony. The revival of agriculture would be instrumental both in creating and distributing wealth, but also in reviving the Christian virtues of fortitude, temperance and prudence. In other words, social relationships as well as economic prosperity would be enhanced if agriculture was improved. The most coherent presentation of the 'agriculture' case on purely economic grounds was by Pierre le Pesant, sieur de Boisguilbert, whose *Détail de la France* (1695–96) called upon the government to stimulate agricultural reform through radical changes to the tax structure; thereby the economy as a whole would benefit as a revitalised agriculture created 'modern' market mechanisms.[43] Around the turn of the century, merchants, moralists and economic thinkers were engaging in imaginative debates which implied the emergence of a 'national' economy characterised by high prices, profits and wages, and sustained by sophisticated market mechanisms. Colbert's initiatives had been governed chiefly by the demands of state power. Without questioning the importance of a sound economy to the power of the state, the new economic thought of the late seventeenth century advocated economic growth also to enhance the prosperity and moral improvement of the subjects of Louis XIV.

Justice

Louis and his ministers regarded justice as one of the primary functions of the king, but it was a subject brimming with problems for there was little uniformity in the codes of law and systems of justice in different parts of the kingdom. In much of southern France the law courts applied written, Roman law, whereas in other parts of the country, customary law was practised. Jurisdictions often overlapped, and law courts disputed each other's competence. The principal courts were the *parlements*, beneath which were the *présidiaux*, the *bailliages* (known as *sénéchaussées* in some parts of the country), and, lower still in the hierarchy, the *prévôtés* or *vigueries*. Alongside the *parlements* stood other courts which were regarded as 'sovereign', that is supreme courts of appeal: the Grand Conseil (which dealt with such matters as the crown referred to it), several Cours des Comptes and Cours des Aides (dealing mainly with fiscal and taxation matters), and the Cour des Monnaies (which judged cases arising out of currency disputes). Then came a host of lesser law courts, including seigneurial, municipal and commercial tribunals. Such a proliferation of courts and legal systems kept the cost of justice high and led to delays as appeals went from one body to another; and since the magistrates and other officers of the sovereign courts were *officiers*, it was in their financial interest to preserve the country's many courts with their contested jurisdictions.

Of course, seventeenth-century notions of justice were not the same as those of the twentieth century, but even contemporaries recognised that in the conduct of many courts in France there were serious deficiencies. Because the judges, lawyers and other staff of local courts were fully integrated into regional society, they too easily exercised justice in the interests of themselves and their friends; they were open to bribery, sometimes had links with leading criminals, and too often passed judgements biased in favour of those whom the judges favoured. Again, because magistrates held their positions as *offices* which were passed from father to son, some courts effectively were the personal instruments of a few families who monopolised the offices within them. Colbert denounced such practices and malpractices in a memoir which he submitted to the king in 1664:

> Justice has this fault above all, which is that, apart from using up the energies of more than seventy thousand men, it imposes a tyrannical and burdensome yoke, in your name, upon all the rest of your peoples; by its chicanery, it occupies a million men and gnaws away at a million others, reducing them to such misery that they can think about no other profession for the rest of their lives.[44]

Molière touched on the problem in one of his finest plays, *Le Misanthrope* (1666). The principal character, Alceste, is involved in a court case which he loses, and in one of the most compelling speeches of the play laments that, 'My cause is just, but I have lost the trial.'[45] This was a cry which many of Louis's subjects could have echoed.

Louis came to the question of justice from two directions. First, he instituted special commissions ('Grands Jours') to investigate alleged corruption. Grands Jours were held at Clermont in 1665 and Le Puy in 1666 to try nobles, lawyers and others whom the crown suspected of tyrannising and abusing the local populace (the 'Grands Jours d'Auvergne'). The trial at Clermont was especially notable in that 692 sentences were handed out, including the execution of some leading nobles; a commemorative medal was struck honouring the king's actions to suppress injustice.[46] Second, in 1665 Louis established a Conseil de Justice to conduct a general enquiry into the state of justice throughout the kingdom. The council, staffed by *conseillers d'état* and senior judges, formed working parties which studied particular aspects of legal reform and, after meeting together for discussion, submitted proposals to a higher committee consisting of some of the most powerful names in the country, such as Colbert, Le Tellier, Séguier, Henri Pussort (Colbert's uncle) and others who met with the king and drafted six great legal codes: the Ordonnance Civile (sometimes known as the 'Code Louis') of 1667 which established greater uniformity in court procedure, the Ordonnance sur les Eaux et Forêts (1669) which aimed to improve communications and the supply of timber for the navy, the Ordonnance Criminelle (1670) which brought greater uniformity into criminal procedure, the Ordonnance de Commerce (1673) which regularised commercial law, the Ordonnance de la Marine Marchande (1681) which laid down regulations on maritime contracts and on the management of the ports of France, and the Ordonnance des Colonies (1685) which defined the legal status of the indigenous populations and the slaves of the colonies. This body of legislation looked impressive, but was far from easy to enforce. The ordinances had to be registered by the various *parlements* and provincial estates, and ran up against vested interests, especially in local and seigneurial courts which could effectively ignore the rulings from Paris. The intendants had to spend much time attending and supervising law courts, cajoling and threatening magistrates, and endeavouring to ensure that the royal ordinances were obeyed. It must be conceded that the intentions of the crown were realised only in part, and Louis XIV never succeeded in eradicating abuses at every level of the judicial system.[47] Throughout his reign, Louis and his ministers continued the drive towards greater uniformity in the law; thus, in 1679 there were established in southern France (the area of Roman law) professorships of 'French law'. One of the functions of these professors was to define 'French law'; accordingly, figures such as Antoine de Martres in Toulouse and Claude Serres in Montpellier conducted historical research into medieval laws and edicts in an attempt to establish a corpus which could be identified as 'French law'. The task of compilation continued into the eighteenth century and may be seen as an early stage of a process which culminated in the Napoleonic Code (1804). Uniformity of law was seen by Louis XIV as a necessary condition of equitable justice; he could not achieve uniformity in his own lifetime, but began a process which, he hoped, would be concluded by his successors.[48]

Social Control

This chapter so far has discussed taxation, economic policy and the law; important as these topics are, we should devote at least a few pages to other aspects of the relationship between Louis and his subjects. It was stated earlier[49] that the French Wars of Religion bequeathed to the Bourbons alarming socio-political divisions: between crown and social elites, but also within the social elites, between the social elites and lower social orders, and within lower social orders. The healing of those divisions was among the most challenging imperatives facing the dynasty. However, the Frondes showed that the process must be handled selectively, for those rebellions had reopened fissures between crown and social elites. Moreover, the latter briefly had joined forces and come close to imposing their will on the government. It was only when the temporary alliance of the Fronde of the Princes and the Fronde of the Parlement of Paris collapsed, that the crown's position was secured. Louis XIV therefore had to maintain rather than overcome social divisions if circumstances so dictated. Social control was an aspect of kingship in which he displayed impressive qualities, for the Frondes proved to be the last great rebellion capable of uniting nobles, *officiers*, urban and rural masses; and the incidence of popular uprisings decreased considerably during the personal reign, even though warfare and its attendant financial exigencies continued almost to 1715. Historians have not yet reached consensus in explaining the diminution of coordinated popular violence during Louis's personal reign, but several hypotheses have been advanced.[50] On the negative side, it is possible that the ruthlessness with which earlier risings had been crushed by the crown deterred further popular insurrection, and that the anarchy which affected Paris and other parts of the country during the Frondes so alarmed the social elites that they repudiated mass risings as a means of resisting the crown. More positively, the government's attempts at more equitable systems of taxation and justice may have taken the edge off popular discontent; and during periods of harvest failures and famine, the government made strenuous efforts to guarantee that grain was taken from the countryside to the towns, especially Paris, to forestall renewed urban rebellion.[51] It has also been argued that the Catholic Church formed an alliance with the crown whereby the church impressed upon the laity the virtues of obedience to the social and political order, and the crown backed the church in its mission to 'christianise' the country and subvert the Huguenots.[52] The enthusiasm with which the church assisted the cause of social control paralleled the steps taken by the government to propagate the image of the king throughout the country by a concerted programme of propaganda.[53] Each of these hypotheses has its merits, but any discussion of social control under Louis XIV must also stress the care with which he disciplined the social elites.

Recent historical thought on this subject has been influenced by the work of the German sociologist, Norbert Elias,[54] who argued that seventeenth-century royal courts inculcated in their members certain modes of behaviour, certain social and political values, and an attachment to the king which overrode all other loyalties. The court, in other words, was a powerful weapon with which seventeenth-century monarchs forged the 'absolutist state'. As factors in the taming of court societies, Elias stressed the importance of the architecture of great palaces, the choice of who did and did not attend court, and the intricacies of etiquette and ceremony, especially as they involved courtiers who attended the person of the king; and in a chapter devoted to the French court,[55] he described how Louis XIV created an elaborate and manipulative environment which at every turn manifested his own magnificence, and accentuated the dependency of the nobles upon him: a dependency of honours, sinecures, provincial posts, marriages. This rigid hierarchy and the strict codes of behaviour went far beyond the confines of Versailles; they were transmitted by courtiers to the social elites of the provinces, who gradually adapted their own conduct and socio-political attitudes to those of the royal court. Elias's thesis pays close attention to the diffusion of courtly values and loyalties within the provinces as a factor in social control after the traumatic 1630s, 1640s and early 1650s.

Another historian has traced a parallel phenomenon in what she terms 'the decline of great noble clientage'.[56] Great nobles resided at Versailles and were absent from their provincial commitments for long periods (Louis-Joseph, Duc de Vendôme, who was appointed Governor of Provence in 1669, had made only three brief visits there by 1702;[57] this might be an extreme case, but it nevertheless illustrates the point); and since they had no need of extensive retinues at their country seats, they pared them to a minimum. Thereby the clientage networks of court nobles steadily contracted in the provinces during Louis XIV's personal reign, and many of the functions in public life which once had been fulfilled by 'clients' of the nobles were assumed by intendants or by appointees of ministers of the crown: in Languedoc after 1670, for example, most important administrative posts were filled by members of the Colbert clan such as the Marquis de Castries, who became lieutenant-general in Lower Languedoc.[58] Noble clientage was not in a state of terminal collapse, for it assumed amended forms in the eighteenth century; for the time being, however, the crown steadily supplanted nobles at the head of 'clientage networks' in the provinces and sought to maintain social control through its own agents and 'clients'.

The extent to which courtly and metropolitan mores were becoming the norm throughout the country may be judged at many levels. In Toulouse, for example, the architecture of large houses, the additions to the episcopal palace and the construction in 1685 of a public square, all reflected the tastes and styles of Versailles and Paris; and when the Duc de Bourgogne was born in 1682, a huge fireworks display was held in Toulouse: the soaring and bursting rockets portrayed fleurs de lys, the insignias of members of the royal family, and other glittering images of royalty in its glory.[59] The palace of Versailles itself was open to the public, and the king was frequently to be seen. Large crowds attended public ceremonies such as royal marriages and births, and it was possible even to gain entry to more intimate occasions. When the English traveller Edward Browne went to France in 1664 he saw Louis XIV leaving the Louvre for Versailles; a few days later he saw the king near Paris, 'in a chariot, two other nobles with him. The chariot was open before and he drove it himself.'[60] Another traveller, Richard Ferrier, recorded that when he went to Versailles in May 1687 he 'had the honour to see the king, Monsieur and the dauphiness at dinner with abundance of the nobility standing round the table'.[61] In 1677 John Locke saw Louis XIV on several occasions at military parades and at the opera; and in December 1678 Locke attended Louis's *grand lever* at Saint Germain:

> there is nothing so remarkable as his great devotion which is very exemplary, for as soon as ever he is dressed, he goes to his bed's side where he kneels down to his prayers, several priests kneeling by him, in which posture he continues for a pretty while, not being disturbed by the noise and buzz of the rest of the chamber, which is full of people standing and talking one to another.[62]

Again, in 1698 the Danish physician Winslow visited Versailles with two German friends. Although Protestants, they were admitted to the chapel of the palace and observed the king attend Mass.[63] It would be wrong to imagine Versailles as a retreat to which Louis withdrew from the public gaze. He led a public life, was frequently on display and through the example of the court which he commanded, instructed his subjects in the virtues of obedience, deference and respect for public order.

Those aspects of Louis's relationship with his subjects which have been discussed corroborate at least some of the judgements of Goubert with which this chapter opened, if with certain necessary qualifications. Louis's pursuit of the interests of the state did impose sacrifices on his people, especially the peasants, but he did attempt to keep the element of sacrifice under control. But one is nevertheless left with an abiding impression of the limitations on the king's capacity materially to improve the lot of his subjects. All-embracing though his theoretical powers were, the demographic and geographic facts of life, the endemic nature of warfare, and the tenacity of financial and legal tradition, all too frequently frustrated his reformist ambitions. Nevertheless, social instability did abate, and France did transcend the upheavals of earlier decades; Louis paid sufficient attention to relations with his subjects, to be able to consign to history the Frondes and the threat of civil war. There was, however, one sphere in which he was unwilling to compromise: that was religion, to which we now turn our attention.

4

LOUIS XIV AND THE CHURCHES

Historical tradition and French constitutional thought together predisposed Louis XIV to preserve the special relationship between crown and Catholic Church, but his religious policies also displayed an intemperance which contrasts with the dispassionate calculation which he sought to bring to other aspects of government. This tendency was most evident when he allowed his personal convictions a formative role in religious policy, and certain of his advisers were not above manipulating the king's spiritual disposition to their own ends. The increasing harshness with which Louis treated religious minorities, especially his Protestant subjects, suggests that the triumphant Catholicism to which he subscribed became a determinant of policy rather than an instrument of government. Louis's personal religious commitment appears to have evolved from the routine Catholic observances of his youth to a fervent piety in his middle and later years, when he was punctilious in his religious observances, attended mass daily, and during the seasons of Advent and Lent listened to cycles of sermons given by some of the finest preachers in the country: Bourdaloue, Gaillard, Mascaron, Bossuet and others. Indeed, one historian has estimated that in the course of his personal reign Louis probably heard over one thousand Advent and Lenten sermons.[1] Louis took his Easter duties seriously: on Maundy Thursday he washed the feet of poor people, attended the adoration of the cross on Good Friday, applied the Royal Touch to sufferers of scrofula, and took communion.[2] The importance of religion to Louis, both as an individual and as King of France, is reflected in the chapel at Versailles. Designed by Jules-Hardouin Mansart, it was begun in 1689, consecrated in 1710 and completed in 1712; it was therefore the product of the last twenty-five years of Louis's reign. There are two levels: a simple ground floor where the altar was situated and where courtiers and other visitors took their seats, and an elaborate upper gallery with a colonnade of Corinthian columns, where the king and his entourage sat. The richly painted ceiling was executed by Antoine Coypel. The chapel was an imposing testimony to the role of religion in the last two and a half decades of Louis's life, and remains one of the focal points of the palace of Versailles.[3] Indeed, after the court and government formally settled there in 1682, representatives of the church were at the nub of activities: members of the royal family, Princes of the Blood and aristocrats were accompanied by their confessors or chaplains, ecclesiastical dignitaries frequently were at Versailles, the papal nuncio or his assistants were regular visitors; the Catholic Church had a strong presence at Versailles, and was fully integrated into the court system.

Louis's spiritual welfare was overseen from many quarters, but a special responsibility rested with his confessors, all of whom were Jesuits. The two longest-serving were Père François Annat from 1654 to 1670, and Père François de la Chaise from 1674 to 1709. The former, one of France's leading theologians, was a prominent opponent of Jansenism who encouraged a similar hostility in Louis XIV. La Chaise's period as confessor coincided with the 'pious' phase of Louis's life and with some of the most controversial aspects of the king's religious policy: the climax of the persecution of the Huguenots, the crown's continuing resistance to Jansenism and problems relating to Gallicanism. He has sometimes been portrayed as a pernicious influence who exploited Louis's tendencies to intolerance, and exerted unwarranted pressure over the appointment of bishops and other prelates. This 'black legend' should be treated with some scepticism. La Chaise undoubtedly favoured the abolition of Protestantism in France, but so did the entire Catholic hierarchy; and although the king consulted him on candidates for leading benefices, Louis made up his own mind on key appointments (for instance, Noailles as Archbishop of Paris was little to La Chaise's liking). La Chaise even checked some of Louis's more extremist tendencies: he attempted to keep the king's antipathy towards Jansenism within limits (it was after La Chaise's death that Louis was most heavy-handed in his treatment of the Jansenists), and he dissuaded the puritanical king of later years from banning the theatre at Versailles. Another prominent figure in Louis's religious development was his morganatic wife, Madame

Scarron (later the 'Marquise de Maintenon'). She first came to his
attention as the person who helped his mistress Madame de
Montespan to care for and educate their children. Madame Scarron
was reserved, cold-mannered and deeply religious, but also alert to
the possibilities of her position. She gradually replaced Madame de
Montespan in the affections of the king, who in 1673 granted her the
estate of Maintenon with the title 'Marquise'. When he broke with
Madame de Montespan in 1680, the Marquise de Maintenon took her
place. After the death of the queen in 1683, she secretly married the
king. Under her influence Louis's Catholicism became ever more
penitential and heartfelt; and while we should recognise that other
figures also swayed his religious thinking, she was uniquely placed to
encourage his religious sensibilities.

The Catholic Church in France[4]

The position which the Catholic Church occupied in French society
was by any measure imposing. About 90 per cent of Louis's subjects
were Catholic, and in everyday life they frequently encountered physical reminders of their faith: cathedrals, churches, monasteries,
convents, shrines, wayside statues of Christ, the Virgin or a saint.
Homes often were adorned with crucifixes and other religious arte-
facts, while more affluent households possessed copies of the Bible
(Bible reading was not an exclusively Protestant activity in France),
prayer books, paintings, engravings, statues and other representations
of religious subjects. Generalisations about the nature and depth of
religious faith are difficult. Among the mass of the rural population,
personal piety could coexist with popular belief in magic, beneficent
or wicked spirits, witches and other inhabitants of the spirit world;[5]
at the other extreme France produced philosophers and theologians
whose devotional and other works formed part of the outstanding
Christian literature of the century. Here we are not concerned with
the religious history of France as such, but if we are to understand
the significance of Louis's religious policies we must grasp that
Catholicism was at the centre of the lives of most of his subjects; it
surrounded them physically and guided them spiritually, morally and
intellectually. Faced with the challenge of stabilising society after the
Protestant revolts of the 1620s and the Frondes of the 1640s and early
1650s, Louis looked to the church for backing. It duly responded: in

their pastoral letters, bishops urged upon the laity their Christian duty to give their fidelity to the lawful secular powers; parish priests likewise regularly preached upon the theme of obedience; in the schools and colleges run by the Oratorians and Jesuits, pupils again were instructed in the virtues of loyalty to the king. Alongside the sustained campaign by the Catholic Church to broaden and deepen its hold over the spiritual life of the nation went a parallel undertaking to assist Louis XIV towards the pacification of society.

The Counter-Reformation had penetrated France in the first half of the century, and in a country emerging from civil war had placed strong emphasis on evangelical activity and social improvement. During the reign of Louis XIII, the Catholic Church devoted considerable resources to missions among the rural and urban masses, to the conversion of Huguenots, education, charitable works among the indigent and the sick, and to the spiritual regeneration of the religious orders. The great names of the Counter-Reformation in France – figures such as St François de Sales, Pierre Bérulle, St Vincent de Paul, and Ste Jeanne de Chantal – epitomised that combination of spiritual regeneration and social action which defined a movement which in many respects was a response to the tragic aftermath of the French Wars of Religion.[6] Their endeavours were remarkably effective, especially among the social elites. In the major towns and cities of France, large numbers of lay men and women including the topmost sections of society joined confraternities devoted to spiritual regeneration, moral improvement and charitable work. One of the most influential was the Compagnie du Saint-Sacrement, founded about 1630 by Henri de Lévis, Duc de Ventadour. The Compagnie attracted royalty and great aristocrats into membership, and quickly became a national movement. It attempted to preserve an air of secrecy in order to resist the temptation towards spiritual and moral pride which a public society might have posed. Ironically it was this very secrecy – which in practice was only partial, since in the tightly knit circles of metropolitan and provincial elites it was known who the members were – which was to bring the reputation of the Compagnie into question. Members extended their influence into the realms of commerce, education, the seminaries, and upon the private lives of ordinary Catholics. At their best, members of the Compagnie manifested in their own lives and encouraged in others a selfless social service and deepening of religious faith, but among their ranks were less worthy figures with reputations as mischievous and prudish

intruders into the affairs of other people. Again, in the tense political atmosphere of the post-Fronde years the government was exceedingly suspicious of a society committed to secrecy, no matter how
exemplary its ideals and purposes. How could the government be
certain that it was not being used as a front by unscrupulous political schemers? Even some bishops were disturbed at the zealotry of
the Compagnie, and feared that it might become a 'church within the
Church'. In 1660 the Archbishop of Rouen presented to Mazarin a
formal complaint against its activities. Mazarin welcomed this opportunity to curb the society, but avoided the controversy which a governmental ban would have created by urging the Parlement of Paris to
take the necessary steps. In 1660 the Parlement, without mentioning
the Compagnie by name, proscribed all assemblies which met without
the king's permission. Although it survived a few more years, the
Compagnie was effectively defunct by the late 1660s.

Apart from its spiritual functions, the Catholic Church wielded
considerable powers in institutional and economic terms. The clergy
was the First Estate of society and thereby enjoyed legal pre-eminence
in the kingdom; this was seen, for example, in the provincial estates
and Estates General, where the clergy enjoyed pre-eminence over the
nobility (the Second Estate) and commoners (the Third Estate).
Because of its legal status the clergy was able to recruit from every
level of society, including the nobility whose social standing ensured
that they received a disproportionate share of bishoprics and prestigious benefices.[7] The clergy possessed financial and legal privileges
including exemption from many taxes and immunity from civil courts.
Churches, monasteries, convents and bishops often were substantial
landowners, and received the *dîme* (tithe) – a proportion of their
produce – from peasants. At least every four years a General Assembly
of the Clergy met to review problems facing the church, and to decide
how much money to vote the king as a *don gratuit*. Most education in
France was in the hands of the clergy: the Jesuits and Oratorians had
colleges throughout the country while, in the universities, Theology
was recognised as the senior faculty. The Catholic Church's social and
institutional functions extended far and wide – for instance, the
church also ran many of the hospitals and charitable institutions of
France – and Louis could be under no illusions as to the economic
and social powers which the church commanded.

Being deeply rooted in the socio-political systems of France, the
Catholic Church was bound to harbour various theological tenden-

cies and factional rivalries. In France, as elsewhere, relations between Jesuits and Dominicans sometimes were strained; appointments to the larger bishoprics and archbishoprics usually implied the strengthening or weakening of one ecclesiastical party or another, and the ease or difficulty with which groups gained access to the ear of the king or one of his ministers could affect their position within the church. In these respects France was typical of the rest of Catholic Europe, for similar comments could be made about the church in Spain, Italy, Germany or elsewhere. However, the Catholic Church in France did claim to be unique in Christendom in that it possessed rights – 'Gallican rights' – which distinguished it from other branches of the church. It formed part of the universal church and shared in the general opportunities and problems of that body, but it also claimed a special status resulting from its rights as the French Catholic Church.

Gallicanism

Gallicanism derived from an alliance between the French ecclesiastical hierarchy, the crown, the Parlement of Paris and the Sorbonne (the Theology Faculty of the University of Paris). Gallican rights had evolved during the Middle Ages, but had been formulated during the Great Schism (1378–1417) when rival popes sat in Rome and Avignon. Assemblies of the French clergy responded to the factionalism into which the papacy had fallen by proclaiming that the authority of general councils of the church was superior to that of the pope, that taxes to the pope ('annates') could be withheld if the French clergy so decided, that vacancies to bishoprics and other benefices should be filled by election, not by papal appointment; and that these 'rights' should be protected by the king. During the fifteenth century successive popes challenged the validity of these rights, but encountered united opposition from crown, Parlement of Paris, Sorbonne and French clergy. A compromise was reached by the Concordat of Bologna (1516), which conceded the right of the king to nominate candidates to senior benefices in France, the pope then instituting the nominees; a financial provision was included (the *droit de régale*): when a benefice was vacant its revenues would go to the king. In return for these papal concessions, the king ensured that annates were paid to Rome as in the past. By the Concordat, the Kings of France exercised control over ecclesiastical patronage: henceforth access to archbishoprics, bishoprics and the most important monasteries and convents was dependent on the royal will.

French jurists continued to assert and define Gallican rights. Two influential statements were by Pierre Pithou whose *Libertés de l'Eglise Gallicane* (1594) listed eighty-three 'liberties', and Pierre Dupuy in *Les Preuves des Libertés de l'Eglise Gallicane* (1639). This latter work reprinted documents to support the arguments presented by Pithou; it was reissued in 1651 with royal approval and became the authoritative statement of Gallican rights down to the Revolution. Dupuy asserted three principles. The first was that the temporal power of the king and his agents was not subject to spiritual authority; the pope could not excommunicate the king or his agents in the exercise of their temporal powers, nor could he dispense the king's subjects from loyalty to him. The second was that the pope did not have absolute authority over the clergy of France in matters of church discipline and the temporal functions of the clergy; in these two areas papal authority must yield to the will of the king; no papal bull, no decree of a general council of the church dealing with disciplinary or temporal affairs was admissible in France without royal consent. The third was that, in the disciplinary and temporal affairs of the church, the King of France rather than the pope exercised supreme authority.

The question of Gallican rights, and especially the *droit de régale*, was raised anew in 1673. Since the beginning of the war against the Dutch Republic (1672), Louis XIV had been seizing church property to help to finance the conflict. In 1673 he went a step further and extended the *droit de régale* to every part of his kingdom, which now was larger than in 1516: provinces such as Béarn, Brittany and Provence had been incorporated, and the frontiers had expanded. Pope Clement X protested against the seizures of property, but remained silent on the extension of *régale*, a silence which Louis interpreted as tacit acquiescence. Louis was further encouraged by the fact that with two exceptions – François-Etienne de Caulet, Bishop of Pamiers, and Nicolas Pavillon, Bishop of Alet – the bishops in France supported him. Pavillon died in 1677, but Caulet appealed to the new pope, Innocent XI, against Louis's action. Innocent stood by Pavillon, announced that the *droit de régale* applied only to the territories comprising France in 1516, and refused to recognise the validity of ecclesiastical appointments in other parts of the country. The affair threatened to get out of hand. A General Assembly of the French Clergy in 1680 reaffirmed 'Gallican rights', and in 1682 a meeting of

French bishops issued four definitive principles: the king was supreme in temporal affairs; in spiritual matters the pope held authority subject to a general council; the traditional liberties of the Gallican church remained valid; and in matters of faith the pope was not infallible, but required the consent of the universal church. Innocent XI rejected the four Articles and in return refused to institute bishops whom Louis nominated. Deadlock set in: by 1688, thirty-five bishoprics in France were vacant, and in that year Innocent secretly informed Louis that he and his ministers were excommunicated. It was in the interests of neither side to take the dispute to its extremes. A settlement was reached in 1693 under the pontificate of Innocent XII: Louis agreed to urge the French bishops to withdraw the four Gallican Articles of 1682 (they duly complied), but in return the pope recognised the king's right to nominate to benefices throughout the modern enlarged kingdom. The Gallican question was to reappear in new guises in the eighteenth century, but for the time being Louis was pleased to have the matter resolved. His disputes with Rome had come at a most inopportune time, for, as will be seen, he was facing a difficult international situation in the 1680s and early 1690s, and the Jansenists and other heterodox Catholic groups were causing him disquiet. The settlement of 1693 enabled Louis to set Gallicanism aside as a source of controversy.

Jansenism[8]

Louis's tendency to become locked in religious controversies of immense complexity, and then to attempt a crude, simplistic 'solution', is illustrated by the question of Jansenism which, unlike Gallicanism, was an international movement of recent origin. It arose from the teaching of Cornelius Jansen, Professor of Theology at the University of Louvain and from 1636 Bishop of Ypres. By the time he died in 1638 his ideas were well known in theological circles, but in 1640 reached a wider audience through his posthumous *Augustinus*, a study of the thought of one of the most influential Fathers of the Church, St Augustine. Jansen developed a theology of predestination according to which, because of the Fall of Man, nobody is capable of contributing to his or her salvation, be it through good works or religious observance. Salvation comes only to those upon whom God confers grace; but in His unfathomable wisdom He bestows it upon some but not upon others. These austere tenets were close to Calvinism, but Jansen maintained that, far from flirting with Protestantism, he was seeking to show Calvinists the way back to Catholicism by demonstrating that on questions of grace and predestination they were at one with Catholic teaching. Many implications followed from Jansen's theology. If most human beings are denied salvation, is the worship which they offer to God of any value, indeed are they members of the church at all? On the answer to this question depended others such as the mission of the church, and its spiritual and social functions. Moreover, if most people remain enslaved to sin, does not their condition make a mockery of any claims to free will and moral responsibility? In these and other matters Jansen challenged what he considered to be a scandalously imprecise position on the part of the Jesuits. Jansenists were particularly critical of the Spanish Jesuit Luis Molina, whose *De Concordia* (1588) also dealt with divine grace. Molina contended that the Fall was not all-embracing; human beings retain a spark of original innocence which can be revived by divine grace. Men and women can choose to accept grace and thereby contribute to their salvation. Unworthy though people may be, the church should readily absolve them from sin and admit them to Mass, for all are capable of responding to grace even if slowly and intermittently. Not all Jesuits went as far as Molina, but the Order repudiated Jansenism on the ground that it concentrated on selected aspects of Augustinian thought, disregarded non-Augustinian interpretations of grace, and built a towering theological edifice on narrow foundations. Rome thought likewise. The papacy traditionally tolerated scholarly speculation on even the most obscure questions, including predestination, but resisted any attempt to bind dogma to one particular school of theology. In 1643 Pope Urban VIII issued the bull *In Eminenti* censuring the *Augustinus*.

The key figure in the introduction of Jansenism into France was Jean Duvergier de Hauranne, Abbé de Saint Cyran, who was a friend of Jansen. He disseminated Jansenism through preaching and writing, but also through his influence on the Cistercian convent of Port Royal whose abbess, Angélique Arnauld, belonged to a well-known family of the *noblesse de robe*. The convent was located in a dank valley, La Vallée du Rhodon, not far from Versailles, but in 1625 Mère Angélique transferred it to the southern outskirts of Paris where the air was more wholesome. In 1633 Saint Cyran became spiritual director to the convent which embraced Jansenism, the nuns following an ascetic

lifestyle of devotion to prayer and contemplation. Port Royal established schools in Paris and attracted laymen who found in Jansenism
a religious ethos responsive to their own needs. These 'solitaires', who
included men of the highest intellectual calibre, regularly went into
religious retreat at the abandoned convent in the country. Prominent
among them were other members of the Arnauld family – notably
Antoine, whose *De la Fréquente Communion* of 1643 was one of the great
texts of Jansenism – and Pierre Nicole who also wrote on religious
themes and was active in the Port Royal schools. In 1648 Mère
Angélique returned to the Vallée du Rhodon with some of the nuns
from Paris. The two centres remained focal points of French
Jansenism down to the 1660s; and although the Paris convent gradually retreated from Jansenism, Port Royal des Champs in the valley
remained faithful until Louis XIV closed the convent in 1709. Port
Royal attracted leading figures from the worlds of literature, the
sciences and the visual arts. In the sciences Blaise Pascal and Denis
Dodart were Jansenists; in literature Jean Racine (who as an orphan
was brought up in a Port Royal school), Boileau, La Fontaine and
Madame de Sévigné had close relations with Port Royal; and in the
visual arts Philippe de Champaigne – one of whose daughters was a
nun there – painted and donated portraits of leading figures in the
convent. Pascal made incisive contributions to the defence of
Jansenism. From 1656 to 1657 he published eighteen *Lettres Provin-
ciales*; written in a brilliant style which blended clarity, elegance and
irony, they upheld the claims of Jansenism against attacks by Jesuits
and became literary best-sellers of enduring fame. Meanwhile
Jansenism received further censure by Rome. In 1651 Pope Innocent X appointed a commission to examine five propositions allegedly
found in the *Augustinus*.[9] The commission concluded that the propositions were heretical, and recommended their condemnation; a papal
bull to that effect was issued in 1653. The Jansenist response was
formulated chiefly by Antoine Arnauld, who agreed that the five
propositions deserved condemnation, but denied that they were to be
found in the *Augustinus*; the papal commission had misconstrued
Jansen's work. Even though Innocent X in 1654 and his successor
Alexander VII in 1656 insisted that the five propositions were
contained within the *Augustinus*, Jansenists persisted in their denial.

Apart from these intricate theological problems, Jansenism carried
political implications which raised the apprehensions of the French
government. Against the view that the institutions of the state were

instruments of the divine will, some Jansenists held that political, legal
and other institutions were no more than Fallen Man's attempts to
preserve elements of civil society; they did not necessarily reflect the
divine order, nor were the actions of the state invariably binding on
Christians. This was a sensitive issue, for as early as the 1630s and
1640s Jansenists were among the foremost critics of Cardinal Richelieu whom they charged with subordinating the church to interests of
state. It was the Frondes, however, which most implicated Jansenists
in resistance to the government. Leading Frondeurs such as the Duc
de Luynes, the Duchesse de Chevreuse and the Duc de la Rochefou-
cauld had close links with Port Royal; so did Robert Arnauld d'Andilly
who wrote one of the most vitriolic attacks on Mazarin, *La Vérité Tout
Nu* [*sic*]. Many Parisian priests of Jansenist leanings were suspected
by Mazarin of supporting the Frondes, while one of his most
implacable enemies, Cardinal de Retz, openly associated with
Jansenists. Mère Angélique and others at Port Royal insisted that they
would not countenance rebellion, but it was unrealistic to suppose
that Jansenism could emerge from the Frondes untainted by the experience. Rome, the French crown and French bishops hostile to
Jansenism took steps to curb the movement. The Assembly of the
Clergy in 1661 adopted a formulary to which all priests, heads of
colleges, and members of religious orders were ordered to subscribe.
It included a promise of obedience to the pope, and the words, 'I
condemn... the five propositions of Cornelius Jansen contained in his
book entitled *Augustinus*.' The formulary was accepted by most priests,
but Jansenists were divided on their response. Some subscribed,
although the nuns of Port Royal refused as did four bishops (including
Caulet and Pavillon). After further talks involving Rome and the
government the bishops subscribed in 1668, but only to a formulary
hedged in qualifications; those nuns who still held out were kept at
Port Royal des Champs. A truce had been achieved by this so-called
'peace of the church'. Rome and Louis XIV were more anxious to
quell controversy than to force Jansenists to conform to the letter of
the formulary. Although the settlement was ambiguous, it provided
temporary respite.

   This episode left Louis with an even stronger distaste for Jansenism.
He perceived in it more than a religious phenomenon, for even after
the 'peace' it continued to attract both lay and clerical support. Missals
and breviaries composed by Jansenists sold profusely; so did Bibles
translated into French, especially that by Le Maître de Sacy. Insofar

as Jansenism upheld the pre-eminence of the individual conscience against external authority (whether that authority be church or state), Louis suspected that it provided a convenient guise for ex-Frondeurs to continue resistance under another name. For some years the 'peace of the church' held, but by the late 1670s the government and ecclesiastical authorities were again making life difficult for Jansenist leaders. In 1679 the 'solitaires' of Port Royal des Champs were dispersed, the convent was forbidden by the Archbishop of Paris to receive any new novices, and Antoine Arnauld was driven into exile in the Dutch Republic. Even so, the influence of Jansenism continued, and found a doughty exponent in the Oratorian priest Pasquier Quesnel. Quesnel was an enigmatic figure in that his Jansenism did not exclude other theological traditions: he wrote in defence of Gallican rights, and in his theology drew upon St Thomas Aquinas as well as St Augustine. In 1684 he went into exile in the Spanish Netherlands, where he expanded and republished in 1692 his most popular work, *Réflexions Morales*, which owed little to the *Augustinus* and reflected a broad range of theological influences. The *Réflexions* received wide praise, including that of Louis-Antoine de Noailles, Archbishop of Paris; its appearance signalled that perhaps Jansenism was returning towards the orthodox fold.

Whether or not this trend would have continued must remain a subject of conjecture, for in 1703 Quesnel – still in the Spanish Netherlands – was arrested at the instigation of the Archbishop of Malines; his papers were seized and made available to agents of the French government. His correspondence not only provided evidence that many Jansenists had never taken the 'peace of the church' seriously – they still appeared to regard themselves as an elect group which in the last resort was answerable neither to pope, episcopacy, nor king – but revealed what looked like an extensive network of Jansenism still operating in France. To modern eyes this 'network' appears a diffuse penumbra around a small, hard core of Jansenists; its significance was cultural rather than religious in the strict sense. By now, however, France was embroiled in the War of the Spanish Succession and Louis was in no mood to be forbearing towards religious deviants. He saw Jansenism as a highly organised movement which still threatened the unity of the church and therefore the safety of the state. In 1705 he persuaded Pope Clement XI to publish the bull *Vineam Domini* which reaffirmed that all Catholics must subscribe to the formulary of 1661 before receiving absolution. Louis sent the bull to the Assembly of the Clergy in 1705 with an injunction to proceed with its adoption as quickly as possible; he also had the bull registered by the Parlement of Paris. Louis had not finished: largely at his instigation the pope in 1708 condemned Quesnel's *Réflexions Morales* as contaminated with Jansenism, and in 1709 Louis announced the closure of Port Royal des Champs. The remaining nuns were dispersed among other convents, the buildings were torn down to prevent them becoming a place of pilgrimage, and the bodies of Pascal and Racine, who had chosen to be buried there, were disinterred and transferred to Paris.

We might assume that, after these hammer-blows against Jansenism, Louis had more than amply demonstrated his orthodox religious credentials, and that his wisest course was to cease paying attention to Jansenism, leaving it to the church to resolve any residual problems. He did not. He continued his pursuit, to the point of creating further and unnecessary difficulties. In 1711 he instructed his ambassador at Rome to request from the pope a new condemnation of Jansenism. Clement XI complied when in 1713 he issued the bull *Unigenitus Dei Filius* which condemned 101 Jansenist propositions allegedly contained in Quesnel's *Réflexions Morales*. That the pope responded in this way doubtless is evidence of Louis's continuing international authority, even at the height of the War of the Spanish Succession, but *Unigenitus*, which passed without much comment elsewhere in Catholic Europe, provoked controversy and opposition in France. Why, then, had Louis sought it? The answer is partly to be found in his own obsessive religious temperament, but also in factions around him which turned his detestation of Jansenism to their own account.

Factional Influences on Louis XIV

One figure who manipulated Louis was his new Jesuit confessor Michel le Tellier (no relation to the minister), whose target was Noailles, Archbishop of Paris. Noailles had often criticised the Jesuits and made no secret of his opinion that their influence in the country was detrimental to the good of the church. Le Tellier replaced La Chaise as royal confessor in 1709, but whereas the latter had been the personification of immaculate manners, elegant comportment and diplomatic language, Le Tellier's conduct was assertive and blunt. He resolved to mount a counter-attack against the archbishop and found an opportune weapon in Noailles's sympathetic response to the *Réflexions Morales*. As early as 1706 Le Tellier had been to Rome to help to organise Jesuit opposition to the *Réflexions Morales*; as confessor to the king he now advised Louis XIV that it was his duty to sustain the campaign against Jansenism. When *Unigenitus* was promulgated it reflected many of Le Tellier's own views, and Noailles perceived in it a thinly disguised attempt to discredit him: if Noailles had failed to see the flaws in a work which contained no less than 101 serious errors, what did that say about his judgement?

Another influence on Louis XIV was Madame de Maintenon and, indirectly, Archbishop Fénelon (a friend of Le Tellier), whose motives for undermining Noailles went back to the Quietist affair. Quietism[10] was a mystic stream within Catholicism which went back to the Middle Ages. In the seventeenth century it was revived by the Spaniard Miguel Molinos, whose *Spiritual Guide* (1675) was translated into several languages. Quietism (Molinism) advocated self-abandonment to the love of God: the Christian should contemplate God rather than engage in customary religious exercises and petitionary prayer, and should approach formal acts of worship as aids to mystical experience rather than meritorious occasions in their own right. In France, Quietism found its principal advocate in a wealthy widow with aristocratic connections, Jeanne Bouvier de la Motte, Madame Guyon. In 1685 she published a guide to Quietist practices entitled *Moyen Court et très Facile pour l'Oraison*, and followed it the following year with *Les Torrents Spirituels*. These works earned her a mixture of notoriety and success: she was detained for a time in a convent in Paris, but through her aristocratic friends was released in 1688. She was invited to court where a coterie of devotees gathered around her, including Madame de Maintenon and the new tutor to the Duc de Bourgogne, François de Salignac de la Mothe-Fénelon (who was appointed Archbishop of Cambrai in 1695). Madame Guyon resided at the convent school of Saint Cyr near Versailles which Madame de Maintenon had founded in 1686 for the daughters of impoverished nobles. Madame Guyon exerted a strong influence there as she encouraged the girls towards mystical religious experiences. Leading ecclesiastics who visited Versailles expressed disquiet at her activities, especially since in 1687 Rome had condemned Molinos's *Spiritual Guide*. Even Madame de Maintenon was made uneasy by the behaviour of Madame Guyon, and had misgivings over the ascendancy she was exerting over the

girls at Saint Cyr. Madame de Maintenon and Fénelon asked Jacques
Bénigne Bossuet, Bishop of Meaux, one of the finest minds in the
French Catholic Church (it was he who had drafted the Gallican articles of 1682), to inquire into Quietism. Assisted by other clerics, among
whom Noailles was prominent, Bossuet conducted the investigation
and concluded that Quietism was incompatible with Catholic orthodoxy. Fénelon was dismayed at the findings of the commission which,
he felt, had gone much too far in turning religious faith into an intellectual exercise; in his view Bossuet and his team had greatly under-
estimated the legitimate role of mystical experience in the Christian
life. In 1697 Fénelon composed his *Explication des Maximes des Saints*
as a rebuttal of Bossuet. However, Madame de Maintenon felt it necessary to distance herself from Fénelon and from Madame Guyon (who
in 1698 was imprisoned, then exiled to Blois). Madame de Maintenon
reverted to strict Catholic orthodoxy and implored the king to protect
the church against deviants. However, she took strong exception to
the fact that Jansenists, among whom she numbered Noailles, had
joined the attack on Quietism: Jansenists accused Madame Guyon and
her supporters of negating that profound sense of penitence without
which salvation was impossible, and of losing themselves in escapist
reveries of dubious spiritual value. Louis XIV was not going to listen
to Jansenists, but he did respect the advice of Bossuet and Madame
de Maintenon. He asked Pope Innocent XII to denounce Fénelon's
defence of Quietism, but the pope was reluctant to do so in conclu-
sive terms, for he had some sympathy with Fénelon's warnings against
an over-intellectualised Christianity. In 1699 the pope condemned
certain aspects of the *Explication des Maximes des Saints*, but in moderate
terms that Fénelon was able to accept. Meanwhile, the archbishop was
ordered back to his archdiocese by the king, and was discharged from
his duties as tutor to the Duc de Bourgogne. Fénelon never returned
to Versailles, but he harboured a sense of betrayal by Bossuet and
Noailles, and was irked that a Jansenist 'sympathiser' should have
been involved in his disgrace. When Le Tellier schemed against
Noailles, he had the support of the Archbishop of Cambrai.

Under such pressure Louis sought and acquired *Unigenitus* in 1713;
however, it split the church in France and led to tensions between
Louis and the Parlement of Paris. The month after its promulgation
Louis called a meeting of bishops to receive the bull. Whereas most
did so, Noailles refused to admit the bull to the archdiocese of Paris,
and was supported by eight other bishops; many of the religious

orders in France, the Sorbonne and the Parlement of Paris also backed Noailles. At the centre of their objections was the suspicion that papal pronouncements on Jansenism, terminating in *Unigenitus*, represented a steady but perceptible undermining of Gallican rights. The role of the Jesuits in the formulation of the bull reinforced these suspicions, for the Jesuits were widely considered to be agents of papal power. Louis, who earlier in his reign had been involved in disputes with Rome over his protection of Gallican rights, now found himself in the ironical position of attempting to make the clergy (or at least an important section of them), the Sorbonne and the Parlement of Paris – three main bodies in the great Gallican 'alliance' – comply with orders from Rome. The Parlement called for a general council of the church to settle questions of doctrine and dogma (Louis's appeals to Rome could be interpreted as concessions to papal infallibility), and in 1714 the Chancellor of France, Pontchartrain, resigned over *Unigenitus*. Under royal pressure both the Sorbonne and the Parlement eventually gave in, but after Louis's death in 1715 the bull was challenged anew by the Parlement of Paris, while the Regency of Louis XV turned a blind eye to renewed Jansenist activity. Jansenism bedevilled the last few years of Louis's reign. Admittedly, it posed complicated dichotomies – predestination as against free will; individual conscience as against ecclesiastical and state authority; the authority of Rome as against Gallican rights – but by attempting to pursue these matters to their logical conclusion, Louis succeeded only in turning Jansenism into a cause which attracted much sympathy and which continued to influence the religious history of France down to the Revolution.

The Huguenots[11]

If Louis's treatment of the Jansenists earned him criticism within some sections of Catholic France, his suppression of the Protestant or Huguenot Church ('La Religion Prétendue Réformée' or RPR in Catholic and governmental parlance) won wide approval. The term 'Huguenot', as signifying 'Protestant', had emerged in the mid-sixteenth century and derived from the Swiss-German word 'Eidgenossen', which signified 'confederates'. Louis regarded the existence of the Huguenots as a shameful reminder of royal weakness during and after the Wars of Religion. In 1598 Henri IV had conceded the Edict of Nantes, defining the position of Protestantism within state and society in the interests of social and political peace. Henri had never envisaged it as a permanent settlement; in spite of his Huguenot upbringing, as King of France he shared the common assumption that a multi-confessional state was vulnerable to faction-alism at home and intervention by foreign states. The surest precon-dition of socio-political stability was one church, but pending that day the Edict of Nantes legally incorporated the Huguenots into the state. The edict defined those parts of the country in which they hence-forth had rights of worship; it recognised their liberty to pursue such careers as they wished; it created special tribunals (*chambres mi-parties* comprising magistrates from both faiths) to adjudicate disputes between Huguenots and Catholics; and as a further assurance of their safety it allowed the Huguenots to fortify certain towns. The Edict of Nantes was not a powerful declaration of the principle of religious toleration; it was a pragmatic response by Henri IV to the crises of the Wars of Religion, and a price he was willing to pay for peace.

How sizeable was the Huguenot population? The most recent esti-mates[12] suggest that in 1610 the Huguenots numbered about 930,000, to which can be added another 100,000–125,000 from the province of Béarn which Louis XIII later incorporated into the kingdom. If we take this combined figure of between 1,030,000 and 1,055,000 in 1610, the Huguenots constituted about 6 or 7 per cent of the popu-lation of France. Thereafter they went into decline: to about 980,000 in 1630, 850,000 in 1660 and 730,000 in 1680, by which time they comprised between 3 and 4 per cent of the population.[13] Some of the reasons for decline were those which affected the whole country – periodic food shortages and disease, and the repressions which followed civil disturbances – but the Huguenots also were under constant pressure from the Catholic Church (including activists from the Compagnie du Saint Sacrement) to convert, and there was a steady seepage from the one church to the other especially on the part of the higher nobility; and when, for example, Marshal Turenne became a convert in 1668, this was regarded as a considerable coup by the Catholic Church. Although there were Huguenots in northern France, most lived south of the Loire, and were concentrated in an arc running from Poitou down the Garonne into Languedoc (with a 'branch line' into Béarn) and across to Dauphiné. In these areas many towns and villages had Protestant majorities; indeed, in the early 1660s about 40 per cent of Huguenots lived in towns with popula-tions over 2000. The Huguenots had a highly organised ecclesiastical structure which served also as a convenient forum for unofficial political debate: the country was divided into sixteen 'provinces' each of which had an annual assembly attended by the pastor and two elders from each congregation; a national synod met in theory every three years, although in practice it did so irregularly. The Huguenots also paid close attention to the education of the young. By 1610 they had established thirty-one academies throughout France (including Béarn): some were in the south-western and south-eastern heartlands of French Protestantism (Bergerac, Montauban, Castres, Montpellier, Nîmes and elsewhere), others were strung along or near the Loire (Saumur, Loudun, Tours, Gergeau and others); in 1659 there was added the famous academy at Sedan which lay in territory acquired by Louis XIV in the Peace of the Pyrenees. The Huguenot academies guaranteed a supply of well-educated pastors able to provide leadership to the church, but in more general terms ensured that Huguenots would be in a position to pursue careers in a wide sphere of activities and, so Huguenots hoped, prove creative and valued subjects of the crown.

As within Catholicism, there were various tendencies within Protestantism ranging from strict Calvinism which brooked no compromise on matters of faith and doctrine, to more 'liberal' attitudes prepared to seek accommodation with Catholicism. Bishop Bossuet hoped to encourage this latter tendency. He held discussions with Pastor Ferry from Metz, and in 1670 published his *Exposition de la Foi Catholique*, a work which aimed to lead Protestants back to Catholicism. French Protestantism still retained its spiritual vigour; the older view expressed by Léonard that, after its initial period of expansion in the sixteenth century, it lost its sense of enterprise, is no longer persuasive. It was not that the Huguenots had settled down to a lukewarm *modus vivendi* in the seventeenth century; it was rather that they were faced by the French Counter-Reformation Church which took seriously its missionary activities against 'heretics' and 'backsliders'. The Catholic Church organised missions among the Huguenots, and against Bossuet's mediatory *Exposition* may be set such anti-Huguenot publications as Pierre Bernard's *Explication de l'Edit de Nantes* (1666) which stressed the ephemeral nature of the edict and reminded the crown that it could revoke the edict as and when necessary; or the numerous writings of Père Meynier: for instance *L'Edit de Nantes Exécuté selon les Intentions d'Henri le Grand* (1670), which called for the most strict application of the terms of the edict.

Politically the Huguenots had ceased to be a problem for the government by the 1660s. Earlier in the century, notably in the 1620s, they had rebelled, but thereafter had come to terms with the Bourbon regime. During the Fronde at Bordeaux some Huguenots supported the risings on an individual basis, but the Huguenots as a body throughout France preserved their allegiance to the crown (a stance publicly acknowledged by Mazarin in 1652). At the beginning of his personal reign, therefore, Louis XIV's Huguenot subjects numerically were in decline and politically presented no danger. However, his entire philosophy of kingship drove him towards the elimination of a religious minority whose existence was incompatible with the adage 'one king, one faith, one law'. To Louis the question of the Huguenots was not 'utilitarian' in nature; it raised a matter of principle before which Louis was capable of only one response. Other voices also urged him to remove this 'stain' on the honour of France. Ever since 1605 the Assembly of the Clergy had regularly formulated accusations against the Huguenots, and demanded the strict application of the terms of the Edict of Nantes; later assemblies regularly petitioned the king to exclude Huguenots from offices or charges, to order the closure of Huguenot churches built in areas not specified in the edict, and to impose a ban on Protestant open-air preachers. In 1661, in response to demands from the Catholic clergy, government commissioners were appointed to investigate the extent to which the Huguenots had exceeded their privileges: each team normally comprised an intendant, a Protestant and a Catholic priest. These commissions insisted on strict adherence to the Edict of Nantes: in the 1660s the commission in Dauphiné closed almost half of the Huguenot churches, while in Languedoc, where the Huguenots were numerically strong, the commission excluded them from the Estates and from many offices (in 1663 municipal offices were reserved for Catholics in Montpellier, Mazamet, Sommières and other towns); it closed Protestant schools and excluded Huguenots from the management of hospitals. Throughout the 1660s, commissions everywhere enacted similar measures, undermining the religious and social foundations of Protestantism. Nevertheless, protests at Huguenot 'misbehaviour' continued to be presented to the crown by Estates and other legal bodies in provinces with large Protestant minorities: thus, the Estates of Languedoc and Parlement of Toulouse frequently sent formal petitions to the king calling upon him to curb the religious activities of the Huguenots. In the first decade of his personal reign, therefore, Louis's policy towards the Huguenots not only developed in accordance with his political and religious philosophy; it responded to Catholic opinion in the provinces.

Over the next twenty-five years Louis, working through the Conseil d'en Haut, enacted a coherent programme of anti-Huguenot legislation which culminated in the Revocation of the Edict of Nantes in 1685. Hundreds of decrees and laws were passed, some of local application only, others being imposed throughout the country. They were organised around three main principles. One aimed to weaken the purely religious basis of French Protestantism. 'Illegal' Huguenot churches continued to be dismantled (there were over 800 Protestant churches in 1660, but only about 240 by the early 1680s) and open-air services were banned; the national synod was forbidden to meet (the last one did so in 1659), and from 1669 provincial synods were not allowed to communicate with each other. As from 1680 the government commissioners attended provincial synods to exercise a watching brief, and Huguenots living in parts of the country where they were a small minority were debarred from migrating to areas where they were in a majority. In 1676 a 'treasury of conversion' was established by the government by which cash payments were made to Protestants who converted. Tax concessions were also available for those who abjured Protestantism (immunity from *taille* for two years), while those who did not were assessed at high rates of *taille*. A second principle aimed to undermine Protestant family life. Intermarriage with Catholics was forbidden if an objection came from the Catholic side; from 1680 the children of mixed marriages were to be brought up as Catholics. In 1681 it was decreed that at the age of seven Huguenot children could convert to Catholicism; they would be taken from their families and placed in Catholic boarding schools. With regard to the rituals central to any family – baptisms, weddings and funerals – those of Huguenots had to take place either early in the morning or late at night with only the immediate family circle as witnesses. In 1680 Catholic magistrates were empowered to visit the death-beds of Huguenots to attempt to secure conversions. The third principle excluded Huguenots from the professions and other careers. Restrictions regarding the curriculum were imposed on Huguenot schools, whose independence was ended in 1685. More and more Huguenots were removed from law courts, town councils, trades guilds and the practice of medicine. The *chambres mi-parties* were suppressed in 1679 which meant that lawsuits involving Catholics and Protestants almost invariably went in favour of the former.

One remarkable feature of these decades is that the legislation was borne by the Huguenots without rebellion, and this acceptance of what was blatantly discriminatory legislation requires explanation. One factor is that by the 1660s and 1670s most Huguenots had become 'royalist' by conviction. They were greatly influenced by St Paul's adjuration: 'Every person must submit to the supreme authorities... anyone who rebels against authority is resisting a divine institution' (Romans 13: 1–2). There was no question that Louis XIV was the legitimate king, hence he must be obeyed. The theories of 'legitimate resistance' which Huguenots had developed during the Wars of Religion when law and order had collapsed, were no longer considered applicable. Huguenots accepted that they must either suffer, convert or leave the country; they must not resist their king. Again, to the majority of Huguenots obedience was also dictated by self-interest. As a declining minority which was losing its noble elites to Catholicism, open resistance to the crown would have been suicidal: it would have had no realistic prospects of effective support from abroad and would have invited the harshest reprisals from the government. On this score, Huguenot leaders were conscious that they still lived under a residual cloud of 'republicanism' deriving from the memory of the execution of Charles I in England by a 'Puritan' Parliament, for in many French Catholic circles the decapitation of Charles led to a crude equation between Protestantism and republicanism. Beginning with people such as Samuel Bochart, whose *Lettre... pour Répondre à Trois Questions du Droit et de la Puissance des Rois* (1651) was a resolute defence of the divine right of kings and a denunciation of regicide, Huguenot leaders had continually declared their loyalty to Louis XIV, even acquiescing in his measures to enforce the Edict of Nantes to the letter. Huguenot leaders hoped that after a period of chastisement by the king a new, if unfavourable, equilibrium might emerge which would allow them to recover their place in French society. Meanwhile, financial inducements, anti-Huguenot legislation and missions organised by the Catholic Church continued to take their toll. The Catholic Church took steps to receive into its ranks the *nouveaux-convertis*, as ex-Huguenots were known, and to instruct them in Catholic doctrine. It was a slow, difficult process. In Languedoc the resources of the Catholic Church were greatly strained, for in that province Occitan rather than French was the common language, and there were insufficient priests versed in Occitan to cope with the conversions.

In 1681 the character of anti-Protestant policy changed and forced at least some Huguenots to revert to the resistance theories of the past. Louis XIV forbade Huguenots from fleeing the country; he thereby reversed what had been European practice since the middle of the sixteenth century. Since the Peace of Augsburg (1555) the governing principle in the religion of European states had been that of *cuius regio, eius religio*: 'he who rules a territory shall decide its religion'. As an unwritten corollary, however, it was understood that those who did not conform to the ruler's religion should be allowed to leave the state if they wished. Louis XIV broke with convention by insisting that his Huguenot subjects must not attempt to flee the country under pain of severe punishment. In short, his policy now was not simply to convert as many Huguenots as possible and to allow the remainder to emigrate; it was to convert all Huguenots.

The other new departure in 1681 was the adoption of violent methods to achieve conversions: the billeting of dragoons (cavalry soldiers) on Huguenot families, known in brief as the infamous *dragonnades*. The initiative for the employment of troops in hastening the conversion of Huguenots came, not from the government, but from René de Marillac the intendant in Poitou; he proposed the idea to Louvois who in turn gave his consent. *Dragonnades* were a tried and tested means of reducing recalcitrant populations to obedience, and had been used in the past against tax evaders, Huguenots (in Aubenas in 1627 and Montauban in 1660) and other 'antisocial' elements. The procedure was that the targeted families were obliged to supply lodging and food for soldiers. This might seem innocuous enough; but the financial drain on a family forced to provide for several soldiers was considerable, and ill-disciplined troops committed atrocities against the persons and property of their hosts. In the case of the Huguenots, the soldiers understood that few questions would be asked about their conduct, and even allowing for exaggeration, it is clear that the Protestants of Poitou (and in due course other provinces) were subjected to widespread intimidation, abuse and atrocities. Indeed, within twelve months Marillac was boasting that some 30,000 Huguenots had converted; conversion meant immunity from the *dragonnades* and two years' exemption from *taille*. It was from this stage that Huguenot emigration accelerated, in spite of the risks involved. Emigrants went mainly to the Netherlands, Germany, Switzerland and England, bearing horror stories of the persecution. Within those countries, pamphlets containing lurid illustrations of unspeakable tortures inflicted on Protestants by soldiers of Louis XIV were disseminated, and the governments of those and other Protestant states began to make formal protests to the French government. Meanwhile the use of troops to secure conversions was extended to Languedoc and Béarn in 1683, and to Provence and the Dauphiné in 1685. It was claimed that during the five years of their use, the *dragonnades* resulted in between 300,000 and 400,000 Huguenots becoming Catholic.[14] Many of these 'conversions' were nothing more than judicious reactions to extreme adversity, and given the inability of the Catholic Church to muster sufficient human resources to cope with this flood of humanity (which was now enjoying tax concessions) a crisis of another kind was developing in 1685: popular Catholic hostility towards a policy which left them to carry a tax burden all the heavier since ex-Huguenots had temporary relief.

The extent to which Louis XIV was *au fait* with the details of the conduct of the *dragonnades* and the violence in the south of the country is still open to question. Glowing statistics of conversions were being submitted to him by Louvois, but he was also receiving protests from foreign governments and information from the intendants via the Conseil d'en Haut; it is hard to believe that somebody as well-informed as the king could have been ignorant of what was happening. Exactly at what point he decided to revoke the Edict of Nantes is uncertain, but it could have been as early as 1683. He was under other pressures which made revocation an attractive possibility. For several decades the Catholic Church had been implementing a form of 'contract' with the crown: for its part the church preached obedience to the crown and thereby assisted the king to stabilise society, but in return it regularly called on him to fetter Protestantism. Revocation was a means whereby Louis could meet that 'debt'. In the 1680s he was enmeshed in the Gallican and Jansenist controversies: a bold act might strengthen his position on these fronts. His relations with Pope Innocent XI were vexatious; revocation might help to cultivate a more benevolent attitude on the part of the pope. Louis's international standing was suffering because he refused to provide military assistance to the Austrian government when Vienna was besieged by the Turks in 1683. After the Emperor Leopold I, with the aid of John Sobieski of Poland, drove back the Turks, Leopold's reputation in Europe soared; revocation might place Louis XIV once again at the centre of European attention. On the domestic front, Louis's second wife Madame de Maintenon, aided by Père la Chaise (whose moderating influence did not extend to Louis's Huguenot policy), was reminding the king of his religious duty; and although she did not take the decision for him, she encouraged him towards revocation. All of these forces worked on the king and predisposed him to the final step; there was, however, one other consideration which persuaded him that the Edict of Nantes should be abrogated. The Huguenots were the last great 'problem' bequeathed by the Wars of Religion and remaining to be solved. The religious wars had imposed deep political and social divisions upon France which were exploited by foreign powers, notably the Spanish Habsburgs. Louis XIII and Louis XIV had assumed the 'historic' task of healing or overcoming those divisions, and rendering France immune from foreign intervention. The process had been long, difficult and on occasion had come close to grief as, for example, during the Frondes; by the 1680s, however, Louis considered the task almost complete: the nobility and aristocracy were no longer a source of political danger, the *parlements*, provincial estates and other great intermediate bodies of state were integrated into the purposes of monarchy, the level of popular resistance to the crown had subsided, and French internal politics no longer were vulnerable to the intrigue of foreign states. What remained were the Huguenots, the last vestige of the heritage of the Wars of Religion; but now in the 1680s Louis was in a position to 'solve' that problem too. The revocation of the Edict of Nantes would mark the culmination of a long phase of French history which went back to the 1560s, and posterity would acknowledge Louis XIV as the king who accomplished the great mission which his revered grandfather had begun.

On 15 October 1685 Louis issued the Edict of Fontainebleau which revoked the Edict of Nantes. The new edict proclaimed that since so many Huguenots had become Catholic there was no need for the remnant to be afforded special status; the Edict of Nantes was redundant. Protestantism legally ceased to exist in France. Nevertheless, the anti-Huguenot legislation remained in force, and the *dragonnades* continued to be employed against Huguenots who refused to convert. During the years of persecution about 200,000 Huguenots (about 27 per cent of the Protestant population) left the country against the orders of the crown. About 60,000 went to the Dutch Republic, 50,000 to Britain and Ireland, 25,000 to Brandenburg, 22,000 to Switzerland, and the remainder elsewhere including other parts of Germany, the Americas and southern Africa. It used to be thought that the economic cost to France of this loss of population was heavy, but that is an exaggerated view.[15] Certainly the emigrants included economically productive people such as those in the cloth trade, but most of the great Protestant financiers, businessmen and industrialists had become *nouveaux-convertis* and remained in France; moreover, they often established new commercial links with their co-religionists now settled elsewhere in Europe.[16] It is also too much to claim that all emigrants automatically turned anti-French and – rather like the noble *émigrés* of the French Revolution a century later – became a permanent political danger to the French government. Some did continue to rail against the king, but most accepted their lot in the hope that Louis's successor might adopt a more moderate position and allow Protestants to return.[17] Among those Protestants who remained in France, some opted for resistance to the crown. In the mountainous regions of Languedoc, pastors and members of the Huguenot churches met clandestinely for worship (they saw themselves as analogues of the Children of Israel spending a period in 'the desert' to reinvigorate their faith). Their secret assemblies were attended by visions, ecstatic outpourings and 'miracles'. Pursued vigorously by the authorities, they burst into violent rebellion in 1702. This 'revolt of the Camisards' was concentrated in the Cévennes mountains and lasted in its main phase until 1704 when a truce was agreed with the government, although intransigent Camisards rejected the settlement and continued sporadic guerrilla warfare down to 1713.

The Revocation of the Edict of Nantes earned Louis XIV fewer plaudits than perhaps he had hoped. He received congratulations from Catholic leaders in France, but Pope Innocent XI, while approving the revocation, denounced the use of violence and did not change his mind in his dispute with Louis over Gallican rights. Elsewhere in Europe – especially the Protestant states – Louis was pilloried as a tyrant, and the anti-French coalitions of the 1680s and 1690s acquired a new sense of purpose as Louis came to be perceived as an ideologue seeking not only to advance the interests of France as any head of state should, but 'universal monarchy' whereby the whole of Europe would be dominated by a France committed to militant Counter-Reformation. From Voltaire onwards, historians of Louis XIV have been almost unanimous in criticising his treatment of his Protestant subjects. Yet when it is set alongside other aspects of his religious policies, the difference appears one of degree rather than of principle. Louis was no theologian, his grasp of the history of the church was sketchy, and although he eventually acquired strong religious convictions, he had difficulty in understanding that other people took their faith equally seriously, and beyond a certain point would not make concessions. If one of the tests of the success of a reign is the extent to which it copes effectively with problems inherited from the past, another is the nature of those which it transmits to posterity. On the first count, by the mid-1680s Louis felt that he had resolved the major issues passed down from his grandfather; but in retrospect we are aware that the 'solutions' which he brought to the sphere of religion were to store up serious difficulties both for state and Catholic Church in the eighteenth century. The blasts which the eighteenth-century Enlightenment was to launch against the relationship between French state and Catholic Church, were in no small measure a reaction against the obsessive orthodoxy of Louis XIV in matters of religion.

5

LOUIS XIV AND
THE DIRECTION OF IDEAS
IN FRANCE

The aim of this chapter is twofold: to discuss aspects of French cultural
life in which the crown displayed a direct interest, and to assess how
far members of the French intelligentsia were beginning to question
principles and practices of the regime by the turn of the century. The
cultural history of France under Louis XIV should be contextualised
in time and in space,[1] for it encompasses scientists, writers, artists and
others whose combined lives span almost the entire period of Bourbon
monarchy down to the Revolution. For example, when the French
Académie des Sciences was founded in 1666 it included among its
members Marin Cureau de la Chambre who was born in 1596 when
the Wars of Religion still had not run their course, while towards the
end of Louis's reign was born Denis Diderot (1713) who was to be
one of the most prominent figures in the French Enlightenment of
the eighteenth century, and died just five years before the Revolution. French cultural history under Louis XIV owed much to scholars
from other parts of Europe. France opened itself to cultural influences from outside, welcoming from abroad famous names in the
sciences, philosophy, the visual, literary and musical arts; likewise
French scholars travelled to other parts of Europe or corresponded
with colleagues elsewhere. The second half of the seventeenth century
was a period when there triumphed among the intellectual elites of
Europe the concept of a *république des lettres*; scholars regarded themselves as 'citizens' of an over-arching 'republic' made up of men and

women of learning in every country, and bound together by the pursuit of knowledge irrespective of religious creed, political commitment or nationality. Subjects of Louis XIV were active in the life of this cosmopolitan community; the phrase 'French culture' should not be interpreted in an exclusively French sense, but should incorporate an international dimension.

The Concept of 'Academies'

Louis XIV inherited a long tradition whereby the crown patronised the visual, literary and musical arts, but in the course of the seventeenth century there flourished in Europe a relatively new form of cultural organisation, the society or academy devoted to one or more branches of learning. The origins of academies went back to the Renaissance when princes, prelates and cities assisted men of learning who grouped together to study Classical scholarship; thus, at the end of the fifteenth century the city of Florence supported the 'Platonic Academy', a circle of scholars devoted to the study and publication of the works of Plato. The Italians remained in the forefront of the 'age of academies'. In 1601 there was founded in Rome the Accademia dei Lincei composed of natural philosophers, and in 1657 the Medici family founded in Florence the Accademia del Cimento which was devoted to the sciences. Seventeenth-century academies were also a response to ideas on epistemology expounded by the English philosopher and statesman Sir Francis Bacon (1561–1626). He championed modern scholarship against ancient, and advocated collaborative approaches to the acquisition of knowledge. In such works as *The Advancement of Learning* (1605) and the *Novum Organum* (1620) he called for sustained and cooperative programmes of 'experimental learning': teams of researchers organised in academies should work on problems in the sciences; the teams would conduct experiments, compile and classify information, establish hypotheses to be tested by yet more experiments. Moreover – and this strengthened the appeal of Baconianism in a century which saw the trial of Galileo – collaborative research would prevent individual scholars from falling into philosophical or theological 'error', and would protect them against attacks by opponents driven by jealousy rather than by genuine scholarly disagreement. The example set by Italy and the spirit of Baconianism inspired the formation of academies in France. Cardinal

Richelieu founded the Académie Française in 1635, mainly from a group of writers gathered around Valentin Conrart. This state literary society was formed partly in response to pressure from writers who contended that if the literary potential of the French language were to be realised, it must be refined, purified and clarified: fixed rules of grammar must be established, spelling regularised, the meanings of words defined and rules of composition agreed. Thereby would be fashioned a linguistic instrument capable of producing the most sublime literature. On his side, Richelieu approved of the formation of a formal literary academy which would confer prestige on the crown. Throughout the century the Académie Française pronounced on matters of literary doctrine and taste, worked towards the publication of a dictionary which would identify and define every word in the language, celebrated great state occasions through verse and prose, and published laudatory works in honour of the king.

During the personal reign of Louis XIV much of the initiative to incorporate other branches of French cultural life into an 'academy' framework came from Colbert who, as Surintendant des Bâtiments du Roi, was ideally placed to advance the process. He was fully attuned to the political benefits to which royal patronage of learning could lead, not only to the crown whose national and international prestige would be enhanced but also to himself as the organising master-mind. However, Colbert was sufficiently realistic to understand that even a country as large as France possessed only a limited amount of outstanding scholarly and artistic ability; he was prepared to cast his net widely and seek talent from far afield. French cultural life would be enriched by the contribution of foreigners, and insofar as Louis XIV became acknowledged as the monarch to whom scholars from all over Europe looked for cultural patronage, his reputation would be enhanced. Colbert sought advice as to who should be sponsored. In the visual arts he relied mainly upon Charles Lebrun, head of the Gobelins and one of France's leading painters, and for the worlds of letters, philosophy and the sciences he turned to Jean Chapelain, poet and member of the Académie Française. From 1662 onwards Chapelain submitted to Colbert lists of writers and scholars in France and abroad who should receive financial grants in recognition of their services to literature and scholarship. In 1663 Colbert announced that the government had created a fund out of which selected scholars would be paid; in return they were expected to extol the virtues of Louis XIV in the works which they created.[2] Louis XIV conferred grants not only upon

French writers such as Corneille and Mézerai, but also foreigners including the Flemish astronomer Hevelius, the Florentine Carlo Dati, and the great Dutch scholars Heinsius and Vossius.[3]

In the early 1660s Colbert was contemplating the creation of a state-sponsored 'General Academy', which would bring together several scholarly and artistic disciplines. Two proposals for such an academy were put to him. One came from the writer Charles Perrault, who suggested that Colbert should oversee the formation of a General Academy which would consist of four sections: literature (grammar, eloquence, poetry), history (including geography), philosophy (which would also cover chemistry, botany, anatomy and physics) and mathematics (algebra, geometry, astronomy). The second came from the Dutch scientist Christiaan Huygens who visited France in the 1650s and early 1660s, and eventually resided there at Colbert's invitation. About 1663 he drew up plans for a 'Company of Sciences and Arts' comprising scientists, architects, painters, sculptors and engineers. It would be devoted to 'applied' knowledge and would invent machines for use in industry and agriculture, search for improved techniques in navigation, industrial processes, the construction of bridges and canals, and would endeavour thereby to serve the practical needs of France. Huygens argued that such a society organised around utilitarian principles would contribute to *la gloire* of Louis XIV even more than an academy devoted exclusively to 'pure' knowledge. Attracted though he was by a General Academy, Colbert gradually retreated from its creation.[4] He was aware that it would meet opposition from established bodies such as the Académie Française, the University of Paris and other educational institutions such as the Jesuit colleges and the Collège Royal, which perceived in a monolithic and powerful General Academy under the direct patronage of the crown a danger to their own independence. Instead he opted for separate academies more limited in scope, but together comprising the disciplines which would have figured in a General Academy. This structure remained in place down to the Revolution, and it was only with the foundation of the Institut de France in 1795 that a body resembling a 'General Academy' was established.

State Academies under Louis XIV: The Visual Arts

Three of the state academies in whose creation Colbert was intimately involved dealt with the visual arts. The first was the Académie des

Inscriptions et Belles-Lettres (1663). This began as a small group of only four members who were responsible for devising the inscriptions and designs for royal medals and monuments. They turned to ancient Rome for their inspiration, and it was through the mediation of this academy that much of the iconography through which Louis XIV was represented in painting, sculpture, medallions and statues, drew upon Roman themes and motifs.

The same year, 1663, there was a reorganisation of the second body to be considered: the Académie Royale de Peinture et de Sculpture which had been founded in 1648 on Italian models. The aim of the academy[5] was to raise the status of painting from that of a 'mere craft' practised by artists who learned their trade as apprentices to master-painters, to that of a theoretically based 'liberal art' involving a study of abstract principles. For some time the academy struggled, for it had the misfortune to be founded in the year in which the Parisian Fronde began, and amidst the turmoil of the late 1640s and early 1650s relatively little could be achieved. Colbert worked with Charles Lebrun to reform the Académie de Peinture et de Sculpture in 1663: it was provided with a Protector (the king), a Vice-Protector (Colbert), a Director (Lebrun), a set of regulations and premises in the Louvre. The academy trained students through lectures, tutorials and practical classes. Students were required to study mathematics, optics, perspective (Leon Battista Alberti's *Della Pittura* [1436] was a basic text) and geometry. The entire tenor of the training emphasised painting and sculpture as intellectual exercises; works of art produced by academicians could be appreciated fully only by those versed in the complex and demanding theory – deriving mostly from Classical antiquity – upon which the painting rested. Lebrun was strongly influenced by Descartes's *Treatise on the Passions of the Soul* (1649) which argued that although our passions are animated by physiological responses to external stimuli, we are capable of distinguishing between desirable and undesirable passions through the exercise of reason. Moreover, we are capable of overcoming undesirable passions by the exercise of the will; moral strength comes through governing the will by reason. This was the thinking behind Lebrun's insistence that under his leadership the Académie de Peinture et de Sculpture would elevate the mind over the senses, and set design above colour in its instruction of young artists: by appealing primarily to the intellect, painting would stimulate the power of reason. This trend was re-affirmed when in 1666 Colbert established a French Academy in Rome under the direction of Charles Errard. At any one time twelve young artists from France (six painters, four sculptors and two architects) would reside there to study at first hand the sculpture and architecture of Classical Rome; once back in their own country they would work exclusively on the royal palaces or such other projects as the crown allotted them.

The third institution in the visual arts was the Académie d'Architecture, founded in 1671 under the direction of François Blondel. Architecture, because it is easily visible (as against paintings or medallions which may be accessible only to a few), was the subject of much debate in France. Mazarin had championed Roman baroque, and a tribute to his taste may still be seen in Paris in the former 'Collège Mazarin' (now the Institut de France) built with money bequeathed in his will. Occupying a choice site facing the Louvre, it was designed by Louis le Vau who adopted two dominant architectural features reminiscent of Roman baroque: an imposing dome and curved wings projecting from the central façade like two enveloping arms. Colbert, although a former protégé of Mazarin, did not follow his taste in architecture. Indeed, when the great Bernini came from Italy to Paris in 1665 and accepted a commission to design an extension to the Louvre, Colbert persuaded Louis XIV to reject Bernini's plans; the pretext was that they would have cost too much to execute, but the real reason was one of architectural taste: Colbert favoured a more austere style which, he felt, was becoming to the King of France. In the event, the extension to the Louvre with its famous eastern colonnade was undertaken by a French architect, Claude Perrault. When the Académie d'Architecture was founded its brief was to evolve a style of architecture which was characteristically 'French', and not simply a derivative of modern Italian fashions; thus, while Colbert and the king acknowledged that in the sciences French scholars would profit from the presence of foreigners, they were resolved that architecture should follow a 'French' style as developed by French architects. It is notable that all the great public works constructed under Louis XIV were by French architects: the Salpêtrière hospital by Le Vau and Libéral Bruant, Les Invalides by Jules Hardouin Mansart and Bruant, the Observatory by Claude Perrault, Versailles by Le Vau and Mansart, and the Porte Saint Denis by François Blondel (the first director of the Académie d'Architecture). Blondel had received no formal architectural training, but had experience of planning military installations in France and in the West Indies. He was steeped in Classical architectural theory and maintained that architecture, like painting, must be based on rules of symmetry, proportion and harmony, every element in a building forming part of a grand design. Blondel later published the lectures which he gave at the academy under the title *Cours d'Architecture* (1675–83). They became the definitive statement of Classical doctrine as taught in the academy during the reigns of Louis XIV and his successors. Blondel was no slavish imitator of Classical rules of architecture: rather he encouraged the modern architect to modify and adapt those rules, but he was emphatic that Classicism provided the theoretical foundation of all good building.

The Académie des Sciences

The three academies in the visual arts which Colbert founded or reformed turned to the Classical past for inspiration, and the principles which they expounded mirrored those being applied to the theatre by writers such as Corneille and Racine who also chose subject-matter from the Classics, adhered to Classical rules of composition, and in their plays explored the complex relationships between reason and the passions in human behaviour.[6] The Académie des Sciences (1666)[7] was very different in conception, formation and purpose: it was rooted in 'modern' not 'Classical' science, and adhered to no over-arching philosophical system. Before it was founded in 1666 there were various informal meetings in Paris of philosophers and scientists; these groups included one which gathered around the Minim friar Marin Mersenne, while others were run by Louis Habert, sieur de Montmor, Melchisédec Thévenot, and Pierre Michon the Abbé Bourdelot. *Habitués* of these circles met Colbert and urged him to found a formal, state society; and, as we have seen, Huygens presented him with a plan for a 'general academy' which would include subjects in the sciences. Still bearing in mind the possibility of a broad-based society, Colbert moved towards the formation of the Académie des Sciences in 1666 when, at various stages throughout the year, he announced the names of twenty-one founder-members who first met in December in premises set aside for them in the Royal Library in Paris. Huygens was the only foreign member, although in 1669 he was joined by the Italian astronomer Cassini; other well-known figures were Roberval the mathematician, Auzout the astronomer, Cureau de la Chambre the physician, and Claude Perrault (who although renowned as an architect, had trained as a physician and was appointed to the medical section of the academy). Unlike the Académie Royale de Peinture, the scientific academy was provided with no regulations or formal structure; Colbert left it to the academicians themselves to decide these matters. During the first few weeks of the existence of the academy the members debated questions of organisation and procedure. Although they refused officially to adopt any particular philosophical or scientific system, they were agreed that the way ahead was through 'experimental learning', and that where possible they should collaborate on programmes of joint research. This Baconianism was to be one of the defining principles of the academy over the next two or three decades. Collaborative research was undertaken alongside the work done by academicians individually; it was long and painstaking and was felt to be especially valuable in life sciences such as botany and zoology. When provisional results were available the government met the cost of the publication of lavish, extensively illustrated volumes including, for example, the *Mémoires pour servir à l'Histoire Naturelle des Animaux* (1671) and the *Mémoires pour servir à l'Histoire des Plantes* (1676). Colbert regarded this academy as a body to which he might turn for advice on practical matters. Accordingly, he provided it with a laboratory (located in the Royal Library), financial support for equipment, pensions for some members, and a magnificent observatory designed by Claude Perrault which was built just to the south of Paris and completed in 1672. The academy advised Colbert on problems relating to navigation, inventions of machines, projects in military and civil engineering, the provision of water supplies to the palace of Versailles and numerous other problems which he brought to its attention. One of the most important aspects of the utilitarian work of the academy was cartography. Existing maps of France were notoriously inaccurate and led to many misconceptions about the size of the country, the geographical relationship of its major cities, and France's relation to other parts of the world. Beginning in the 1660s Jean Picard and other academicians began a long-term project to extend the Paris meridian, and then gradually to calculate the longitude and latitude of major cities with greater accuracy than in the past. The work was slow and expensive, but by the time the academy was able to publish a new atlas of France in 1684 many serious errors in existing maps had been eradicated.

Other Academies

By the 1670s the regime was patronising several state academies
through which it could influence extensive tracts of French cultural
life. It would be wrong to think of the government as imposing a
dead hand of conformity on writers, painters, architects, scientists and
others. Quite the reverse: competition for membership of these academies was fierce, and the government left it largely to the academies
themselves to decide such issues as taste, rules and style in literature
and the visual arts; and although Charles Lebrun, for example,
expected his artists and sculptors to work within a defined canon,
they still had ample scope for individualism and invention.[8] French
cultural life flourished under the regime of the academies and proved
as innovative, imaginative and creative as that of any other part of
Europe. Yet more academies were founded: the Académie de Danse
(1661) and the Académie de Musique (1672). This latter institution
was the brainchild of the composer Jean-Baptiste Lully, an Italian by
birth. Lully moved to France at the age of eleven and proved to be
a musician of outstanding talent and versatility; he also possessed a
ruthless, domineering personality which took him into royal service
where, in 1653, he was appointed composer of instrumental music.
In 1661 he was promoted to Surintendant de la Musique: he collaborated with Molière in the production of *comédies-ballets*, developed a
'French' style of opera, and managed the elaborate musical life of the
court. The musical academy which he founded in Paris in 1672 organised musical concerts at court and elsewhere, but also provided
training – in singing and in stringed and wind instruments – for
young musicians who hoped to gain access to one of the troupes of
musicians at court.

Universities and Colleges

One problematic area was the relationship between the state academies and other institutions with a cultural role. The universities and
colleges were especially important, for between them they educated
almost the whole of the social and political elites, and the knowledge,
approaches to learning, the moral and religious values which they
instilled into their students, were bound to have implications for the
wider cultural life of the nation.[9] Some indication of the availability

of higher education is suggested by the fact that by the middle of the seventeenth century there were fourteen universities in France, rising to nineteen by 1715 (the additional universities were acquired through the conquest of neighbouring territories); in addition there were over 200 colleges run by religious orders such as the Jesuits and Oratorians, or by the Huguenots before the Revocation of the Edict of Nantes. With the exception of the Académie des Sciences, several of whose members were professors in the Faculty of Medicine of the University of Paris, academicians generally functioned outside of the universities and colleges. In some senses the state academies may be seen as representing a 'counter-culture' to that of the universities and colleges: modern literature, painting and music were minority interests in the universities and colleges, although it is fair to say that the academies of painting and architecture, to the extent that they taught mathematics and geometry, overlapped with these older institutions.

Broadly speaking, the history of universities in seventeenth-century France was one of decline; the state responded by steadily extending its control over the universities at the expense of that of the church. The Wars of Religion had serious effects on many universities including Paris. Whereas at any one time in the early 1500s about 10,000 students were enrolled in the Faculty of Arts of the University of Paris, by the early 1600s the figure had declined to some 2000; and although a period of recovery followed, the rate was slow. Even at the beginning of the personal reign of Louis XIV, every university with the exception of Paris had less than 1000 students; Toulouse, one of the largest, had only about 800.[10] In 1598 the government turned its attention to the University of Paris which received new statutes: the authority of the crown and of the Parlement of Paris within the university was increased, the students henceforth were obliged to spend six hours a day in class, and the statutes specified the Classical authors whom the students must study. State intervention in universities continued throughout the seventeenth century (in 1603 the government reconstituted the University of Aix). During Louis XIV's personal reign, Colbert in 1667 ordered the intendants to inquire into the condition of the universities and colleges in their regions, and Louvois followed this up with a similar investigation in 1685: the intendants were ordered to draw up inventories of the resources of the universities and colleges, and to establish statistics of student numbers.

In spite of its problems the University of Paris, with about forty colleges, was by far the largest and most prestigious of the universities. It also received two further assets of importance in the seven-teenth century: Richelieu paid for a splendid chapel at the Faculty of Theology (the Sorbonne), and as was stated earlier Mazarin bequeathed a new college to the university, known popularly as the 'Collège Mazarin' but more formally as the 'Collège des Quatre Nations'.[11] Students in the universities began their studies in arts[12] which were taught in the colleges (the Faculty of Arts was an exam-ining body which conferred its *licence* upon successful graduates), and having qualified therein moved on to one of the senior faculties of Theology, Law or Medicine. The Law Faculty was of particular interest to the government in view of the Fronde which had pitted magistrates against the crown. Until 1679 the Faculty of Law in Paris taught only canon law, not civil law; in 1679 Louis XIV ended this prohibition, allowing civil law to be taught in Paris as elsewhere. In the same year he established Chairs of French Law throughout the universities of the country; the holders were paid directly by the crown and were, in effect, the king's direct representatives in the formation of future generations of lawyers. Since in one sense 'French law' did not exist (there were many legal systems operating in the kingdom), the profes-sors tended to teach and comment upon selected laws and edicts which the crown had issued.

The universities continued to manifest deep-rooted problems. Buildings were usually in a lamentable state: for every well-maintained college in the University of Paris, several were in poor condition if not abandoned altogether (by the 1660s the once-illustrious Collège Coqueret was destitute, and the Collège de Boncourt had been merged with the Collège de Navarre). Discipline was notoriously lax and abuses common, especially among *boursiers* (students with schol-arships) in the faculties of Theology, Law and Medicine. In 1679, for example, *boursiers* from the Collège Maître-Gervais assaulted the prin-cipal of the college, dragged him off to a drinking den to make him drunk and forced him to sign promises of money.[13] Many *boursiers* were 'perpetual' students, holding on to their scholarships as long as fifteen or twenty years by missing examinations or by carefully calcu-lating the frequency with which examinations could be failed before it was necessary to pass and proceed to the next stage of studies in order to keep the scholarship. The quality of teaching in the univer-sities was often indifferent, and some provincial universities such as Cahors or Rheims were known as 'easy' institutions which seemed to regard the award of a degree as a certificate of attendance rather than of academic achievement. Curricula had changed little since the Middle Ages; the Arts were based on Latin, Greek, philosophy and rhetoric; history, geography, modern literature were scarcely touched upon, and scientific subjects generally received only cursory treatment. Without being anachronistic by accusing them of failing to act like their twentieth-century counterparts, it is still hard to avoid the conclusion that, in spite of the efforts of Louis XIV's government, seventeenth-century French universities remained in a state of crisis, and that as 'cultural agencies' they are to be differentiated sharply from the state academies.

On the whole, the colleges run by the religious orders were in a better condition: discipline among the students was more rigorous and the curriculum more innovative than in the universities. Many orders had colleges or academies, but it was the Jesuits and Oratorians who led the way in 'modern' approaches to education; by the late 1600s the Jesuits had almost 100 colleges under their control and the Oratorians had twenty-five. Jesuit colleges were to be found in the cities and larger towns of France, and in the Collège de Clermont the Jesuits possessed one of the most prestigious colleges in the University of Paris. Their educational methods derived from the *Ratio Studiorum*, a pedagogical manual drafted for the order in 1599 and emphasising not only the importance of Classical languages, but also modern languages and sciences. During the seventeenth century some of the Jesuit colleges were larger than most universities: several colleges had over 500 students, while those at La Flèche and Bordeaux had over 1000, and Rouen had about 2000. The Jesuit colleges taught classical languages, philosophy and rhetoric as did other institutions, but also drama, modern literature, mathematics and physics. The Oratorians too had a 'modern' curriculum. Their schools were less numerous than those of the Jesuits and were located in the smaller towns of France; their students therefore came from lower social ranks than those of the Jesuits. Their 'model' college, founded in 1637, was at Juilly about twenty miles east of Paris. Oratorian education was based on Latin, which was taught through French up to the fourth year, and thereafter through Latin itself; from 1640 Juilly and other colleges based their Latin courses on a manual, the *Nouvelle Méthode Latine*, drawn up that year by Charles de Condren, the Superior-General of the Oratory. The philosophy courses of the Oratorian colleges went up to modern times, and even included Descartes in spite of his heterodox reputation. Oratorian colleges taught French history; they concentrated on biographical studies of monarchs and the wars which they fought. Mathematics formed part of the curriculum, and although the levels attained by the students varied from elementary to advanced, the Oratorians endeavoured to assure at least a basic numeracy in their pupils.

Books and Printing

The principle that educational institutions shaped not only the intellectual powers of future generations, but their religious, moral and political attitudes as well, was fully grasped by the government. The demands of social control allied to the paternalistic tradition of French monarchy predisposed Louis and his ministers to keep a cautious watch on education in France; and a similar concern extended to the realm of printing. The greatest philosophers, theologians, political thinkers and scientists of France undoubtedly enhanced the prestige of the country and the king, but since at least the sixteenth century it had been evident that unorthodox ideas in these and other spheres could, when widely propagated through the medium of printing, have widespread social and political consequences; and during the Frondes the clandestine publication of thousands of 'Mazarinades' – antigovernment pamphlets – had fuelled popular violence. It followed that the state must equip itself with instruments for controlling the dissemination of knowledge and information.[14] During the sixteenth and seventeenth century regulations had accumulated by which all books published in France had to receive a licence from the crown before being printed. Royal censors, many of whom were magistrates or theologians attached to the Sorbonne, read and approved manuscripts before allowing them to be printed. Censors sometimes turned books down because their content was judged unsound on political, moral or religious grounds, but often because they were considered unscholarly. Censorship was not simply a means of upholding orthodox thought: it aimed also to ensure reasonable standards of scholarly or literary quality. Another purpose was to afford authors a degree of protection against plagiarism: a manuscript which simply reproduced the content of a book already in print would not receive a licence. Further control over printing was exercised through guilds. Printers, binders and booksellers belonged to guilds governed by elaborate regulations, although in practice books and pamphlets sometimes were published clandestinely as happened during the Parisian Fronde; pro-Jansenist pamphlets were also secretly printed in defiance of the law. On these and similar occasions printers either withheld their normal printer's identification mark, or published books under a false mark (attributing it perhaps to a foreign source). Colbert attempted to tighten the control of printing through the Conseil de Police which sat from 1666 to 1667. In this latter year the council drew up a list of all Parisian printers and their employees, the number of printers was reduced to thirty and the regulations under which they operated were redefined. In 1667 the council also created a *lieutenant de police* for Paris; the system was extended to the rest of France in 1699. The first *lieutenant* was Gabriel Nicolas de la Reynie who exercised his office until 1697. He worked closely with the king, the Chancellor and the Parlement of Paris in addressing problems of crime and security in Paris, and among his responsibilities was the application of laws on printing. He and his staff kept printers under close scrutiny to ensure as far as possible that they were not transgressing the rules. The question of printing became especially sensitive in the 1690s and early 1700s when social distress was rising because of natural disasters exacerbated by the fiscal consequences of warfare. Criticism of the king, his ministers and members of the royal family again began to appear in print.[15] Some of the hostile pamphlet material was written by foreigners or Huguenot refugees abroad, such as the pastor Pierre Jurieu whose works were smuggled into France, but within France too Louis was being lampooned through pamphlets and engravings. For obvious reasons the authors chose to remain anonymous, but a few have been identified: they include Nicolas Larmessin, a Parisian bookseller-engraver, and Franz Paul von Lisola, a lawyer in Franche-Comté.[16] Critics accused Louis of tyranny, ambition, vanity, licentiousness and a host of other failings.

'Fin-de-Siècle' and the Regime of Louis XIV

From the point of view of the government, scurrilous literature was a nuisance rather than a danger; what is far more significant historically is the emergence in the last two decades of the seventeenth century of serious socio-political comment subjecting to sceptical scrutiny many principles and assumptions which had guided the government since the 1660s. Sometimes this is interpreted as signs of 'opposition' to Louis XIV or the 'decline' of the reign,[17] but it is equally valid to argue that it forms part of a wider process of self-examination and preparation for the next reign in which the government itself was engaged. Louis was nearing his sixtieth year in the 1690s and was sufficiently realistic to know that he must begin to prepare the kingdom for his successor. There was an international dimension to this process which will be discussed in the next chapter, but on the domestic front change was in the air by the 1690s. Fresh faces were brought into the Conseil d'en Haut: Seignelay and Pontchartrain in 1689, Beauvillier, Le Pelletier and Pomponne in 1691, Torcy and Chamillart in 1700. They helped the king towards such original measures as the capitation and the *dixième*, the drawing up of an inventory of the country's cereal supplies in 1694 and 1695, and from 1697 a comprehensive review of socio-economic conditions in the provinces by the intendants. This ethos of reform extended to cultural spheres. In 1699, for example, the Académie des Sciences underwent fundamental restructuring under the direction of its president, the Abbé Jean-Paul Bignon. A nephew of Pontchartrain, he was brought into the Académie by his uncle in 1691 specifically to rejuvenate what had become a moribund institution. Bignon expanded the membership in the 1690s, but in 1699 secured from the crown a set of statutes which reorganised the academy, raised its membership to seventy (before that membership was usually about thirty), defined in detail its functions, procedures, relations with scientists elsewhere, the conduct of its business, and the nature of crown support. A new class of honorary members was created to which were appointed aristocrats and ministers of the crown. Bignon thereby saw the Académie des Sciences as a link between the worlds of politics and scientific research; ministers of the crown would be exposed to the 'enlightening' influence of the sciences and would learn to bring to political decision-making those habits of mind and methodologies which had served the sciences so well. While it is true that by the turn of the century the regime of Louis XIV was the subject of criticism from inside the country, it would be a mistake to suppose that the regime was resistant to calls for change.

Reference has already been made to the economic debates of the late 1600s and early 1700s in which proposals for change accompanied criticism of existing conditions;[18] they found their counterpart in the world of letters which between 1687 and the end of the century was dominated by the quarrel between the ancients and moderns.[19]

This dispute began in 1687 when Charles Perrault read to the
Académie Française his *Poème sur le Siècle de Louis le Grand* in which
he criticised 'ancient' writers, praised his contemporaries, and
acclaimed the reign of Louis XIV as superior to that of Caesar
Augustus in political and cultural achievement. Some academicians,
notably Boileau and La Bruyère, were offended by what they
regarded as disparaging remarks on the 'ancients' and published
stern rejoinders to Perrault, Fontenelle and other 'moderns'. This
acrimonious quarrel subsided in the mid-1690s without resolution,
but was symptomatic of the critical spirit that was in the air towards
the end of the century. This spirit was evident in the historiography
of the late seventeenth century. Even writers who regarded themselves as royalists were composing historical texts as instruments of
'loyal' criticism of Louis XIV. The Jesuit priest, Père Gabriel Daniel,
for example, used his *Dissertations Préliminaires pour une Nouvelle
Histoire de France* (1696) and his *Histoire de France* (1713), as the occasion for praising those French monarchs whose moral and religious
commitments came close to Catholic ideals, and for reprimanding
those whose love of war imposed suffering on their subjects. In similar
vein, Louis le Gendre's *Essai de l'Histoire du Règne de Louis le Grand*
(1697) stressed the need for international peace and fiscal reform
within France.[20]

One influential group which turned a sceptical gaze on the regime
comprised figures gathered around Louis's eldest grandson, Louis
Duc de Bourgogne: it included Paul Comte de Saint-Aignan and later
Duc de Beauvillier, governor to Bourgogne (it was he who drafted
the questionnaire with which the intendants conducted their national
survey in 1697), Fénelon who was tutor to Bourgogne until he was
dismissed because of his implication in the Quietist controversy, and
Louis de Rouvroy, Duc de Saint-Simon, the great memoirist. This
coterie aspired to shape the future monarchy and government of
France. Louis XIV, its members calculated, would be succeeded by
the Grand Dauphin as 'Louis XV', who in turn would be followed by
the Duc de Bourgogne as 'Louis XVI'. It was the presumptive
'Louis XVI' whom they aimed to turn into a 'modern' monarch
equipped to rule the France of the eighteenth century. In retrospect
we know that their plans were frustrated by the deaths of the Dauphin
and the Duc de Bourgogne respectively in 1711 and 1712, but this
does not invalidate the seriousness of the intention to inculcate Bourgogne with political principles which, they felt, were appropriate to

the coming century. In so far as this didactic process involved adverse judgements on aspects of the rule of Louis XIV, it had to be handled sensitively; all the more so since, from 1699, the king introduced his grandson to the procedures of government by allowing him to attend meetings of central administrative councils, and in 1702 of the Conseil d'en Haut itself. As befitted an heir to the crown, Bourgogne acquired military experience during the War of the Spanish Succession, although his performance as a general was at best mediocre.

The thinking of the 'Bourgogne group' may be traced through two of its central figures, Fénelon and Saint-Simon, each of whom expressed his thoughts through literary works of outstanding quality although of very different genres.

Fénelon

Fénelon was appointed tutor to Bourgogne in 1689 because of his reputation as a brilliant teacher. In 1678 he was appointed Superior of the Congrégation des Nouvelles Catholiques (young girls who had converted from Protestantism to Catholicism), and was responsible for instructing them in the Catholic faith; and from 1685 to 1687, at the invitation of Bossuet, he conducted missions among ex-Huguenots in Saintonge. In both of these tasks he was deemed an outstanding success by Bossuet and others. Fénelon forswore heavy-handed, peremptory treatment both of his pupils and of adult *nouveaux-convertis*; instead he expressed respect for the sincerity of their Protestant faith, and sought to lead them slowly and sensitively towards Catholicism. On his return from Saintonge he published his *Traité de l'Education des Filles* (1678) which explained the rationale behind his methods. He also served as spiritual adviser to the Duchesse de Beauvillier and the Duchesse de Chevreuse (both daughters of Colbert), and to them he brought this same admixture of intuitive understanding and benevolent if firm direction. The husband of the former, who had been appointed governor to the Duc de Bourgogne, recognised Fénelon's exceptional qualities and in 1689 appointed him tutor to Bourgogne. Fénelon had few materials with which to educate the young prince and so composed his own; they included his *Dialogues des Morts* (conversations in which great figures from distant and recent history discuss the human condition), and his most famous prose work, *Les Aventures de Télémaque* which was composed in 1695 and published in 1699.

The background to *Les Aventures* is Homer's *Odyssey* wherein is recounted the adventures of Ulysses on his journey home after the fall of Troy. In his own story Fénelon draws freely upon Classical authors, and introduces into the tale battles, storms, athletic trials, dreams and mythology. Telemachus, son of Ulysses, sets out to find his father, and is accompanied by a wise counsellor, Mentor, who is in fact the goddess Minerva who has assumed human form. They visit fabulous lands, some mythical and others which are authentic, such as Egypt. In Egypt (Book 2 of the *Aventures*) the enlightened administration of Sesostris is held up by Mentor/Fénelon as an object-lesson in kingship. After admiring abundant signs of prosperity in the land, Mentor points out the moral to Telemachus/Bourgogne: 'How happy is a people led by a wise king! It enjoys abundance, lives happily, and loves him to whom it owes its well-being. Telemachus, this is how you should reign... Love your people like your children; enjoy the pleasure of being loved by them.' In due course Telemachus and Mentor meet Sesostris who laments that, although he strives to rule justly, he has too many self-interested advisers:

> How unfortunate it is to be set above other people. Often one cannot see the truth with one's own eyes; one is surrounded by people who prevent the truth reaching he who commands; everyone has an interest in deceiving him; everyone hides ambition behind apparent zeal. They make a show of loving the king, but only love him for the wealth which he provides. They love him so little that, in order to acquire his favours, they flatter and betray him.

The text of *Les Aventures* is peppered with political aphorisms. In Book 5, when Telemachus and Mentor are on the island of Crete, Mentor treats his pupil to a disquisition on kingship:

> [The king] has absolute power to do good, but his hands are tied when he wants to do evil. The laws confer his people upon him as the most precious of all gifts, but on condition that he be the father of his subjects. The laws require that one man should serve the well-being of the many by wisdom and moderation; not that the many, by their poverty and cowardly servitude, should flatter the pride and idleness of one man... The king should not have more wealth and pleasure than other men, but more wisdom, virtue and glory. He must be the defender of the country abroad by

commanding his armies; at home he must be the judge of the
people in order to make them good, wise and happy. It is not for
his own benefit that the gods have made him king...; he owes the
people all of his time, labour and affection: and he is worthy of
kingship only in so far as he forgets himself and sacrifices himself
to the public good.

The novel expounds a philosophy of kingship which implicitly finds
Louis XIV wanting. It accuses him of waging unnecessary and aggressive wars, gross expenditure on an ostentatious court at Versailles,
susceptibility to flatterers and time-servers, an inability to perceive his
true political interest, and disturbing tendencies to despotism.
Fénelon's ideal monarch as revealed in the novel is a Christian
philosopher-king who rules by divine right, subjects himself to the
law of God, takes only wise counsellors into government, devises his
policies rationally and patiently, devotes himself to the well-being of
his subjects, oversees their protection by just and equitable laws,
generates prosperity by keeping taxes low and by stimulating
commerce and agriculture; in his relations with other states he resorts
to war only when all other options have been exhausted, and in order
to forestall armed conflict he maintains a well-organised diplomatic
service which, by cooperating with those of other states, preserves
international harmony. The vision of kingship which Fénelon develops
in *Les Aventures de Télémaque* is close to that which Louis XIV expounds
in his *Mémoires*. Fénelon's charge against Louis is not that the king's
reign was based on erroneous principles, but that it had departed
from the principles which Louis expressed early in his personal reign;
if France is to recover peace, prosperity and justice they must be reaffirmed. Fénelon was a conservative critic who urged the Duc de
Bourgogne to abjure the errant ways of his grandfather and return
to paths of godliness, purity and sagacity.

Saint-Simon

Born in 1675,[21] Saint-Simon was of a younger generation than
Fénelon; but whereas the latter was priest, theologian and didact,
Saint-Simon was soldier and courtier. He had a genius for observing
the conduct of his fellow courtiers at Versailles and other royal palaces.
His memoirs, written in the 1740s from extensive notes and jottings

drafted earlier, are a wonderful evocation of the court of Louis XIV and the post-1715 Regency, and although they have to be treated with a certain scepticism, for Saint-Simon was an acerbic and opinionated writer, they provide an unrivalled account of the personalities and intrigues of that remarkable court society. Like most nobles Saint-Simon was inordinately proud of his ancestry, which he claimed could be traced to Charlemagne. He spent several years in the army but, having been passed over for promotion in 1702, resigned his commission and thereafter spent most of his time at court in the entourage of the Duc de Bourgogne. His other principal ally was the Duc d'Orléans who became Regent of France in 1715; on the death of Orléans in 1723, Saint-Simon retired to his estates near Chartres where he wrote his memoirs. They cover the period from 1691 to 1723, and are renowned not only for the detail and panache of their narrative, but for their character-portraits and incomparable accounts of the ritual and ceremonial of court. They are, however, much more than a record of events: they are the vehicle for a political philosophy which Saint-Simon also expressed in his *Projets de Gouvernement du Duc de Bourgogne* which he composed in 1714 or 1715 after the death of Bourgogne. This latter text purports to contain the principles which the Duc de Bourgogne would have adopted had he succeeded to the throne. Taken in conjunction with the memoirs, it constitutes both a critique of the reign of Louis XIV and an exposition of monarchic government as Saint-Simon envisaged it.

Saint-Simon was a thorough-going monarchist who nevertheless held that the aristocracy ought to resume the 'natural' role in government from which Louis XIV had excluded it. He concurred in the conventional view of monarchy resting on legitimate descent and the divine right of kings. Like Louis XIV himself, Saint-Simon conceded that kings are answerable to God alone. Again like Louis XIV, Saint-Simon acknowledged fundamental laws within which monarchy should function and to whose defence it should commit itself; one of his most bitter accusations against Louis XIV was that the king flouted the fundamental laws not only by legitimising some of his illegitimate children, but by conferring rights of succession upon illegitimate males. The king unquestionably enjoyed unique status in that he alone embodied sovereignty, but he needed devoted and honourable advisers before deciding policy. Saint-Simon contended that the king's capacity to govern effectively was endangered from three sources: a chief minister, court favourites and mistresses. On the first count, Louis XIV, Saint-Simon believed, never fully liberated himself from the influence of Mazarin even though the cardinal died in 1661; on the second, the king was consistently susceptible to flatterers at court; and on the third, he allowed Madame de Maintenon a disgraceful degree of influence over himself and his policies. Madame de Maintenon was one of Saint-Simon's *bêtes noires*. He regarded her as an inveterate schemer whose religious piety was conditional upon her exercising power over the king. Her ambition unfortunately was accompanied by average intelligence and limited experience of the world which left her vulnerable to every latest intellectual fad, especially in matters of religion. This vain, hypocritical and inconsistent woman nevertheless had the power to sway the policies of the king, to manipulate ministers of the crown, and browbeat members of the royal family. Her influence over the king, believed Saint-Simon, was malign and contrary to the best interest of crown and country. This was not all. The king's ministers and secretaries of state failed to give him the disinterested service which he required. Louis thought to preserve his authority in government by drawing his ministers from modest social backgrounds on the mistaken assumption that they would serve him submissively; correspondingly he excluded from government Princes of the Blood and great aristocrats in the belief that they could not be trusted to fulfil his will. Here, Saint-Simon argued, Louis XIV committed a lamentable error: he failed to understand that ministers and secretaries of state of 'bourgeois' origins were interested chiefly in self-promotion, in exercising power with minimal reference to the king, in acquiring wealth, titles, estates, and good marriages for their children. The king did not receive objective advice from his ministers since they would not risk his displeasure and possible political disgrace by disagreeing with him. For reasons of self-interest the ministers allowed the king to pursue disastrous policies for which France paid heavily. Had Louis taken Princes of the Blood and aristocrats as advisers it would have been otherwise: by nature they were born to serve in government; and since in their own right they were already wealthy and in possession of great estates, they did not have to temper their advice to the king in the light of his pleasure or disapprobation. In Saint-Simon's opinion, the king's policies would have been more perspicacious and more conducive to the well-being of France had he followed 'nature' instead of his perverse will in his choice of ministers.

In the *Projets de Gouvernement du Duc de Bourgogne*, Saint-Simon outlined a strategy for the future government of France. The key lay in restoring the social pre-eminence of the traditional nobility, and bringing the aristocracy back into government. He advocated a governmental structure based on seven councils: ecclesiastical affairs, war, the navy, foreign affairs, finance, despatches and 'orders'. This last would be particularly important. Headed by a peer of the realm, it would be composed of aristocrats who would devise measures to re-establish unambiguous distinctions between the different orders of society. The council would confirm rules of precedence and oversee the protocol to be observed towards each other by people of varying social rank; in short, the Council of Orders would rehabilitate those social distinctions which Saint-Simon considered to be a prerequisite of good government, but which had become indistinct under Louis XIV. Like that of Fénelon, Saint-Simon's critique of the government of Louis XIV reflected a conservative cast of mind; and it envisaged the restoration of a golden age when king, Princes of the Blood and aristocrats supposedly had collaborated in a form of government which was 'natural', balanced and appropriate to the needs and character of the kingdom. His plans should not be dismissed as hopeless utopianism, for after the death of Louis XIV, the Duc d'Orléans as regent created a system of councils remarkably similar to that advocated by Saint-Simon.[22] For a time at least, the government of France conformed to the principles of the 'Bourgogne group'.

The political principles associated with Louis XIV not only required his regime to extend its authority into the realm of 'high culture', but were the subject of critical evaluation by contemporary literature, music, painting and other forms of cultural expression. The student who aspires to understand this period of French history should know something of, for example, the literature of the period, for therein were conducted 'political' debates of the greatest importance. The plays of Corneille and Racine, the correspondence of Madame de Sévigné, and the piercing, ironical *Caractères* of La Bruyère, as well as the works of Fénelon and Saint-Simon discussed above, raised questions such as: what is the nature of just or unjust monarchy, what constitutes heroic or unworthy behaviour by the king, how far do the practical demands of monarchy conflict with royal honour, to what extent are kings subjected to forces beyond their control, how far is the pursuit of *la gloire* consistent with the demands of Christian humility, and what fate does a king who abuses his power deserve?

French writers, artists, composers and others upheld the tradition that they had a duty to question and even challenge the regime of Louis XIV; not in a spirit of negative resistance, but one of positive didacticism. Louis XIV and his advisers recognised the validity of, and indeed the necessity for, constructive criticism. The control of cultural life which they channelled through state academies, for example, was not intended to impose a crushing orthodoxy, but rather create circumstances in which the best creative talent within the kingdom could find expression under royal patronage. This is not to say that modern notions of 'freedom of expression' pertained, but the relationship between crown and the movement of ideas in France was, on balance, healthy and productive.

6

LOUIS XIV AND EUROPE

Louis XIV's vision of kingship ascribed a high priority to international relations. In some senses his approach to foreign affairs seems to abound in inconsistencies: it combined idealism with pragmatism, generosity with ruthlessness, an obsessive sensitivity regarding his reputation with an indifference to international vilification, a punctilious regard for the legality of his actions with cynically calculated *raison d'état*, expressions of a yearning for peace with an assiduous pursuit of warfare for its own sake. Yet in its essentials Louis's conduct was no different from that of his fellow heads of state. Whatever their constitutional foundations – monarchic, theocratic, autocratic, republican or other – the behaviour of European governments in the international arena was of a piece. If the France of Louis XIV was able to dominate western Europe for long periods, it was because he was able to bring to bear upon a propitious international context the immense human, military and financial resources at his disposal, not because he conducted foreign policy in original ways. The principles, purposes and dynamics of his foreign policy have long exercised historians. Some have interpreted his policy as another facet of his state-building, others have emphasised his pursuit of *la gloire*, while an alleged long-term intention to secure the Spanish throne for the house of Bourbon has even been advanced as the key to his foreign policy.[1] Present-day scholars are less inclined to search for all-embracing explanations of Louis's foreign policy; they emphasise instead the role of accident and unforeseen circumstances in shaping his policies, his need to adjust his plans in the light of political events abroad. Louis, by this view, was not a free agent manipulating western Europe according to some master plan; he was but one contestant – albeit an important and powerful one – in the rough house of European international relations. This is not to say that he did not have certain broad purposes: like any head of state, he was committed to the security of the kingdom, and to creating as far as possible an international situation favourable to France. But this is different from claiming that, from the beginning of the personal reign, he had a blueprint for action which governed the whole direction and execution of his foreign policy.

Geopolitical factors constrained his actions. It was an axiom of French foreign policy throughout much of the seventeenth century that Spain on the southern frontier and Spanish territories on the eastern and northern frontiers (Franche-Comté and the Spanish Netherlands) were inherently hostile to French interests, and that the Spanish ruling family, the Habsburgs, could normally rely upon the backing of their Austrian cousins in their disputes with France. One thread never far from the surface of French foreign policy involved the search for measures to frustrate Habsburg intentions. Elsewhere the situation was less clear-cut: Savoy on the south-eastern frontier blew hot and cold in its approach to France; relations between France and the two chief maritime powers, England and the Dutch Republic, likewise fluctuated.[2] Even Franco-Swedish relations, which generally were good because the Swedish government was heavily dependent on French money, had their ups and downs. The north-eastern frontier was especially problematic. Between Franche-Comté and the Spanish Netherlands lay a chain of duchies and ecclesiastical territories, including Lorraine, Alsace, Bar, Luxembourg, Metz and Toul, which could be viewed as 'gates' or 'alleys' providing access to and egress from France. Richelieu had regarded the security of these 'gates' as a major priority, and their preservation remained at the centre of Louis XIV's policy. As regards Europe beyond the French frontier regions, Louis often had a wide range of policy options available to him; but he had no choice over the concentration of a high proportion of his diplomatic and military resources on the defence of the frontiers.

The Instruments of Policy

What instruments were available to him for deciding and implementing policy? It should be emphasised that, as with every other branch of government, it was Louis himself who decided policy, but

only after lengthy discussion in the Conseil d'en Haut. Foreign policy
was a subject for which he displayed prodigious enthusiasm, and
since warfare was a principal instrument through which policy was
implemented, he showed an equal passion for military affairs. The
Secretaries of State for Foreign Affairs and for War had ready access
to him beyond the regular meetings of the Conseil d'en Haut.[3] Louis
devoted many hours to private conversations with them, and over
the years acquired considerable expertise in international relations.
In the council itself lengthy discussions were devoted to foreign
affairs as Louis endeavoured to ensure that he was well informed
not only on the international situation at any one time, but on the
personal qualities of other heads of state, their strengths and weaknesses, those of their ministers and other advisers, and the state of
their domestic politics.

For the implementation of policy and the maintenance of regular
contact with other states Louis possessed a diplomatic service which
was among the most highly developed of the age.[4] It upheld his interests through the normal intercourse of diplomatic relations with other
governments, but also through agents, spies and the judicious distribution of financial gifts to foreign statesmen who supplied useful
information. Sophisticated though it was by seventeenth-century standards, we should not imagine that the French diplomatic service bore
comparison with that of a modern state. The French government
normally maintained permanent embassies only in Rome, Spain,
England, Venice, the Dutch Republic and Savoy (although not Austria,
for reasons that will become apparent); elsewhere it used less senior
'residents' or temporary missions despatched for particular purposes.
Even though the number of French ambassadors increased during
the personal reign of Louis XIV, by 1715 they still numbered only
fifteen; in addition there were two 'residents' and fifteen 'envoyés' on
foreign postings.[5] There existed no formal procedure for training
diplomats, and since ambassadors usually had to bear the cost of their
postings themselves, only claiming reimbursement from the French
government later, they were often chosen as much for their financial
standing as for their diplomatic skills. One function of Louis's diplomatic agents was to bind 'client' states to France through financial
gifts. In 1661 the Swedish government agreed to receive French subsidies in return for backing French policies towards Poland; in 1664
the Elector of Saxony was allied to France in return for French gold;
in like manner the Elector of the Palatinate, the Archbishop of

Cologne and the Bishop of Münster were brought into the French orbit. From 1680 Denmark was in receipt of funds from France, and in 1683 subventions were being paid to England, Brandenburg, the Palatinate, and the Archbishops of Mainz and Cologne, not to mention other prelates in Germany and several princes in Italy.

Warfare, the Army and Navy

Warfare loomed large in Louis's foreign relations: he was at war or involved in military conflict for almost fifty of the seventy-two years of his reign. Of all the traditions surrounding European monarchy, that of 'the king as warrior' was among the most ancient. The social values of the seventeenth century were such that monarchs and nobles regarded warfare as an honourable activity worthy of the social elites,[6] and it was considered axiomatic that the most glorious kings appeared on the battlefield. Both Louis's grandfather and father experienced warfare at first hand, and Louis XIV was resolved that he too would command his troops in battle. Accordingly he attended and helped to direct sieges on various occasions, and from time to time observed battles from positions which placed his life in danger. In 1692, for example, he took much of the royal court with him to the siege of Namur, a city which boasted that it had never been captured; for several weeks Louis camped with his army, visited the trenches to encourage his troops, observed and made suggestions as to the conduct of the siege, and on several occasions approached close to enemy lines. To Louis's elation the city and citadel fell; he was jubilant at being the first warrior to overcome the formidable defences of Namur. The French nobility shared this military ideal. Almost all officers in the army were nobles, for military commissions conferred enormous social prestige. Families whose noble titles were of recent origin felt it especially necessary to prove their status: of the 167 generals who commanded Louis's armies during his reign, some 40 per cent belonged to families whose titles went back only a hundred years or so.[7]

Under Louis XIV the army underwent considerable modernisation chiefly at the hands of two Secretaries of State for War, Le Tellier and his son Louvois.[8] Although they did not initiate reform – in many respects they continued processes which began under Richelieu and Mazarin – they acted with urgency and vigour. They increased the size of the army, improved its organisation and quality of equipment, tightened discipline, and turned it into a fighting force capable of matching the best in Europe. Whereas the French army in the 1620s and early 1630s numbered at most 20,000, by the late 1630s it had grown to over 150,000 and was up to 400,000 by 1690; it remained at 350,000 or thereabouts down to the early 1760s.[9] This expansion took place chiefly in the infantry, which by the late 1600s outnumbered the cavalry by about five to one.[10] The emphasis on infantry reflected shifts in the conduct of warfare. The quality and standardisation of firearms and cannon was constantly being enhanced, placing the foot-soldier at an advantage over cavalry. Siege warfare was becoming increasingly common, and whether a position was being defended or attacked it was infantrymen rather than cavalry who generally decided the outcome. The French government recognised the growing importance of siege warfare and accordingly recruited more military engineers into the army. In 1611 there were only eleven attached to the army, but by 1630 the number had risen to thirty-six. The drive to train and use more engineers came from Sébastien le Prestre, Comte de Vauban, the great military engineer and architect of defensive fortifications. In 1676 a corps of engineers was placed under his direction; by 1691 numbers had risen to over 270, and in the eighteenth century there were usually between and 300 and 380 engineers attached to the French army.[11]

Of course, the larger the army, the greater the problems of organisation and control. One traditional problem which led to disputes and inefficiency was that of precedence between the officer ranks of different regiments. This was a most sensitive subject which raised issues of regimental and personal pride. In the 1650s the government published a series of ordinances aiming to impose a modicum of order, and in 1661 a general ordinance was issued grading all the ranks in the army. Arguments still occurred, but the situation was much improved.[12] The use of uniforms became more common. Their purpose was to enhance *esprit de corps*, improve discipline and make desertion more difficult. In support of the army, Le Tellier and Louvois established arsenals, metallurgical and powder factories in the frontier provinces. Medical services were improved with the foundation of military hospitals, notably that of Les Invalides near Paris. In the administration of the army, Le Tellier and Louvois inherited *intendants d'armée* and *commissaires* from Richelieu.[13] Louvois in particular imposed a rigid authority on these agents whose function was to oversee military logistics, especially the supervision of wages and ordnance. At the Ministry of War he developed five bureaux dealing with different aspects of military administration.

The navy too was expanded under Louis XIV.[14] Earlier in the century Richelieu had built up the fleet, but it was Colbert, who in 1669 took over responsibility for the navy, who modernised the fleet and provided it with organisational and ordnance support. Toulon, Rochefort, Le Havre, Dunkirk and Brest were developed as arsenal ports with warehouses, breakwaters, improved road links to the interior, better anchorages, construction and repair facilities and all the necessities of an up-to-date naval base. A programme of shipbuilding raised the strength of the fleet to 120 ships of the line by 1689: in that year the English fleet numbered 100 and the Dutch had sixty-six ships.[15] Recruitment to the navy was regularised through a system whereby lists of sailors were drawn up – 'maritime classes' – from which crews for the king's ships were to be taken; ingenious as the scheme was on paper, its expectations were not matched by the outcome.[16] The administrative support available to the navy was improved through the use of intendants and commissioners similar to those attached to the army. These were impressive developments, but the navy nevertheless remained the junior service: in the 1690s and early 1700s government expenditure on the navy was usually only about one-sixth of that on the army.

Principles Underlying Louis's Foreign Policy

Given the size and wealth of the state, and the effectiveness of the diplomatic and military resources at his disposal, Louis XIV could afford to think of foreign relations in ambitious terms. Granted that geopolitical realities were bound to influence his foreign policy, how far was it shaped by other factors? The answer must be, only to a limited extent. In a reign of such length, the international context within which the king operated changed frequently, forcing him to modify or adjust his policies. Louis's *Mémoires* discuss the international situation of the early 1660s, and conclude that an auspicious climate then existed. Spain had been weakened by sustained warfare and was content to preserve its 1659 peace treaty with France; the Holy Roman Emperor was preoccupied with internal affairs rather than with international relations; domestic problems also ensured that the Dutch,

English and various Italian states desired a period of peace.[17]
However, the *Mémoires* also recognise the transience of these advantageous circumstances, and avoid any suggestion of fixed principles
which should govern French policy in every eventuality. Louis's
foreign policy, when seen in its totality, suggests that he had no blueprint for Europe, no 'grand design' which purportedly wove the many
strands of his foreign policy into a coherent whole.[18] In so far as
patterns may be discerned, they are the product of modern historical
research rather than the conscious intent of Louis XIV. All things
considered, it is hardly likely that any seventeenth-century monarch
consistently could have pursued foreign policy according to a preconceived master plan. Like his contemporaries, Louis often had to
formulate policy on scanty information (in spite of the efforts of his
diplomatic service), while at the same time attempting to fathom the
often circuitous actions of his rivals. Broad geopolitical considerations
aside, foreign policy perforce was often governed by short-term
factors, for even alliances could not be taken for granted; today's
enemy could be tomorrow's friend and vice versa. Thus, whereas
France was allied to England from 1656 to 1659 and from 1672 to
1674, from 1688 onwards they were enemies; and while the French
and the Dutch Republic usually were allied from 1635 onwards, they
fought each other from 1672 to 1678 and on other occasions thereafter.[19] There was also a personal dimension to international relations
which rendered implausible any likelihood of foreign policy being
governed by over-arching principles. Louis XIV was not alone in
using the European arena in pursuit of *la gloire*. In their own way
William III of England, Charles XII of Sweden, the Emperor
Leopold I and other monarchs allowed questions of reputation to
influence policy. Conflicts over dynastic claims resulting from acci-
dents of birth, marriage and death, complicated international relations. Disputes over claims could range from minor affairs of no great
consequence, to the most portentous issue of the second half of the
seventeenth century: the Spanish Succession. The relentless pursuit
of dynastic rights was among the most vexatious problems in international affairs, and Louis too was to play his part by asserting claims
(or those of his queen) to Spanish possessions. By the second half of
the century, however, there had emerged a concept – to which Louis
subscribed – aiming to diminish the destabilising effect on international relations of lengthy conflicts over rival dynastic claims,
namely that of 'equivalence': to avert long wars, one side would defer

to the claims of the other in return for 'equivalent' rights or territory elsewhere. For example, in 1667 at the time of the Devolution crisis, Louis XIV wrote to the Spanish government proclaiming that he had no intention of asserting a claim to anything 'other than that which belongs to us, *or its equivalent*'.[20]

One scholar, looking back to earlier decades of the seventeenth century, has argued that Richelieu's foreign policy incorporated a vision of peace wherein Europe, liberated from the danger of Habsburg hegemony, would live in harmony and equilibrium under the benevolent leadership of the King of France.[21] However sound this interpretation, it surely cannot be applied to Louis XIV. International relations in the second half of the seventeenth century were governed by *raison d'état*, not ideals of international fraternity. Some of Louis's enemies were to accuse him of ambitions to exercise a 'universal monarchy' over the whole of Europe. Even this is a highly exaggerated and distorted response to his policies. Louis was not an ideologue; he was a man attuned to the norms and practices of his time. It is in these terms that he should be interpreted, and any judgements, if judgements there must be, should adopt the value-systems of the late 1600s, not those of the late 1900s.

Louis and Europe in the Early 1660s

During the last few years of his life Mazarin was instrumental in securing a favourable international position for France. He established good relations with Protestant, republican England and in so doing remained faithful to Richelieu's precept that foreign policy must not be subjected to confessional or ideological constraints. By the Peace of Westminster (1655), Mazarin and Cromwell settled outstanding differences between their two countries, and the following year entered into military alliance. In 1658 there was formed in Germany the League of the Rhine, chiefly at the instigation of the Archbishop of Mainz; its purpose was to preserve the neutrality of the Rhineland especially against Austrian Habsburg meddling. In addition to several German territories the league was joined by Sweden, and accepted the 'protection' of France. The league expanded when Denmark joined in 1663 and Brandenburg in 1665. In 1659 Mazarin negotiated the Peace of the Pyrenees, thereby ending the war against Spain which had begun in 1635.[22] His death made little difference to the course of French foreign policy in the 1660s, for Louis XIV relied heavily on the Secretary of State for Foreign Affairs, Lionne, for guidance. Lionne had been groomed in international relations by Mazarin: he had been one of the cardinal's right-hand men during the negotiations at Westphalia (1648), and had been closely involved in the formation of the League of the Rhine and in the Peace of the Pyrenees.

In 1662 Louis made two territorial acquisitions. First, he reinforced France's position on the North Sea coast by purchasing Dunkirk from England for 5 million livres. Second, by the Treaty of Montmartre, Charles IV of Lorraine ceded his duchy to France in return for an annual subsidy and recognition of him and his successors as French Princes of the Blood with rights of succession to the French throne. The treaty with Lorraine was a major success, for this was a region where French governments traditionally felt militarily vulnerable; now that it was closely bound to France, that section of the frontier was rendered more secure. Again in 1662 Louis signed an alliance with the Dutch Republic, which thereby entered France's network of international agreements. Within a few years the Dutch placed Louis in a difficult position, for in 1665 they went to war against England and called on the French for help. Louis did intervene, but in view of developments in Spain – to be discussed shortly – greatly welcomed the Peace of Breda which ended the Anglo-Dutch conflict in 1667.

Louis proved captious on the matter of diplomatic precedence. This was a most sensitive issue, for the order and precedence observed by diplomatic representatives in foreign courts carried heavy implications for the prestige and status of their governments. In 1661 Louis informed all of his ambassadors that they must insist on being accorded precedence over their Spanish counterparts. On 10 October 1661, the Spanish Ambassador to London refused to concede seniority to the French Ambassador, and a violent altercation took place involving their respective entourages. When informed of the incident, Louis XIV expelled the Spanish Ambassador from the French court and demanded from the Spanish government an explanation for the fracas in London. After acrimonious negotiations, the Spanish yielded and conceded French diplomatic precedence abroad. However, the Austrian Habsburgs refused to be bound by the agreement and continued, as before, to afford pride of place to the Spanish Ambassador at the court of Vienna. It was for this reason that Louis XIV never sent an ambassador to Vienna, only representatives of a lower rank.

The Spanish Succession and War of Devolution

The extent to which external events could force Louis's hand is seen
in the first manifestation of the Spanish Succession problem in 1665.
It arose from the marriage between Louis XIV and Maria Teresa,
agreed by the terms of the Peace of the Pyrenees.[23] Several Franco-
Spanish royal marriages had taken place in the sixteenth and seventeenth centuries, including two in 1615: Louis XIII to Anne of Austria,
and Elisabeth of France to Philip IV of Spain. The union between
Louis XIV and Maria Teresa upheld a well-established tradition. Their
marriage contract was similar to that of Louis XIII and Anne of
Austria, but also contained differences out of which disputes arose.
One contentious issue was Maria Teresa's dowry. After much hard
bargaining, the French and Spanish negotiators agreed that she
should have a dowry of the same size as that of Anne of Austria and
Elisabeth of France in 1615: 500,000 gold écus (worth about 3 million
livres). It was to be paid in three instalments and within eighteen
months of the consummation of the marriage (a form of wording
which left room for flexibility). The chief importance of the dowry
was not financial – after all, 500,000 gold écus in no way represented
the true financial worth of a Spanish princess – but political: it was a
sign that in legal and constitutional terms Maria Teresa ceased to be
Spanish. The dowry was linked to an associated issue: Maria Teresa
renounced her claim to the throne of Spain and its territories. This
was a clause without which the Spanish would not have consented to
the marriage, for they regarded it as imperative that the French must
not be allowed a pretext for claiming the throne of Spain. French
negotiators nevertheless succeeded in inserting a crucial word into the
contract, namely that the renunciation was 'conditional upon'
('moyennant') the payment of the dowry. The principle of Maria
Teresa's renunciation was not new, for when Anne of Austria married
Louis XIII a similar clause was written into the contract. Through
renunciation Maria Teresa surrendered her succession rights, not only
because politically she had ceased to be 'Spanish' as the dowry signified, but because as Queen of France she would automatically acquire
a new set of 'French' rights in place of her former Spanish claims,
and it was rights to the French succession which she and her husband
would pass on to their progeny (to whom her renunciation of the
Spanish throne also applied). In order to reassure the Spanish,
Louis XIV agreed that, after their wedding, he and his queen would

confirm the renunciation and have it registered by the Parlement of Paris. On the Spanish side an equivalent post-marital procedure was envisaged, but Philip IV committed what proved to be a disastrous mistake. In 1618 the Spanish Cortes had affirmed the exclusion of Anne of Austria from the Spanish throne, but had also extended her renunciation in perpetuity to her descendants; this debarred her son Louis XIV and his children from claiming all or part of the possessions of the Spanish crown. In view of this act of 1618, Philip IV did not feel it necessary once more to turn to the Cortes. By this omission he left the way open for Louis XIV later to assert the 'Spanish' claims of his descendants; not through his mother Anne of Austria (the validity of whose renunciation he did not question), and not through himself, but through his wife whose renunciation had never been endorsed by the Cortes.[24] Neither Louis XIV nor Philip IV fully met his obligations by the terms of the marriage contract. Philip IV refused to pay his daughter's dowry because Louis XIV would not allow his wife to reiterate, or the Parlement of Paris to register, her renunciation; and Louis would not recognise his wife's renunciation as binding until the Spanish paid the dowry.

The problem became urgent in 1665, for on 17 September Philip IV of Spain died, leaving as his heir an infant son, Charles II, who was still a few weeks short of his fourth birthday. The child's health was poor and he was not expected to survive into adulthood; what then would become of Spain and its vast territories in Europe and the New World? Such an eventuality had been foreseen by the Spanish and Austrian Habsburgs. In order to meet it they had a family compact whereby, in each generation, a Spanish Habsburg princess would marry an Austrian cousin. Should the male line in Spain expire, the relevant princess would succeed as Queen of Spain (unlike France, but as in England and Scotland, females could reign) and her consort also would be Habsburg. Accordingly, Margaret, the younger sister of Maria Teresa, was betrothed to Leopold I, the Holy Roman Emperor (they married in 1666), Margaret retaining her claim to the throne of Spain. In 1665 and the years immediately following, the assumption in the Spanish government was that, if the infant Charles II died, Margaret and Leopold would succeed him. Louis XIV rejected this analysis. On hearing of Philip IV's death, he proclaimed that his wife's renunciation was invalid since her dowry remained unpaid, and that in the event of the decease of Charles II, Maria Teresa, not Margaret, was rightful Queen of Spain. Louis followed up this assertion with a second: that because his wife's renunciation was null and void, it was she and not her brother Charles II who ought to succeed immediately to the Spanish Netherlands. The basis of this proposition was the so-called 'Law of Devolution'. In Brabant and a few other places in the Spanish Netherlands, inheritance rights were governed by the 'Law of Devolution' according to which the children of a first marriage had priority over those of a second. Maria Teresa was the daughter of Philip IV by his first marriage, whereas Charles II and Margaret were the children of his second; by invoking this Brabantine law Louis XIV made an immediate claim on the Spanish Netherlands in the name of his wife. He publicised his case as widely as possible, authorising the publication of pamphlets explaining the 'legality' of his claim; they included the *Traité des Droits de la Reine Très-Chrétienne sur Divers Etats de la Monarchie d'Espagne* (1667) which outlined claims both to the Spanish Netherlands forthwith, and to the throne of Spain should Charles II die childless. The Spanish replied in kind, issuing publications denouncing the 'illegality' of the French position and accusing Louis XIV of blatant territorial aggression. Meanwhile Louis XIV took steps to seize his wife's 'inheritance' by force. In May 1667 he personally led an army into the Spanish Netherlands, where several frontier towns were captured including Lille. In February 1668 a second army (which Louis again accompanied) invaded and speedily occupied Franche-Comté, a Spanish territory on France's eastern frontier.

These rapidly evolving events had implications for the Austrians, Dutch, Swedes, Rhineland principalities and English as well as the Spanish. The Emperor Leopold I's main concern was the Spanish Succession: if Charles II died, would he and Louis XIV have to fight a full-scale war over Spain? Such a course would be disastrous, for even if one side achieved emphatic victory (an unlikely outcome since the war inevitably would be internationalised and could turn into military deadlock), the other would seek redress at the earliest opportunity. Hence there took place between French and Austrian representatives one of the most remarkable secret negotiations of the century resulting in the Treaty of Grémonville in January 1668: if Charles II died childless, the Spanish Succession would be partitioned between the Bourbons and the Austrian Habsburgs. The principal French portions would be the Spanish Netherlands, Franche-Comté, Navarre, Naples and Sicily; the remainder (Spain, its other European possessions and the New World) would go to Leopold's wife, Margaret.

The treaty was a remarkable achievement. It marked a breach in the traditional Habsburg unity of purpose over the great international issues of the day, for Leopold now regarded agreement with France as more important than the preservation of the whole Spanish Succession. Furthermore, the treaty implied that Louis XIV's claims on behalf of Maria Teresa possessed a certain validity; in particular, the Austrians would not stand in the way of French annexation of the Spanish Netherlands. Grémonville exemplified the readiness of both sides to exercise the principle of 'equivalence', even if blended with hard-headed *raison d'état*: in order to avoid a protracted, ruinous and probably indecisive war, they preferred partition of the Spanish Succession to an all-or-nothing stance over their respective dynastic claims.

Meanwhile, the Dutch government, unaware of the Austro-French treaty, was alarmed at the implications of a French occupation of the Spanish Netherlands: how secure would Dutch frontiers be, how safe the Rhineland, and what effects would it have on the maritime balance in the North Sea? In January 1668, the Dutch Republic and England signed the Treaty of the Hague, and were joined in April by Sweden. The publicly stated aim of this Triple Alliance was to mediate peace between France and Spain, but the members had secretly agreed that if the French refused to negotiate, they would ally with Spain and attempt to restore the frontiers of the Peace of the Pyrenees. Louis expressed conciliatory sentiments and accepted the mediation of the Triple Alliance: he signed the Peace of Aix-la-Chapelle with Spain in May 1668. France returned Franche-Comté to Spain and withdrew from most of the Spanish Netherlands, nevertheless retaining some frontier towns including Lille. Louis conceded generous terms to the Spanish not because he was cowed by the Triple Alliance, but because of his secret treaty with Leopold. Charles II of Spain's health continued to cause disquiet (in fact he lasted until 1700) and on his death, expected at any time, the Spanish Netherlands and Franche-Comté would pass into Louis's possession with the support of Leopold; in the face of Franco-Austrian resolution the Triple Alliance would be helpless. However, the events of 1668 did bring home certain lessons to Louis. His erstwhile allies – the Dutch, English and Swedes – had united to frustrate his purposes towards the Spanish Netherlands, and presumably would attempt to do so again when, as he expected, the Netherlands came into his wife's possession. The Dutch in particular had been the prime movers in organising the Triple Alliance, and it made sense to take steps to dismantle the alliance and undermine its linchpin, the Dutch Republic. As regards the alliance, Louis judged rightly that the English in particular felt little natural affiliation with the Dutch, against whom they had fought wars in recent years; by the secret Treaty of Dover (1670), Charles II of England accepted financial subsidies from Louis XIV in return for a promise to support France in a war against the Dutch. Sweden too returned to the French fold in 1672 in return for French money. The Triple Alliance had collapsed.

The Origins and Outcome of the Dutch War, 1672–78

Louis XIV embarked on the second war of his personal reign – against the Dutch Republic (or United Provinces) – in 1672. The most recent reassessment of the outbreak of the war by Sonnino[25] has challenged the view that it followed logically and inevitably from the peace of Aix-la-Chapelle: instead the war owed much to Louis's personal penchant for military campaigning, and to personality conflicts and other divisions within the Conseil d'en Haut. Louis had come to relish the excitement and exhilaration of warfare, and was encouraged to indulge his tastes by Louvois and Marshal Turenne. Lionne and Colbert were more cautious, although not inherently opposed to warfare; the former in particular argued that diplomacy ought to be the principal means of action adopted by a modern state. However, French diplomacy suffered setbacks at the turn of the decade, notably in its failure to secure the election of the French candidate, the Duc de Condé, as King of Poland in 1669;[26] this contrasted with the success of French arms in 1668. Lionne died in 1671, and although his successor as Secretary of State for Foreign Affairs, Pomponne (a former ambassador to the Dutch Republic and Sweden), sought to exercise a moderating influence in the Conseil d'en Haut, he was the newest member of the council and lacked the authority of Lionne. Louis was itching to fight another war, but under three conditions: first, the enemy must be 'worthy' of France (a minor German prince, for example, would not suffice); second, the war must involve splendid military campaigns and result in glorious victory; third, it must be short, and so impose as few financial strains as possible on the treasury. Two potential victims were deemed appropriate: Spain and the Dutch Republic. They were both 'honourable' enemies and, in the opinion of Louvois and Turenne, could be defeated quickly. The choice fell on the United Provinces. In Sonnino's view, it was not because their republicanism and Protestantism represented an ideological danger to France (they did not; moreover, France and the Dutch Republic had been allies a few years before), and not because of economic necessity, although it is true that France and the Dutch Republic had been locked in a tariff war since 1667. France fought the Dutch Republic because the French government calculated that such a war would cause fewer international complications than one against Spain: a Spanish war risked alienating Austria and could provoke another anti-French coalition.

War was declared by Louis in April 1672 and passed through three main phases. The first, lasting to the end of that year, was marked by dramatic French advances. Louis had made careful diplomatic preparations, reaching agreements with several Rhineland territories which allowed his troops passage to the Dutch Republic. He had an army of some 120,000 which was well equipped and led by some of the finest military minds of the age: Turenne, Condé, Luxembourg and Vauban. The Dutch had only 27,000 troops (rapidly raised to 80,000 during 1672) and one uncertain ally, Brandenburg. The Republic was attacked on two fronts: at sea by the English as allies of the French, and through the Rhineland by the armies of Louis XIV and his allies, the Archbishop of Cologne and the Bishop of Münster. The outnumbered and outmanœuvred Dutch could do little other than retreat, until by midsummer most of the Republic was under French control. In July the Dutch sued for peace before the French seized Amsterdam; but Louis demanded terms so humiliating that the Dutch rejected them (the cession to France of all captured territory, the end of anti-French tariffs, the admission of public Catholic worship, the appointment of Catholics to public posts, an annual Dutch embassy to France acknowledging submission to Louis XIV, and a payment of 24 million livres). The Dutch prolonged the talks to allow their most desperate measure to take effect: they opened dykes at Muiden, allowing the incoming seawater to flood extensive tracts of land between Amsterdam and the French forces, effectively turning Amsterdam into an island. A new political and military leader was appointed, William III of Orange (later to be William III of England) with extensive powers to organise national defence. By late 1672 the French still controlled most of the Republic, but had not forced the government into surrender. During phase two in 1673 there were more French successes (especially the capture of Maas-

tricht), but the war became internationalised by the entry of Spain
and Austria in support of the Dutch. The Spanish government was
alarmed at the implications of total French victory, and the Austrians
feared for the future of the Rhineland; their joint coalition with the
Dutch was joined by Brandenburg, by several smaller German territories and later by Denmark and Saxony. Conversely, Louis's allies
began to desert him: Cologne and Münster withdrew in 1673, and
England in 1674. The intervention of the coalition changed the
complexion of the war: by the end of 1673 the French had withdrawn
their troops from the Dutch Republic, and were concentrating their
efforts against the Spanish Netherlands and the Rhineland.

In its third phase the war was fought both in mainland Europe and
the Mediterranean. In 1674 the French secured their own frontiers
by reoccupying Franche-Comté, establishing control over most of
Alsace, and by their victory at Senef (near Charleroi) in August 1674
which prevented invasion from the north. In 1675 and 1676, the
Rhineland, Alsace, Franche-Comté, and the frontier between France
and the Spanish Netherlands remained the principal war zones, but
there were significant developments elsewhere. In 1674 Sicilian rebels
against the King of Spain called on Louis XIV for help. French ships
managed to run the Spanish blockade of Messina and transport
supplies to the Sicilians, and in 1675 French troops landed to provide
military assistance. A joint Dutch–Spanish fleet under the celebrated
admiral De Ruyter was despatched to Sicily in 1676, but in two brilliant actions the French fleet commanded by Duquesne defeated De
Ruyter and secured French maritime supremacy in the Mediterranean. The flow and counter-flow of the war confirmed that, in spite
of brilliant battles and campaigns, neither side had the capacity to
inflict decisive defeat on the other. Moreover, all the belligerents were
finding the financial cost of the war out of all proportion to the diplomatic or territorial gains which victory might bring. Warfare imposed
internal social strains, rebellion breaking out in several parts of
Europe including France, where there were risings in Roussillon,
Guyenne and Brittany in 1674 and 1675. After careful diplomatic
soundings in 1675, peace negotiations opened in Nijmegen in 1676.[27]
The discussions were bound to be difficult since so many states were
involved, but they resulted in a series of treaties from 1678 to 1679
known collectively as 'the Peace of Nijmegen'. The French were
involved in three major settlements. The first was with the Dutch.
Louis XIV restored Maastricht, ended the tariff war and agreed to a

treaty of commerce. Next came agreement with the Spanish. Louis retained Franche-Comté, Artois and several towns in the east and north (including Valenciennes and Cambrai) which would act as a barrier between France and the Spanish Netherlands. The settlement with the Austrians came in 1679. Louis restored parts of Alsace in return for bridgeheads across the Rhine.

The Dutch war was probably the greatest mistake that Louis XIV made in international affairs. None of the criteria which he had set was met: after some early French victories, the Dutch proved to be a much tougher military prospect than Louis expected, and the coalition which joined them transformed the war into a European conflict which was neither short nor unambiguously victorious. In 1678 adulatory medals were struck in France to celebrate the peace, and public festivities were organised to acclaim the 'glorious' achievements of the king; but there was no disguising the fact that the most powerful monarch in Europe, who in 1672 had an overwhelming military advantage over the small and poorly armed Dutch Republic, had bungled the invasion and failed to achieve the rapid, decisive victory which he sought. Louis paid a heavy international price for this war. France came to be perceived abroad as the principal danger to stability in western Europe, and before long Louis had to face further anti-French coalitions. The violent and destructive conduct of French troops against civilians, crops, livestock, buildings, whole towns and villages in the Dutch Republic and in the Rhineland, shocked even hardened contemporary opinion; there was created a popular Francophobia in those regions which lasted well into the eighteenth century, and was to be instrumental in pulling down the Bonapartist Empire. The fiscal and social effects of the war on France were disastrous: French state debt increased, taxes were raised, violent social protest broke out and the economy suffered. Yet Louis had intended the war to be brief precisely to avoid adverse consequences for his subjects. Nevertheless, the peace settlement did have positive results for France. Franche-Comté was an important acquisition, for it added human and economic resources to the kingdom, and strengthened the eastern frontier. Again, some of the frontier towns which France acquired in 1678 were integrated by Vauban into a chain of fortifications along the northern and eastern frontiers as a barrier against would-be invaders. Much as France had suffered, others had done so too. The international position of Spain had been seriously undermined by the war, and its financial and economic situation was very weak. The Emperor Leopold could derive little satisfaction from Nijmegen: he was left internationally isolated at a time when his eastern frontier was coming under pressure from the Turks, and he was facing rebellion in Hungary. As regards the Dutch Republic, by preserving its independence and sustaining war against the most powerful state in western Europe, it had enhanced its prestige abroad and inculcated patriotic pride at home. However, the war had been financially and economically ruinous for the Dutch Republic, which never recovered the economic pre-eminence of earlier decades. Moreover, in 1677 William III of Orange, the stadholder (chief executive officer of the Republic), married Princess Mary, daughter of James, Duke of York and later James II of England. In 1689 William and Mary became King and Queen of the three kingdoms of England, Scotland and Ireland. William III drew heavily on the financial and military resources both of England and the Dutch Republic in later wars against the French, and thereby placed further strain on the economy of the Republic. To the extent that Louis XIV had perceived the Dutch war as a means of subverting the economy of the Republic, it might be said that he succeeded, although not in the way he expected. Indeed, a final assessment of the international configuration of western Europe in 1679 would have to concede that France was now the dominant power. When Louis invaded the Dutch Republic in 1672 he had not been thinking in such strategic terms; although he had intended fighting a short, victorious war, the actual war proved to be so costly that it left the other great powers even more exhausted than France. Louis XIV inadvertently had created a 'French preponderance' in western Europe by 1679.

The concept of frontiers which the French now developed marks a significant step in French geopolitical thought. Since the days of Richelieu the notion of 'gates' had dominated the attitude to the frontiers, but by the late 1670s Vauban and Louvois had come to favour a 'linear' strategy: as far as possible the frontier should run in an uninterrupted line from the North Sea to the Mediterranean, and should be defined and protected by strongly fortified towns. We should not interpret this philosophy as a search for 'natural' boundaries, for it was not until the late eighteenth and nineteenth centuries that 'nature' was deemed a suitable determinant of frontiers. The 'linear' concept was based on the latest military technology which enabled engineers and architects to construct fortifications which were thought to be almost impregnable. In order to give further substance to the line, Louis engaged in a series of 'reunions' in the early 1680s which added territorially to potential weak points. He appointed four *chambres de réunion* to examine the major peace treaties in which France recently had been involved – Westphalia (1648), the Pyrenees (1659), and Nijmegen (1678–79) – in order to identify any territories to which he might lay claim. It was the custom, in peace treaties, to employ a terminology according to which territory was transferred from one government to another with the territory's 'dependencies'; an ambiguous term which usually was left undefined. The *chambres de réunion* scoured the peace treaties as a prelude to claiming 'dependencies' of French acquisitions since 1648. The *chambres de réunion* sat at Tournai to develop claims in the Netherlands, Metz for claims in Lorraine, Breisach for those in Alsace, and Besançon for those in Franche-Comté. The *chambres* worked quickly, and on the basis of their recommendations the French between 1680 and 1684 forcibly occupied and annexed much of the region between the Moselle and the Rhine, including most of Luxembourg and Alsace, and in 1681 the city of Strasbourg. When the process was complete by the end of 1684, the north-eastern segment of the frontier had been strengthened. These acts of 'piracy', as they were seen by other governments, provoked protests. By the Treaty of the Hague (1681), the Dutch and Swedish governments, joined by the Austrian and Spanish the next year, formed an association to guarantee the peace treaties of 1648 and 1678. However, they were reluctant actually to go to war against the French; and in 1683 the Austrians in particular were diverted when Vienna was besieged by the Turks. Only the Spanish took action: in 1683 they attempted to relieve Luxembourg by force, but found no international support. By the truce of Ratisbon, mediated by Leopold of Austria in 1684, they consented to France retaining the 'reunions' for twenty years. In a Europe still suffering post-war exhaustion, Louis's audacity triumphed.

The War of the League of Augsburg (The Nine Years' War)

The year 1684 turned out to be the apogee of Louis XIV's fortunes in international affairs. Thereafter he suffered the consequences of having alienated other powers; in place of governments which were hesitant and deeply suspicious of each other, he increasingly faced organised opposition. For most of the last thirty years of his reign

France was at war and suffered fearful socio-economic consequences. Huguenots, fleeing to other parts of Europe, brought horror stories of the persecution which they had undergone, and after the Revocation of the Edict of Nantes the Protestant states which joined anti-French coalitions were inspired in part by a desire to avenge the suffering of their fellow Protestants. Two other developments help to explain Louis's reversal of fortunes. First, after driving back the Turks in 1683 and 1684, the Austrians were able to bring greater military forces to bear on western Europe, especially since the Hungarian rising was also crushed. Second, in 1688 James II of England was overthrown in favour of William III and Mary. England now moved resolutely into the anti-French camp, and formed with the Dutch Republic an axis of military and financial power committed to overcoming French ambitions. Meanwhile in Germany a growing spirit of resistance to French aggression expressed itself in the creation of the League of Augsburg (1686), which comprised Austria, Spain, Sweden, Saxony and Bavaria, the signatories promising mutual assistance in case of French attack.

The immediate problems which triggered the War of the League of Augsburg (or Nine Years' War) were the successions to the Palatinate and the Archbishopric of Cologne. In 1685 the Elector Charles of the Palatinate died childless; his sister Charlotte-Elisabeth was married to Louis XIV's brother, Philippe d'Orléans. By Charles's will and the succession laws of the Holy Roman Empire she was bypassed in favour of Philip William of Neuburg, father-in-law of the Emperor Leopold. Louis XIV protested and claimed part of the succession for Charlotte-Elisabeth. Next, on 3 June 1688 the pro-French Archbishop of Cologne, Maximilian Henry of Bavaria, died. Louis XIV's intention was to have him replaced by another French partisan, William Egon von Fürstenberg, Bishop of Strasbourg; but a rival existed in the form of the seventeen-year-old Joseph Clement of Bavaria, Bishop of Freising and Regensburg, nephew of the deceased archbishop and the candidate of the Emperor Leopold. After much intrigue and diplomatic manœuvring the papal choice fell on Joseph Clement. Louis decided on a course of action which, he hoped, would intimidate his opponents: on 24 September 1688 he issued a manifesto demanding first, that the truce of Ratisbon be transformed into a full and binding treaty, second, that Charlotte-Elisabeth be paid a cash indemnity in return for her renouncing her claim to the Palatinate (another example of 'equivalence'), and third, that Fürstenberg be appointed

Archbishop of Cologne. In the meantime he ordered his troops to occupy part of Cologne and the Palatinate. French forces marched into these territories, also capturing the fortress of Phillipsburg in October 1688.[28] The League of Augsburg interpreted these moves as precisely the kind of aggression which they had resolved to resist, and raised an army to protect the Rhineland against further French incursions. Meanwhile, word arrived from England that James II had fled and that William and Mary had replaced him. Under orders from their government, the French armies laid waste to much of the Rhineland, especially the Palatinate and adjacent territories. Heidelberg, Worms, Speyer and other towns were destroyed, and the city of Mannheim was left a smouldering heap. The countryside too was devastated. This process of systematic destruction continued until the early summer of 1689 and in Germany brought forth many protests against the 'barbarity' of the 'French Attila'. In 1689 there was formed a large anti-French coalition of England, the Dutch Republic, Austria, Spain and the German signatories to the League of Augsburg: its aim was to return France to its frontiers of 1659.

Europe entered upon a war which was to last nine years and prove even more destructive than the Dutch War. The armies of both sides were larger than ever before at about 400,000 men. That the French were able to muster forces of this size is a testimony to their military organisation (although the fiscal costs were colossal), and that the coalition did so too showed that its members understood that international collaboration was the only answer to the immense military resources of the French. On mainland Europe the war, as in the 1670s, was fought mainly in and around the Netherlands, Flanders and the Rhineland, with an offshoot in Ireland where James II, with French help, landed in 1689 as a prelude to regaining the English throne; his defeat at the battle of the Boyne in 1690 effectively ended the enterprise and allowed William III to concentrate on the continental struggle. There were two other areas of fighting in Europe: one was northern Italy for the control of the key fortresses of Casale and Pinerolo which governed access between France and Italy, and the other was Spain itself, for in 1694 a French army invaded Catalonia and in 1697 occupied Barcelona. At sea, the victory of the French over an Anglo-Dutch fleet at Beachy Head in 1690 was reversed by an Anglo-Dutch victory at La Hougue near Cherbourg in 1692, with neither side thereafter establishing decisive naval superiority. In the colonies, there was fighting in the West Indies and North America;

the French and English also fought in India. As in the Dutch War there were major battles and sieges, but again overwhelming victory was beyond the capacity of either side. On several occasions the coalition armies attempted to invade France from Flanders, but were stopped in battles at Fleurus (1690), Steinkirk (1692) and Neerwinden (1693). Louis made several visits to the war zone (including the siege of Namur in 1692), but after his return to Versailles from the front in June 1693 he never again commanded his armies in person.

As early as 1693 French diplomats had made overtures of peace, but it was not until 1696 that serious talks began. In that year Louis signed a separate peace with the Duke of Savoy who was promised Casale and Pinerolo. Because this treaty both threatened the future unity of the coalition (of which Savoy had been a member) and released French forces in Italy to go north, the Austrians, Spanish, Dutch and English agreed to talks. The Swedes offered to mediate a settlement, which was negotiated in 1697 in a villa belonging to William III at Ryswick, a village near The Hague. The French made concessions to the English. Louis recognised William III as King of England (Mary had died in 1694) and promised to withdraw support from the Stuarts. Colonial territory which the English and French had taken from each other was exchanged. In the settlement with the Dutch, Louis agreed to a commercial treaty favourable to the Republic; he also agreed to the Dutch occupation of eleven fortified towns on the frontier between France and the Spanish Netherlands (they included Courtrai, Mons and Charleroi). Louis treated the Spanish generously: the French withdrew from Catalonia and returned all the 'reunions' on the frontier with the Spanish Netherlands, plus Luxembourg and other territory captured during the recent war. In the Rhineland, the French gave way on the successions to the Palatinate and the Archbishopric of Cologne, and agreed to return the 'reunions' with one major exception: Alsace (including the city of Strasbourg) remained French. The Austrians opposed the loss of Alsace, but since the British, Dutch and Spanish signed peace on 20 September 1697, they had no option but to agree and sign peace on 30 October.

The peace terms implied that Louis had accepted two major realities, although there was no guarantee that he would not renege on his promises in future. First, it seemed that he was reconciled to William III on the throne of England. However, William and Mary had no children; when William died, James II (who was exiled in

France under Louis's protection) or his son might attempt a restoration. How would Louis then respond? Second, at Ryswick Louis apparently recognised that he would not be permitted to acquire the Spanish Netherlands by force, for the Dutch 'barrier forts' along his northern frontier affirmed international resolution on this point. But given Spain's poor record of defending the Netherlands against the French in recent times, and given the fluidity of international relations, the barrier forts by themselves might prove to be an insufficient deterrent to future French intentions. Ryswick was notable for the magnanimity with which Louis handled the Spanish. Louis was benevolent because of the question of the successor to Charles II of Spain. Against all medical expectations Charles II still survived, but was childless. Louis and Leopold had signed a partition agreement in 1668, but by 1697 it was redundant, partly because of a changed international configuration, but also because Leopold now had children whose succession rights he was bound to uphold. If the Spanish Succession were to be resolved on terms agreeable to the French, it was essential that Louis cultivate a pro-French faction at the Spanish court; hence the prudence with which Louis treated Spain at Ryswick.

The War of the Spanish Succession

Information from Spain indicated that a disease-ridden Charles II could not survive much longer, but the governments of post-war western Europe were anxious for the succession to be settled peacefully. William III of England, for example, who in 1689 had agreed to support Austrian claims to Spain, was now much less enthusiastic if that meant renewed conflict with France. The Spanish court was divided over the future of the country,[29] but a powerful group headed by Luis Fernandez Portocarrero, Archbishop of Toledo, held to one principle adamantly: Spain and its possessions must remain intact; there must be no question of partition. This was a stance which Charles himself adopted. There were three candidates for the throne of Spain, but the claims of all were compromised by 'renunciations'. One was Philippe, Duc d'Anjou, the younger grandson of Louis XIV and Maria Teresa; his claim derived from his grandmother whose renunciation to the Spanish Succession the French government still did not acknowledge. A second was Charles, younger son of the Emperor Leopold. Leopold had married twice. By his first marriage he had a daughter,

Maria Antonia (d.1692), who in turn married Maximilian Emmanuel of Bavaria. At her father's insistence, Maria Antonia renounced her claim to the throne of Spain. Leopold had two sons by his second marriage: the elder, Joseph, was groomed to succeed his father as Holy Roman Emperor (and did so in 1705), but the younger, the Archduke Charles, was intended for the throne of Spain; however, this arrangement was conditional on his half-sister's renunciation. If her renunciation proved invalid, then a third candidate came into play: Prince Joseph Ferdinand, son of Maria Antonia and Maximilian Emmanuel, who could claim the Spanish throne through his mother.

The bewildering legal and constitutional problems surrounding each of the claimants could have employed teams of lawyers for many years, but Charles II was dying and a solution had to be found quickly. Urgent international diplomatic manœuvres took place in an attempt to prevent a Franco-Austrian war – which inevitably would involve other states – over the Spanish Succession. Such was the need to find a solution that principle was sacrificed to *realpolitik*. In 1698, the English and Dutch signed a treaty with the French (the Austrians and Spanish were not consulted) based on the principle of partition. It stated that when Charles II died the throne of Spain would go neither to the French nor to the Austrian claimant, but to Prince Joseph Ferdinand. France and Austria would be compensated mainly from Spanish possessions in Italy: France would receive Naples and Sicily, and Austria would obtain Milan. Joseph Ferdinand would therefore inherit Spain, the Spanish Netherlands and other European possessions, and the Spanish colonies in the Americas. Whether Spain and Austria could have been persuaded to accept this arrangement is open to question, for Joseph Ferdinand died in 1699; alternative proposals were needed. In 1700 the English, Dutch and French signed a second Partition Treaty: Leopold's son, Charles, would replace Joseph Ferdinand as successor to the Spanish throne (thus satisfying Leopold, it was hoped), while France would be compensated not only with Naples and Sicily, but also Milan. When they heard of this treaty, both the Spanish government (which rejected the principle of partition) and the Austrian (which would not tolerate French domination of Italy) objected. In October 1700 news spread that Charles II of Spain had written a will containing his decision on the succession. Leopold, assuming that his son the Archduke Charles had been nominated, warned Louis XIV that Austria and Spain together would fight to preserve an undivided succession; Leopold was confident that the

Dutch and English would abandon the French, who would have no option but to recognise 'Charles III' of Spain. Charles II died on 1 November 1700, but his will named not the Austrian candidate, but Philippe, Duc d'Anjou as next King of Spain. Charles II too had thought in terms of reality rather than principle. He conceded the argument which the French consistently had maintained – that Maria Teresa's renunciation in 1660 was invalid – because he concluded that only the French had the resources to preserve the Spanish Succession intact. In short, Charles II put the unity of the Spanish Empire ahead of the legal ambiguities surrounding the Duc d'Anjou.

Louis received the news on 9 November. On 16 November he formally accepted the terms of the will, but only after intense debates in the Conseil d'en Haut.[30] Arguing from a position of *raison d'état*, some ministers urged Louis to reject the will and enforce the 1700 Partition Treaty. France would gain strategic territory in Italy, good relations with the English and Dutch would be preserved, and after ritual protests the emperor would agree, especially since his son would be King of Spain. If France accepted Charles's will (so this argument went), the Dutch and English would feel betrayed and might join the Austrians in a war to drive 'Philip V' from the Spanish throne. Other ministers, supported by the Dauphin and Madame de Maintenon, argued the contrary case, that Louis should accept the will. Justice required it. Had not Louis been insisting since 1660 that Maria Teresa's renunciation was null and void, and that the Spanish Succession legally belonged to the Bourbons? If Louis now abandoned this stance he would, with much justification, be seen at home and abroad as a hypocrite. A religious argument also was employed. As *le roi très-chrétien* Louis was bound to obey the will of God, and what clearer proof could there be of the divine intention than that the Duc d'Anjou should be King of Spain? There was also a geopolitical case in favour of accepting the will: the Spanish Netherlands, for so long a danger to French security, would in effect become a protective cordon sanitaire behind which northern France would be safe. Louis made his decision on 16 November, but sought to make it palatable to other governments by adding that France was making a sacrifice by relinquishing the opportunity offered by the 1700 Partition Treaty to annex territory in Italy. Arrangements were set in hand to prepare the Duc d'Anjou for his new role, and he went to Spain in January 1701.

Even at this stage a war was not inevitable, for it did not break out until May 1702. Hence the question arises of what happened in the intervening period? The brief answer is that, at a time when the international atmosphere was extremely tense and the most delicate conduct of diplomacy was needed, Louis committed several provocative acts which convinced the Austrians, Dutch and English that he had plans to create a Franco-Spanish bloc against whose political, military and economic powers the rest of western Europe would be helpless. Modern historians argue that Louis had no such apocalyptic intentions,[31] but in the exceedingly distrustful international setting of 1701 the actions taken by Louis XIV were interpreted by other governments as evidence of malign intent. Three measures in particular, all taken in February 1701, paved the way to war. First, Louis announced that the new King of Spain retained his claim to the throne of France. This raised fears that Louis envisaged the union of the two kingdoms. In fact he had no such prospect in mind; indeed, Charles II's will – which Louis publicly had accepted – expressly debarred a union. Louis was affirming the sacrosanct nature of French succession law, according to which a French prince could not be denied his succession rights. Louis assumed that in the unlikely event of Anjou becoming King of France, he would abdicate from the Spanish throne. Be that as it may, the timing of the announcement was inept and could do no other than dismay other governments. Second, French troops occupied the 'barrier forts' which the Dutch had acquired at Ryswick. The French did so at the 'invitation' of Philip V whose accession to the Spanish throne was not received with universal acclamation in the Spanish Netherlands. Louis and Philip feared that the Dutch (who as yet had not recognised the new King of Spain) might use the barrier forts as the base from which to encourage an independence movement in the Spanish Netherlands. French occupation of the forts served to warn both the Spanish Netherlands and the Dutch Republic of the finality of the succession; indeed, the Republic recognised Philip V shortly afterwards. Nevertheless, the seizure of the forts, which coincided with the proclamation on Philip's succession rights, augmented the fears of foreign governments. The third provocative measure which Louis XIV took was to secure a monopoly on the provision of slaves to the Spanish American colonies (the *Asiento*), for a French company. This, added to the fact that several French 'advisers' were in Madrid helping Philip V to govern his new kingdom, created the possibility of the integration of Franco-Spanish colonial policy: the two countries would dominate the Americas as they threatened to do Europe.

The Austrian government was the first to decide that an immediate war was the only means of thwarting a Franco-Spanish bloc. In 1701 the Emperor Leopold despatched troops into northern Italy where they captured Spanish territory; he also built up an alliance joined first by several German states (Brandenburg, Hanover, the Palatinate) then, by the Treaty of the Hague in September, by the Dutch Republic and England (the Grand Alliance). The English government became even more convinced of Louis's duplicity. On 16 September the exiled James II died at Saint Germain, where he and his court resided. Louis XIV recognised his son as 'James III', and in so doing asserted the primacy of 'legitimate succession' over 'usurpation', even though he had recognised William III at the Peace of Ryswick. Within this declaration (for which he was congratulated by the pope) there was an element of calculation: he was seeking to regain his prestige as leader of Catholic Europe at the expense of Leopold, now allied to Protestant states. The timing of this particular announcement, coming so soon after the formation of the Grand Alliance, suggests that Louis had accepted that war was imminent; after all, there was no need publicly to recognise 'James III' at this stage, for James was only thirteen years old and could have been quietly informed that recognition would come in due course. As it was, Louis's action stimulated a war fever in the English Parliament; all the more so since Parliament had passed the Act of Settlement (1701) which debarred Catholics from the English throne. On William III's death, Anne, younger sister of Mary, William III's deceased wife, would succeed him. William died in March 1702, but the English government nevertheless joined the rest of the Grand Alliance in a declaration of war on France on 15 May 1702.

Aims and Course of the War

At the outset of the War of the Spanish Succession the principal aims of the allies may be summarised thus: the Austrians sought to replace Philip V by a Habsburg, but to annex Milan at the expense of Spain; they were also intent on protecting the Rhineland from French domination. The Dutch and English were less concerned about removing Philip V than to keep the Spanish Netherlands out of French hands, and to prevent Franco-Spanish colonial integration. The English also aimed to win from Louis XIV a renewed pledge to honour the English

Succession as designed by Parliament, and to withdraw his support from 'James III'. Louis's aims were partly dynastic – to keep his grandson on the throne of Spain – and partly territorial: to preserve the security of the frontiers.

After a slow start the war spread across the Netherlands, Germany, northern Italy, Spain and into France itself, and was conducted also in the Americas. Naval battles and privateering took place in the European seas, the Atlantic and Caribbean. Financially this, the longest war of Louis's personal reign, proved calamitous; at one stage Louis ordered the silver plate of Versailles to be melted down and converted into coinage to pay for the war. The French armies rose to between 300,000 and 400,000 once more, while the combined forces of the allies were of a similar order. Britain recruited an army of 70,000; the Dutch Republic raised one of over 100,000 (an astonishing feat for so small a country), and the Austrian army numbered some 150,000; other allies put significant, if individually smaller, forces into the field. The quality of the allied armies was high. The Austrians in particular had learnt much against the Turks, and in the Duke of Marlborough and Prince Eugene of Savoy the allies had the outstanding generals of the war. Their victories at Blenheim (1704) and Oudenaarde (1708), and that of Marlborough at Ramillies (1706), rank among the great military triumphs of the period. On the other hand, although the battle of Malplaquet (1709) for control of Mons in a formal sense was won by Marlborough and Eugene (they succeeded in capturing the town and the French withdrew from the field), they lost almost twice as many men as the French, whose General Villars at least could claim to have halted their advance. The line of fortifications which Vauban had constructed along the French northern and eastern frontiers did its work well: the allies might drive the French out of the Netherlands and the Rhineland, but they had great difficulty in penetrating France itself. When Prince Eugene's army broke through the northern frontier in 1712 and advanced towards Paris, Villars mustered a piecemeal army and, in one of the most imaginative military manœuvres of the war, inflicted defeat on Eugene at Denain. By 1709 both sides were suffering financial and socio-economic effects of the war, the infamous winter of 1709 exacerbating what was already a calamitous situation in many parts of Europe. Two sets of negotiations were attempted at The Hague in 1709 and Gertruydenberg in 1710. Louis's position in 1709 was exceedingly weak and he was ready to make large territorial concessions; but on each occasion the allies made demands which would have humiliated him, and the talks broke down (the allies required him not only to advise Philip V to abdicate, but to depose him forcibly should Philip refuse).

Thereafter, the political balance began to swing in Louis's favour. In England the election of 1710 brought to power a Tory government opposed to war; in 1711 they began discussions with the French. In Austria the Emperor Leopold had died in 1705 and had been succeeded by his elder son Joseph; but when Joseph died in 1711 his younger brother Charles, hitherto the Austrian candidate to replace Philip V as King of Spain, became emperor. Even he accepted that there was little prospect of his occupying both thrones; Philip V was likely to remain King of Spain. However, events in France caused further confusion. In 1711 and 1712 there occurred the deaths of the Dauphin and of his elder son the Duc de Bourgogne. Louis XIV's successor now was his great-grandson the infant Louis, Duc d'Anjou (later Louis XV); but should this child die, Philip V of Spain was next in line. Would he then abdicate from the Spanish throne, or would he attempt a union of the two countries? Here was a potential crisis which could drive Europe into another decade of warfare unless a definitive resolution to these succession questions was found. The Austrians and Dutch, sensing that the new British government was amenable to a separate peace with France, made overtures for a general conference.

It gathered at Utrecht in January 1712. A series of treaties was signed in 1713 and 1714 which together comprised the Peace of Utrecht, to which was added the Treaty of Rastadt between France and Austria in 1714. One of the most important agreements in the 'package' affirmed that the thrones of France and Spain would remain separate. Philip V renounced his claim to the throne of France and in return was recognised as King of Spain by the other powers. Britain emerged from Utrecht with important political and territorial advantages. Louis XIV endorsed the Protestant succession in England and withdrew recognition from the Stuarts. He ceded overseas territory to Britain, including Nova Scotia and Newfoundland (nevertheless retaining fishing rights in the region). Spain too surrendered territory to Britain: Gibraltar and Minorca, two bases which gave Britain a significant naval presence in the Mediterranean. The French monopoly on supplying slaves to Spanish America was transferred to Britain, which henceforth used the *Asiento* as a means of expanding commerce with the Spanish colonies. Austria too acquired territory, at the expense of Spain: the Spanish Netherlands, Milan, Naples and Sardinia. The implications of these transfers for future international relations were considerable: France once more had a potential enemy on its northern frontier, and Austria was now deeply committed to curbing possible French ambition in the Low Countries and Italy. The Dutch Republic, given the enormous financial and military role which it had played in the war, could derive little satisfaction from the settlements. Its right to occupy most of the barrier forts in the former Spanish (now the Austrian) Netherlands was reaffirmed, otherwise the Republic got little at Utrecht. Spain too lost heavily, for its empire in effect had been partitioned. Charles II's calculation that the Bourbons had the wherewithal to hold Spain's possessions together had proved mistaken. Spain withdrew from north-western Europe and Italy, although within a few years it took steps to re-establish its presence in this latter region. Spain preserved its overseas colonies, but in Europe was now a Mediterranean rather than a continental power. The French could view Utrecht with much satisfaction. Louis's grandson remained King of Spain, and the French 'linear' frontier in the north and east was upheld. France did surrender its conquests on the right bank of the Rhine, but retained Alsace including Strasbourg. The losses in Canada were eased by the retention of the highly profitable fishing rights at the mouth of the St Lawrence.

When Louis XIV died in 1715 France remained the most powerful state in western Europe in spite of the crippling financial and social toll exacted by warfare. Louis had proved to be obdurate in defence of what he regarded as France's fundamental interests (especially the creation of a secure frontier), but flexible and ready to accept 'equivalences' in other matters. The Spanish Succession fell into the latter category. The partition treaties which he signed with the Austrians (1668), and the Dutch and English (1698 and 1700) showed that he was willing to compromise on this dynastic issue, and it is ironic that the last great war of his reign was one which he attempted to avoid: he was drawn into the War of the Spanish Succession through a combination of mistakes on his part and the intensely felt suspicions of his enemies. As he surveyed Europe after the 1713 settlements, Louis could be contented that Spain now had a French ruling family; on the other hand, the Dutch, English and Austrians had succeeded in keeping the former Spanish Netherlands out of his hands. The creation of secure frontiers was Louis XIV's most positive bequest to his kingdom in the realm of international affairs. Whether the same result could have been engineered through alternative and less belligerent means is a hypothetical question to which a definitive answer is impossible. However, it has been argued that the long wars in which Louis XIV's France was engaged were not entirely his responsibility: they may also have been a deliberate ploy by other governments who concluded that the only way to cope with this giant was to waste French financial and economic resources through attrition.[32] If this proposition is sound, it must also be admitted that France's natural resources were such that within a couple of decades of Louis's death, the kingdom had undergone remarkable recovery.

7

CONCLUDING DISCUSSION

Since at least Voltaire's *Le Siècle de Louis XIV* (1751) historians have interpreted and reinterpreted the character, purposes and significance of Louis XIV's reign. Louis has been deplored by detractors, approved by apologists, and variously assessed by those who admit no inclination either way; and we simply have to cast an eye over the incessant outpouring of books and articles on the man and his reign to appreciate what an attraction he continues to exert on the historical imagination. Any short study of Louis can claim only to be provisional in the conclusions which it reaches, for today's orthodox interpretations will look dated in a few years' time as new lines of research require scholars to continue reviewing their ideas. The preceding chapters have attempted to depict some developments in modern Louis XIV studies, but must avoid any impression that a scholarly finality has been reached. In the course of drawing together the principal conclusions of this book, it is appropriate to draw attention to some of the wider historical discussions in which scholars are engaged, and which are of relevance to our understanding of Louis XIV.

One theme to which historians have devoted much attention in recent years is that of 'absolutism', a term which has been employed in historical literature since the early nineteenth century, but which is now widely challenged as a valid epithet encapsulating the reality of seventeenth-century government.[1] Indeed, at least two historians, Collins and Henshall, have gone so far as to proclaim 'absolutism' a myth, and look forward to the day when it has vanished from historical vocabulary. Whether or not such an eventuality is ever realised, the student nevertheless should be familiar with at least some of the arguments surrounding 'absolutism'. Two distinctions should be made at the outset. The first is between 'absolutism' and 'absolute monarchy'. The term 'absolutism' was devised in France in the ideologically charged 1790s by revolutionaries seeking to disparage *ancien régime* government. 'Absolutism' was an expression of opprobrium which signified an allegedly overbearing, despotic government which oppressed its subjects, undermined their rights, and concentrated political power in the hands of the king and his ministers. It gained wider currency in the nineteenth century to denote regimes in seventeenth- and eighteenth-century Europe which supposedly strove to create all-powerful, centralised states based upon a distinctive sociopolitical philosophy, equipped with wide-ranging powers of coercion, well-organised bureaucracies and permanent armies. 'Absolutism' also involved a sustained assault by governments against such traditionalist obstacles as law courts, provincial assemblies, regional administrations, all of which had to be brought under state control and subjected to the will of the government. 'Absolutism', by this measure, was a phase of European history which lasted roughly two and a half centuries from the early 1600s to the late 1700s, and was a formative stage in the transformation of the 'medieval' polities of Europe into the centralised, bureaucratic states of the nineteenth and twentieth centuries. It is this linear, tendentious interpretation of 'absolutism' which has lost its prestige among historians. The more that present-day scholars examine, for example, the relations between the French crown and provincial assemblies, the less convincing becomes the 'centralising' and 'bureaucratising' school of thought. The accumulation of detailed studies of the interaction between the crown and its subjects – some of which will be referred to shortly – have further undermined the notion of 'absolutism', to the point of leading to the calls noted above for its suspension as a category of historical explanation.

The phrase 'absolute monarchy', on the other hand, has retained its standing among historians for, unlike the word 'absolutism', it was commonly used in the sixteenth and seventeenth centuries and on that count alone demands to be analysed. It is here that the second distinction must be drawn between 'absolute monarchy' as a set of principles, and 'absolute monarchy' as a form of government. As a set of principles it has made numerous appearances in this book, but most explicitly in the passages on Louis XIV's *Mémoires*. The *Mémoires* constitute a coherent body of thought on the nature, rights and functions of French kingship, yet the themes and ideas which they developed were neither new nor peculiar to the reign of Louis XIV. They went back many decades and may be traced, in their first systematic exposition, to a work which appeared in 1576 and which identified and investigated all the great problems surrounding 'absolute monarchy': the *Six Livres de la République* by Jean Bodin. This remarkable piece of political literature became a classic going through ten editions by the time of Bodin's death in 1596; it was reissued on many occasions thereafter, as well as being translated into several other languages.[2] The *Six Livres de la République* is not an easy work to understand, for it is organised in a manner which many modern readers find perplexing. The arguments often are intricate (not to say circular and involving much back-tracking), the text is peppered with references to astrology and magic, and the language is often abstruse. Nevertheless, it remains the first great theoretical affirmation of absolute monarchy, and became 'required reading' for seventeenth-century political philosophers such as Cardin le Bret, Charles Loyseau and Bossuet; and the *Mémoires* of Louis XIV likewise reflect the influence of Bodin in the arguments and principles which they advance.[3] It is appropriate to dwell upon Bodin, for all the seventeenth-century and present-day arguments over 'absolute monarchy' drew upon his ideas to a greater or lesser extent.

Jean Bodin and the *Six Livres de la République*

For Bodin, the basic unit of any viable political community was the family. Indeed, he defined the state as '...the rightly ordered government of a number of families... by a sovereign power'.[4] Correspondingly, the family could be understood as a microcosm of the state: 'the well ordered family is a true image of the commonwealth, and domestic [authority is] comparable with sovereign authority'.[5] A stable family or state, he maintained, was only possible where there existed a sovereign power, by which he meant the absolute, unconditional power to which everybody was subject; as he put it, 'the principal mark of sovereign majesty and absolute power is the right to impose laws generally on all subjects regardless of their consent...'.[6] Sovereignty was a precondition of orderly political life. Sovereignty could be vested in a single person, in which case the state was ruled by a monarchy; it could be located in a minority, which is to say government by aristocracy; or it could pertain to the people as a whole in a democracy. Each of these forms of government had its advantages and drawbacks, but to Bodin the most desirable was a monarchy. Aristocracy, in his view, was vulnerable to factionalism, and democracy too easily led to anarchy. Monarchy avoided these dangers: there was no question as to where sovereignty lay, and a king or queen was the most effective antidote to anarchy. Moreover, a hereditary monarchy was to be preferred to an elective, for the latter might imply that sovereignty was shared with the electors. Just as it would be absurd to give the son equal rights and powers to those of the father (this would destroy the relationship between father and son, and perhaps even the family itself), so it would be absurd to give subjects equal rights and powers to those of the monarch, since this would nullify the relationship between ruler and ruled, and perhaps even lead to the collapse of the state itself.

Bodin acknowledged the objection that under certain conditions a monarch might turn into a despot and impose arbitrary government. This he considered an unlikely prospect. He emphasised the limits (difficult to establish with precision though they were) within which the monarch exercised sovereignty. The monarch did not possess universal sovereign powers, only sovereign powers within his legitimate spheres of activity. Bodin wrote of 'the mutual obligation between subject and sovereign, by which, in return for the faith and obedience rendered to him, the sovereign must do justice and give counsel, assistance, encouragement, and protection to the subject'.[7] Beyond the king's sovereign powers lay a host of rights and privileges belonging to his subjects, and which were not dependent on the king except in the sense that he was obliged to defend as well as respect them, especially rights of property and the sanctity of the family. There were other constraints on the monarch's exercise of sovereignty. The law of God, the commitments into which the king or his predecessors had entered, and 'the constitutional laws of the realm, especially those that concern the king's estate being, like the Salic law, annexed and united to the crown, [which] cannot be infringed by the prince'.[8] Moreover, the duties which sovereignty imposed were so numerous and onerous, that to fulfil them would stretch even the most conscientious of rulers; the king had no self-interest in acting despotically or arbitrarily, for to do so would merely multiply his problems and result in conflict with his subjects. In short, despotism was not implicit in 'absolute monarchy'. Should a king nevertheless overstep the limits and rule unjustly, his subjects might not legally resist him. Disagreeable as life under a despot might be, sovereignty was still vested in him, and attempts to depose him easily resulted in civil war. It was better to endure the temporary rule of a despotic but mortal ruler, than to undertake resistance which could have disastrous consequences.

During the French Wars of Religion the question of religious division and conflict carried profound social and political implications. It was a subject which generated much contemporary literature, and in the *Six Livres de la République* Bodin too developed his ideas in this most controversial area. Although his personal religious beliefs were far from clear-cut, for at one stage of his life he flirted with Protestantism, on one point he was adamant: religious fanaticism and intolerance must be shunned at all costs. He expressed a strong preference for a state in which only one religion existed, for thereby social harmony was enhanced. Since the early 1560s, events in France had demonstrated that if a sizeable religious minority were allowed to develop, it could plunge the state into chaos. The king should take steps to prevent the growth of religious minorities, but in so doing should employ only peaceful methods. Heavy-handed persecution simply made minorities more stubborn and drove them into violent resistance. Bodin argued that if Huguenots refused to return to Catholicism in spite of all efforts of persuasion, they ought to be tolerated; not as a matter of principle, but on the pragmatic ground that religious coexistence was the only acceptable alternative to civil war.

The *Six Livres de la République* were not composed in an atmosphere of dispassionate calm. As the preceding paragraph implies, they arose out of Bodin's preoccupation with the Wars of Religion, and especially his horrified reaction to the bloodiest of all episodes, namely the Massacre of St Bartholomew's Day (24 August 1572) when thousands of Huguenots were killed by Catholic mobs and factions. The massacre left him with a despairing view of human nature, according to which human beings have a natural tendency towards conflict and mutual destruction. This must be checked by some transcendent sovereign authority with the power to impose social control (incidentally, the English political philosopher Thomas Hobbes, also writing in a context of civil war some seventy-five years later, reached similar conclusions). Bodin's observations of the factionalism and rivalries which bedevilled French political life reinforced this belief. He was a member of the household of François, Duc d'Alençon, brother of King Henri III, and witnessed at first hand the scheming and treachery which surrounded the royal court and government. He also attended the Estates General of 1576 as a member of the Third Estate, where again he encountered the socio-political divisions which were making a mockery of the authority of the crown.[9] The *Six Livres de la République* were embedded in, and were a product of, the tragic historical circumstances of the Wars of Religion. Indeed, it can be said more broadly that 'absolute monarchy' as a whole, in both its theoretical and practical manifestations, continued to be conditioned by historical context. The principles underpinning 'absolute monarchy' were not the product of abstract reasoning by Bodin or any other political philosopher. The defining themes of 'absolute monarchy' – the nature of sovereignty, the forms which it might adopt, the limits within which it should be exercised, the distinctions between what the king can, ought or has the right to do, the rights and privileges of subjects and of provincial and other institutions, the relationship between political reliability and religious conformity, the problem of how to respond to religious minorities – arose out of, and were discussed within, particular historical circumstances. Bodin, Loyseau, Le Bret, Bossuet, Louis XIV and others who asserted the claims of absolute monarchy did so precisely because they saw no acceptable alternative; between a France governed by an absolute monarch and a France plunged into what Louis XIV called 'le désordre', there was no third way.

Continuing Debates concerning 'Absolute Monarchy'

Bodin's distinction between 'absolute' and 'despotic' monarchy was upheld in Louis XIV's *Mémoires*, which argued that in so far as he exercised the powers of 'absolute' monarchy, it was within his legitimate spheres of activity. Bodin had stated that sovereignty could be vested in several forms of government of which monarchy was but one; moreover, monarchy was not necessarily 'absolute', for it was conceivable that it might share sovereignty with some other body. Louis XIV's stress upon the Divine Right of Kings precluded any possibility of 'shared' or 'mixed' sovereignty. Divine Right, with its insistence that God had chosen the king directly, posited an 'absolute' monarch as a matter of logical necessity. However, even if the principle was widely accepted in France that the king was 'absolute', this nevertheless incorporated the principle that he exercised sovereign

powers within limits; but what were those limits, who was to establish
them, and how were they to be enforced? There existed no supra-
political or supra-judicial body with the authority to adjudicate these
sensitive matters. In practice it was the law courts, especially the
parlements, which attempted to do so. When faced with royal legislation which they considered an infringement of the rights and privileges of the king's subjects, the *parlements* exercised the right of
remonstrance; even the lesser courts had to exercise judgement on
disputes arising from royal legislation, and to this extent contributed
to the debate over the limits of royal sovereign powers. According to
one historian, we can think of the law courts of France conducting
lengthy and sustained 'negotiations' with the crown through a combination of their rulings and remonstrances.[10] The theoretical limits of
absolute monarchy in the seventeenth century resembled a flexible
open frontier which shifted according to circumstance, rather than an
immovable defensive wall which the crown (or the *parlements*,
depending on circumstances) defended to the last fragment of brick
and mortar.

The question of royal sovereignty also ran throughout the tangled
web of the Frondes. These insurrections were the occasion of widespread socio-political conflicts as magistrates, aristocrats, urban and
rural masses locked in combat with the royal court and occasionally
with each other. However, one consistent theme was the doubtful
legality of many of the fiscal practices indulged in by the crown since
the ministry of Richelieu. The meetings in the Chambre Saint Louis
(1648), for example, may be interpreted as an attempt to identify with
greater exactitude than hitherto the limits within which the sovereign
powers of an absolute monarch could be exercised. The provincial
Frondes were driven by the defence of regional 'rights and privileges'
against the 'illegal' incursions of ministers of the crown; even the
'Ormistes' of Bordeaux, for all their flirtation with English republi-
cans, were fighting chiefly to defend provincial rights. Until the declaration of Louis XIV's majority in 1651, it was possible for Frondeurs
to accuse Richelieu and Mazarin of having misled absolute monarchy
into paths of despotic monarchy, and to portray themselves as faithful
subjects serving the young king by showing him the way back to
absolute monarchy. After the declaration of his majority, however, the
distinction between Louis's authority and the actions taken by Mazarin
was difficult to sustain; and since Louis himself upheld Mazarin as
his chief minister, the question of royal sovereignty and its limits was

subsumed in the struggle over the political fate of the cardinal-minister. The Frondes collapsed, but it would be a mistake to suppose that the 'constitutional' issues which they raised fell into abeyance; once the agitation and passions had exhausted themselves, cooler heads were able to recognise the validity of at least some of the demands of the Frondeurs. The chapter on 'Louis XIV and his Subjects' argued that after 1661 Louis XIV tacitly conceded as much; in the matter of extraordinary financial transactions, for example, he attempted to diminish his reliance upon this highly controversial aspect of policy and sought a tax regime which was more equitable than in the past.

Royal sovereignty and the obligations which it placed on the king continued to exercise the minds of political thinkers during the reign of Louis XIV. Some – of whom this book takes Fénelon and Saint-Simon as examples – came from within 'royalist' traditions, but nevertheless found Louis XIV vulnerable to criticism in certain important respects. They portrayed a king who, in spite of his undoubted achievements, all too often had departed from the path of true 'absolute monarchy', chiefly by disregarding his responsibilities towards his subjects and by devoting excessive time, energy and resources to the pursuit of the transient glory occasioned by warfare. From their differing perspectives, Fénelon, Saint-Simon and some others who observed Louis XIV from close quarters, sought to stand against the massive personality cult and adulatory propaganda which surrounded Louis XIV. The king himself they could not hope to influence (and we should recall that Fénelon eventually was banished from court and ordered to remain in his archdiocese), but they did aspire to prepare the Duc de Bourgogne to be a more 'enlightened' monarch than his grandfather; his death in 1712 frustrated their ambitions and left them pessimistic about the future.

Absolute Monarchy and Government

So much may be said about the theoretical framework of absolute monarchy, but it should also be considered as a system of government. It is on this subject that some of the most radical revisions of older historical interpretations have been made in recent years. Whether they examine relations between crown and a particular province,[11] between crown and social elites,[12] or the crown's methods

of government in a wider historical and European context,[13] historians increasingly draw attention to the limitations rather than the
strengths of monarchic power under Louis XIV. For all that the decision-making process at the centre was reasonably efficient (although
on this score too, it should be remembered that policies were often
decided within the Conseil d'en Haut on the basis of information that
was far from comprehensive), Louis's government did not possess
mechanisms capable of imposing policies effectively and uniformly
throughout the kingdom. Modern historians have come to emphasise
the remarkable extent to which Louis XIV sought cooperation rather
than confrontation with provincial bodies and social elites; 'absolute
monarchy' preferred to exert its theoretical authority through carefully managed cooperation rather than confrontation and coercion.
The history of France from the 1560s to the early 1650s contained
too many object-lessons in the calamitous consequences of the failure
of the crown to maintain harmony between itself and the elites, for
the government of Louis XIV to neglect the goodwill of the middle
orders and elites of society. Resistance to royal authority could be
extremely effective, for most provincial administration was run by
local officials, while the magistrates of France were well practised in
defending what they regarded as their legitimate interests. On the
other hand, the Frondes, especially because of their tendencies
towards anarchy or towards aristocratic feuding and infighting, had
alarmed 'solid' Parisian and provincial opinion, as well as the elites.
As Louis XIV made cooperative overtures towards the leaders of
Parisian and provincial society after 1661, he found a ready response
from people who also preferred social stability to the kinds of
upheavals which occurred during the Frondes. Through the judicious
use of intendants, careful management of the provincial governors,
and sensitive handling of provincial estates, law courts and other
bodies, the central government sought a community of purpose with
provincial leaders which preserved Louis from having to test the
claims of absolute monarchy to the full.

If there was any domain in which Louis was able to give full rein
to his powers as absolute monarch, it was that of the persecution of
the Huguenots. The mounting pressure which he imposed on the
Huguenots won the approval of most of his Catholic subjects,
including the senior hierarchy of the Catholic Church. From Louis's
point of view his anti-Protestant policy proved to be one of the most
successful of his entire reign. Protestantism ceased legally to exist in

France in 1685 (with the exception of Alsace where it had special status) and remained proscribed until 1787. This was one area of policy in which Louis could claim to have made no compromises, but rather to have exercised his sovereign powers to the full. In so doing he had fulfilled his coronation oath to defend the interests of the church, and had responded positively to appeals regularly made by the General Assembly of the Clergy to have the stain of heresy removed from France. In 1685 Louis in a sense restored the mono-religious state for which Bodin had expressed a preference, and was able to do so because he carried the majority of public opinion with him. The suppression of Protestantism by Louis offered a tantalising prospect of how conclusively absolute monarchy could 'solve' even the most persistent problems under favourable circumstances. As a declining minority with a history of involvement in rebellion and civil war (even though they had been loyal since the 1630s), the Huguenots were an inviting and perhaps inevitable target for Louis's absolutist ambitions. His persecution of the Huguenots was the product of numerous forces, but they simply augmented a palpable determination on his part to fix on at least one area of policy where he could act unhindered as an absolute monarch. In so many spheres of government Louis had to temper the exercise of his theoretical powers in the light of circumstance; no such impediment hindered his policy towards the Huguenots, who correspondingly bore the full weight of his absolute authority.

The reservations which modern historians express concerning some older interpretations of Louis XIV as an 'absolute monarch', extend beyond the realms of constitutional thought and governmental prac-tice. The contention that the mercantilist economic policies of Louis XIV constituted a decisive stage in the decline of feudalism and the rise of capitalism in France, has been questioned; instead, the French economy under Louis XIV has recently been deemed to have suffered from 'arrested development', the economic policies of the crown apparently having had relatively little impact on the totality of French economic activity.[14] This is not to deny that Colbert's economic plans were conceived with the interests of the state in mind; but it is to maintain that, given the realities of seventeenth-century means of economic production, distribution and consumption, even the best efforts of a minister as energetic as Colbert were incapable of altering French economic life in its essentials. Again, the hierarchical struc-tures of French society, far from undergoing 'modernisation' by a regime which supposedly favoured the 'bourgeoisie' (however that term is interpreted), remained implacably traditional; the ability of Louis XIV's regime to transform society was limited. Indeed, it is extremely doubtful as to whether it had any intention of doing so. Louis's personal social values and attitudes were strictly traditional, and in so far as he contemplated social change, it was in the direction of restoring an idealised past rather than working towards some unprecedented future. In his thought-world it was inconceivable that the social status of the nobility should be diminished. He could envisage a social mobility which allowed commoners to aspire to, and even to enter, the social stratosphere of the nobility; but even in this regard his purpose was to revitalise and give new purpose to the rank of nobility. One topic on which Louis expressed a strong desire to effect change for the better was that of 'le soulagement du peuple'. His respect for the paternal traditions of French monarchy, and his profound sense that Divine Right imposed on him the duty to afford protection and sustenance to his subjects, weighed heavily on him. Nevertheless, it is difficult to avoid the conclusion that, on balance, his reign afforded little by way of 'soulagement' to the French masses. The many decades of warfare in which France was involved exacerbated the effects of natural disasters including famine, and negated the positive effects of such moves as Louis made (for example, in the realm of taxation). France continued to suffer endemic social problems. Unemployment, crime, poverty, disease, famine, violence and insurrection continued. The absolute monarchy of Louis XIV, by collaborating with social elites, was reasonably proficient in ensuring that widespread socio-economic malaise did not turn into coordinated socio-political resistance and conflict, but it proved incapable of alleviating the condition of the mass of 'le peuple' to any marked extent.

Indeed, throughout this survey, it has become evident that in so many aspects of his reign Louis had to respond to realities which either were outside his control, or were only partially susceptible to his actions. Foreign policy in particular tested his ability to react to events as well as initiate them, yet ironically this was yet another domain in which he could act as an absolute monarch with minimum restraints placed on him by 'fundamental laws' or other time-honoured conventions. He was in no sense answerable to his subjects for the course which his foreign policy took; he might seek to explain a growing burden of taxation by pointing to the fiscal consequences of foreign policy or warfare, but policy itself was decided by him –

after consulting the Conseil d'en Haut – without having to take into account 'fundamental laws' or the 'rights and privileges' of his subjects. Underlying many of his foreign policy initiatives was the principle of *raison d'état* which, in brief, contended that, should the safety of the state be placed in serious jeopardy, the king was obliged to adopt whatever measures were necessary to protect it.[15] In so doing he might contravene even the fundamental laws of the kingdom, but was within his rights in so doing; once the crisis was surmounted, however, he must return to conventional absolute monarchy. However, in a reign which experienced decades of warfare which, by its very nature, often exposed the kingdom to invasion, the distinctions between 'absolute' monarchy and '*raison d'état*' monarchy remained blurred for years at a time. It was precisely the fears occasioned by this tendency for '*raison d'état*' to encroach upon 'absolute' monarchy that inspired some of the critical literature examined in Chapter 5. Even Louis himself came to accept that in this respect he had sinned: he interpreted the disastrous winter of 1709, French defeats in the War of the Spanish Succession, and the premature deaths of grand-children and great-grandchildren, as the judgements of an austere God greatly displeased at His unworthy servant, Louis XIV.

Louis XIV and France have been the focus of these concluding remarks, but it is important to acknowledge that absolute monarchy and the controversies which it raised were international in character. Louis XIV may have been the most impressive embodiment of absolute monarchy in the seventeenth and early eighteenth centuries, but he was not unique. Although other kingdoms had their own expe-riences, Spain, Sweden, Brandenburg-Prussia, the territories of the Austrian Habsburgs and Russia all developed into forms of absolute monarchy.[16] Britain is somewhat more problematic, for the position of the crown in England, Scotland and Ireland was not exactly the same; and we should remember that the first two kingdoms were not united until 1707, while the third was not brought into the union until 1801. The argument that, in the seventeenth century, the English Parliament prevented the Stuart kings and their successors from turning into anglicised models of 'Louis XIV' still has much to commend it; but we should also be clear that in many respects the institutions of the English state (based upon crown in Parliament) were just as powerful as those of Louis XIV in France.[17] With regard to Scotland and Ireland, however, their social systems were different from that of England, and the Parliaments of those countries did not exactly correspond to the English body. The Stuart and Orange dynasties had to develop approaches to Scotland and Ireland which were more reminiscent of those pursued by governments in France, Spain, the Habsburg lands and elsewhere, and to this extent came to resemble continental absolute monarchy.[18]

The more historians approach Louis XIV and his government from seventeenth-century perspectives and pursue the multifarious programmes of research which constitute present-day 'Louis XIV studies', the more conscious they become of the difficulties and dilemmas with which he had to contend. Modern scholars can claim, with much justice, to have dispelled some of the grosser interpretations which once surrounded Louis XIV, and in so doing have liberated themselves from older habits of mind which sought to situate him in one or another 'historical process'. Nevertheless, insofar as they seek to understand Louis 'historically', they do not deny, still less ignore, his causative links with the course of later French and European history; on the contrary, they aspire thereby to move towards a more sophisticated understanding of how the present has been shaped by the past. Yet in spite of the sustained programmes of research into Louis and his reign, there is little danger that the subject risks exhaustion. Ever increasingly historians and their colleagues in other disciplines need to study aspects of regional history, the mechanisms of central and local government and administration, the complicated interplay of courtly, noble and other factions, Louis's ministers, taxation, social, cultural and economic history, and a host of other subject-areas. While French colleagues obviously fulfil a major role in the enterprise, it is demonstrably true that non-French historians, including many from the English-speaking world, have made, and will continue to make, distinguished contributions. The discovery of new bodies of information, the evolution of historical methodologies, and the desire to investigate the causal dimensions of seventeenth-century history, suggest that for many years to come we may anticipate further developments in the historical interpretation of *le roi soleil*.

NOTES AND REFERENCES

1 LOUIS XIV AND FRENCH MONARCHY

1. H. Carré, *The Early Life of Louis XIV* (London, 1951), 99; on Mézerai, see O. Ranum, *Artisans of Glory: Writers and Historical Thought in Seventeenth-Century France* (Chapel Hill, 1980), 197–232; the essays in J.C. Rule (ed.), *Louis XIV and the Craft of Kingship* (Ohio, 1969) cover much of the material discussed in this chapter.
2. J. Orcibal, 'Louis XIV and the Edict of Nantes', in R. Hatton (ed.), *Louis XIV and Absolutism* (London, 1976), 156.
3. M. Tyvaert, 'L'Image du Roi: Légitimité et Moralité Royales dans les Histoires de France au XVIIe Siècle', in *Revue d'Histoire Moderne et Contemporaine*, xxi (1974), 521–3.
4. R. Doucet, *Les Institutions de la France au XVI Siècle* (2 vols, Paris, 1948), i, 80–1.
5. E. H. Kantorowicz, *The King's Two Bodies: A Study in Mediaeval Political Theology* (Princeton, 1957).
6. R. Jackson, *Vive le Roi! A History of the French Coronation from Charles V to Charles X* (Chapel Hill, 1984), 32–3.
7. The classic work on the Royal Touch is M. Bloch, *The Royal Touch: Sacred Monarchy and Scrofula in England and France* (London, reissued 1973).
8. See J.H.M. Salmon, *Society in Crisis: France in the Sixteenth Century* (London, 1975).
9. See M. Wolfe, *The Conversion of Henri IV: Politics, Power and Religious Belief in Early Modern France* (Cambridge, Mass., 1993).
10. Jackson, *Vive le Roi!*, 45–6.
11. See P. Sonnino, 'The Dating and Authorship of Louis XIV's *Mémoires*', in *French Historical Studies*, iii, no.3 (1964), 303–37. An English translation of the *Mémoires*, with a historical introduction, has been published by Sonnino, under the title, *Mémoires for the Instruction of the Dauphin by Louis XIV* (New York, 1970). The French edition used by the present writer is J. Longnon (ed.), *Mémoires pour les Années 1661 et 1666* (Paris, 1923).
12. See *Seventeenth-Century French Studies*, xiii (1991), whose articles are devoted to aspects of historical composition in the seventeenth century.
13. The *Mémoires* probably covered 1665 also, but the manuscript has been lost (Sonnino [ed.], *Mémoires*, 115–18).
14. Sonnino, 'The Dating and Authorship'; Ranum, *Artisans of Glory*, 259–68.
15. Longnon (ed.), *Mémoires*, 255.
16. Ibid., 13–14.

17. Ibid., 15.
18. Ibid., 34.
19. Ibid., 21.
20. Ibid., 40.
21. Ibid., 14.
22. Ibid., 15.
23. Ibid., 20.
24. Ibid., 228.
25. There is an extensive literature on monarchic ritual; of special relevance are: L.M. Bryant, *The French Royal Entry Ceremony* (Geneva, 1985); S. Hanley, *The* Lit de Justice *of the Kings of France: Constitutional Ideology in Legend, Ritual, and Discourse* (Princeton, 1983); Jackson, *Vive le Roi!*; S. Wilentz (ed.), *Rites of Power: Symbolism, Ritual and Politics Since the Middle Ages* (Philadelphia, 1985). The journal *Annales ESC*, 41e année, no. 3 (1986) devotes an entire section to French monarchic ritual; A. Boureau, 'Les Cérémonies Royales Françaises entre Performance Juridique et Compétence Liturgique', in *Annales ESC*, 46e année, no. 6 (1991), 1253–64 provides a critical review of essential literature; see also D. Kertzer, *Ritual, Politics and Power* (London, 1988) which raises general questions regarding the significance of ritual.
26. C. Geertz, 'Centers, Kings, and Charisma: Reflections on the Symbolics of Power', in Wilentz (ed.), *Rites of Power*, 15.
27. On the development of Paris in the first half of the seventeenth century, see H. Bannon, *The Paris of Henri IV: Architecture and Urbanism* (New York, 1991); R. Pillorget, *Paris sous les Premiers Bourbons, 1594–1661* (Paris, 1988); on the century as a whole, see O. Ranum, *Paris in the Age of Absolutism* (London, 1968); much information is also available in A. Blunt, *Art and Architecture in France, 1500–1700* (London, 1953).
28. This theme is explored by M. Martin, *Les Monuments Equestres de Louis XIV: Une Grande Entreprise de Propagande Monarchique* (Paris, 1986).
29. The literature on Versailles and the court is immense. N. Mitford, *The Sun King* (London, 1966) and G. Walton, *Louis XIV's Versailles* (London, 1986) relate the king to the palace; on the public representations of the king, and the court and its wider significance, see P. Burke, *The Fabrication of Louis XIV* (London, 1992), N. Elias, *The Court Society* (London, 1983), L. Marin, *Portrait of the King* (London, 1988) and J-F. Solnon, *La Cour de France* (Paris, 1987); on the gardens of Versailles, their relationship to the palace, see K. Woodbridge, *Princely Gardens: The Origins and Development of the French Formal Style* (London, 1986); on the wider significance of the court see J.M. Apostolides, *Le Roi-Machine: Spectacle et Politique au Temps de Louis XIV* (Paris, 1982).
30. J. Cornette, *Absolutisme et Lumières, 1652–1783* (Paris, 1993), 52–3.
31. A.G. Dickens, 'The Tudor-Percy Emblem in Royal MSS. 18 D ii', in A.G. Dickens, *Reformation Studies* (London, 1982), 41–4; on the iconography of Versailles, see J.P. Néraudau, *L'Olympe du Roi-Soleil* (Paris, 1986).
32. For a discussion of the king's observance of his courtiers and further afield into the country, see J.M. Smith, '"Our Sovereign's Gaze": Kings, Nobles, and State Formation in Seventeenth-Century France', in *French Historical Studies*, 18, no. 2 (1993), 396–415.

2 LOUIS XIV AND THE GOVERNMENT OF FRANCE

1. A good short study of Richelieu, with a critical bibliography is R.J. Knecht, *Richelieu* (London, 1991).
2. On these two figures, see, R. Kleinmann, *Anne of Austria, Queen of France* (Ohio UP, 1987) and G.R.R. Treasure, *Mazarin: The Crisis of Absolutism in France* (London, 1995).
3. G. Parker, *The Thirty Years War* (London, 1984), 179–89; A. Osiander, *The States System of Europe, 1640–1990: Peacemaking and the Conditions of International Stability* (Oxford, 1994), Chapter 2.
4. There is an extensive literature on the Frondes; the most recent study (with a good bibliography) is O. Ranum, *The Fronde: A French Revolution, 1648–1652* (New York, 1993); a concise survey is in R. Knecht, *The Fronde* (London, 1975); essays on different aspects of the Frondes are in R. Bonney, *The Limits of Absolutism in* ancien régime *France* (Aldershot, 1995).
5. Good introductions to ideas on the 'general crisis' are: T. Aston (ed.), *Crisis in Europe 1560–1660* (London, 1965), G. Parker and L.M. Smith (eds), *The General Crisis of the Seventeenth Century* (London, 1978), and T.K. Rabb, *The Struggle for Stability in Early Modern Europe* (Oxford, 1978).
6. On the intendants, see below, p. 46–9.
7. On Mazarin see P. Goubert, *Mazarin* (Paris, 1991).
8. On the Mazarinades see: C. Jouhaud, *Mazarinades: La Fronde des Mots* (Paris, 1985) and H. Carrier, *La Presse de la Fronde 1648–1653. Les Mazarinades,* i, *La Conquête de l'Opinion* (Paris, 1989).
9. For a comparison between the Frondes and the civil wars in England see R. Bonney, 'The English and French Civil Wars', in *History*, 65 (1980), 365–82; reprinted in Bonney, *The Limits of Absolutism*.
10. On this see A.L. Moote, *The Revolt of the Judges: the Parlement of Paris and the Fronde 1643–52* (Princeton, 1971); it should be noted that some of Moote's views on the Fronde were challenged by P. Goubert; see Goubert's lecture/essay entitled 'La Fronde et le Problème des Révolutions du XVIIe Siècle', reprinted in his *Le Siècle de Louis XIV* (Paris, 1996), 147–64.
11. R. Pillorget and S. Pillorget, *France Baroque, France Classique, 1589–1715* (2 vols, Paris, 1995), i, 530–9.
12. The most thorough study of this affair is D. Dessert, *Fouquet* (Paris, 1987); in addition to the political advantages which Louis derived from Fouquet's overthrow, there were financial ones: the disgrace of Fouquet provided the pretext for Louis XIV to renege on government debts to financiers with whom Fouquet had negotiated loans.
13. The idea of a 'royal revolution' has been advanced by, among others, M. Antoine, *Le Conseil du Roi sous le Règne de Louis XV* (Paris, 1970), and P. Goubert, *L'Avènement du Roi-Soleil* (Paris, 1967); arguments for and against are covered in D. Dessert, *Louis XIV prend le Pouvoir: Naissance d'un Mythe?* (Paris, 1989); see also the discussion by R. Bonney, 'The Fouquet–Colbert Rivalry and the "Revolution" of 1661', in C. Cameron and E. Woodrough (eds), *Ethics and Politics in Seventeenth-Century France: Essays in Honour of Derek A. Watts* (Exeter, 1996), 107–18.
14. This theme is developed by F. Bluche, *Louis XIV* (Oxford, 1990); see for example Chapter 8.
15. Pillorget, *France Baroque, France Classique*, i, 502–4.

16. E. Lavisse, *Histoire de France depuis les Origines jusqu'à la Révolution* (9 vols, Paris, 1903–11), vols 7 and 8; a modern version with an introductory essay by R. and S. Pillorget, is E. Lavisse, *Louis XIV* (Paris, 1989).

17. Sceptical views are expressed by R. Mettam, *Power and Faction in Louis XIV's France* (Oxford, 1988) and D. Parker, *The Making of French Absolutism* (London, 1983).

18. Mettam, *Power and Faction*, 177–80.

19. On this institution see J. Shennan, *The Parlement of Paris* (London, 1968); on the Parlement after the Fronde, A.N. Hamscher, *The Parlement of Paris after the Fronde, 1653–1673* (Pittsburgh, 1976).

20. Parker, *The Making of French Absolutism*, 106–8.

21. Shennan, *The Parlement of Paris*, 278–9.

22. Ibid., 278, 282–3.

23. R. Pillorget, *Les Mouvements Insurrectionnels de Provence entre 1596 et 1715* (Paris, 1975), Introduction.

24. This is a subject explored by S. Kettering in several works: *Judicial Politics and Urban Revolt in Seventeenth-Century France: The Parlement of Aix, 1629–1659* (Princeton, 1978); also *Patrons, Brokers, and Clients in Seventeenth-Century France* (Oxford, 1986); 'The Decline of Great Noble Clientage during the Reign of Louis XIV', in *Canadian Journal of History*, 24, no. 2 (1989), 157–77; and 'Patronage and Kinship in Early Modern France', in *French Historical Studies*, 19 (1989), 408–35.

25. See for example, W. Beik, *Absolutism and Society in Seventeenth-Century France: State Power and Provincial Aristocracy in Languedoc* (Cambridge, 1985), Mettam, *Power and Faction*, J.B. Collins, *Classes, Estates, and Order in Early Modern Brittany* (Cambridge, 1994), J. Russell Major, *Representative Government in Early Modern France* (London, 1980), and Pillorget, *Les Mouvements Insurrectionnels*.

26. Beik, *Absolutism and Society*, Chapter 11 has financial details.

27. For example Bluche, *Louis XIV*, 136–8; J. Lough, *An Introduction to Seventeenth-century France* (London, 1973), 140–2.

28. Re-evaluations have been presented in A. Smedley-Weill, *Correspondance des Intendants avec le Contrôleur Général des Finances, 1677–1689. Naissance d'une Administration* (3 vols, Paris, 1989–91), and A. Smedley-Weill, *Les Intendants sous Louis XIV* (Paris, 1995).

29. The *contrôleurs généraux* were: Colbert 1665–83, Le Pelletier 1683–89, Pontchartrain 1689–99, Chamillart 1699–1708 and Desmarets 1708–15.

30. R. Bonney, *Political Change in France under Richelieu and Mazarin, 1624–1661* (Oxford, 1978), 427–8.

31. Smedley-Weill, *Correspondance des Intendants*; also the older classics, P. Clément, *Lettres, Instructions et Mémoires de Jean-Baptiste Colbert* (10 vols, Paris, 1861–82), and G-B. Depping, *Correspondance Administrative sous Louis XIV* (4 vols, Paris, 1850–70).

32. Colbert to Creil, Intendant at Rouen, 3 Feb. 1673 (R. Mettam, *Government and Society in Louis XIV's France* [London, 1977], 25).

33. J-C. Petitfils, *Louis XIV* (Paris, 1995), 229.

3   LOUIS XIV AND HIS SUBJECTS

1. The English translation, *Louis XIV and Twenty Million Frenchmen*, appeared in 1970.

2. *Annaliste*, so-called after the journal *Annales E.S.C.*, which was founded in 1929 by Marc Bloch (1886–1944) and Lucien Febvre (1878–1956). This 'school' of historians emphasises the importance of economic and social history, and seeks to understand historical causation, not through the inter-action of short-term 'events', but through the steady unfolding of deep historical forces ('les forces profondes') over long periods of time ('la longue durée'). *Annales E.S.C.* is still committed to this strategy, and a quick perusal of its contents will give the reader a flavour of *Annaliste* history.

3. The chief work on the French population is J. Dupâquier (ed.), *Histoire de la Population Française* (4 vols, Paris, 1988), ii *De la Renaissance à 1789*; the figures given in this section are from this source. For a general assessment see, W. Roosen, 'The Demographic History of the Reign', in Sonnino (ed.), *The Reign of Louis XIV*, 9–26.

4. P. Benedict (ed.), *Cities and Social Change in Early Modern France* (London, 1989), 24.

5. G.N. Clark, *The Seventeenth Century* (Oxford, 1960), 8; T. Munck, *Seventeenth Century Europe, 1598–1700* (London, 1990), 82.

6. These figures include the extraordinary expenses of the crown; if the extraordinary expenses are excluded, the percentage of regular expenditure devoted to warfare during Louis's reign was usually between 70 and 80 per cent (source: R. Bonney, 'Jean-Roland Malet: Historian of the Finances of the French Monarchy', in *French History*, 5, no. 2 [1991], 227–8).

7. For a discussion of the problems see 'The State and its Revenues in *ancien régime* France', in R. Bonney, *The Limits of Absolutism in* Ancien Régime *France* (Aldershot, 1995), XII.

8. The sources for these figures are: Bonney, 'Malet', 214; and E. Labrousse *et al.* (eds), *Histoire Économique et Sociale de la France*, ii, *Des Derniers Temps de l'Age Seigneurial aux Préludes de l'Age Industriel (1660–1789)* (Paris, 1970), 270.

9. A concise outline of these sources is R. Bonney, *The King's Debts: Finance and Politics in France, 1589–1661* (Oxford, 1981), 15–18, 293–6, and D. Dessert, *Argent, Pouvoir et Société au Grand Siècle* (Paris, 1984), Chapter 1.

10. J. Ellul, *Histoire des Institutions de l'Epoque Franque à la Révolution* (Paris, 1962), 495–6.

11. Mettam, *Power and Faction*, 271–6.

12. P. Clément (ed.), *Lettres, Instructions et Mémoires de Jean-Baptiste Colbert* (8 vols, Paris, 1861–82), ii, 96–7.

13. Ibid., 98–9.

14. Petitfils, *Louis XIV*, 253.

15. See A. Guéry, 'Etat, Classification Sociale et Compromis sous Louis XIV: La Capitation de 1695', in *Annales ESC*, no. 5 (1986), 1041–60.

16. 'The State and its Revenues in *ancien régime* France', in Bonney, *The Limits of Absolutism*, XII, 162.

17. Ibid., 166.

18. Cornette, *Absolutisme et Lumières*, 92.

19. R. and S. Pillorget, *France Baroque, France Classique, 1589–1715* (2 vols, Paris, 1995), ii *Dictionnaire*, 'Gabelle'.

20. R. Mousnier, *Les Institutions de la France sous la Monarchie Absolue* (2 vols, Paris, 1974–80), ii, 430–1.
21. R. Bonney, 'The Failure of the French Revenue Farms', in *The Limits of Absolutism*, XI, 11.
22. R. Briggs, *Early Modern France, 1560–1715* (Oxford, 1977), Graph 6.
23. Dessert, *Argent, Pouvoir et Société au Grand Siècle*.
24. Cornette, *Absolutisme et Lumières*, 92–3.
25. On the 1675 rising in Brittany, see R. Mousnier, *Peasant Uprisings in Seventeenth Century France, Russia and China* (London, 1960), Chapter 6; also Mettam, *Power and Faction*, 237–55 (which contains documents illustrating the course of the rebellion and its suppression).
26. H.L. Root, *Peasants and King in Burgundy: Agrarian Foundations of French Absolutism* (London, 1987), 22.
27. This was argued by Labrousse in *Esquisse du Mouvement des Prix et des Revenus en France au XVIIIe Siècle* (2 vols, Paris, 1984); also by F. Braudel in many of his works, such as *Afterthoughts on Material Civilization and Capitalism* (Baltimore, 1977); by P. Goubert, *Beauvais et le Beauvaisis, 1600–1730* (Paris, 1960), and E. Le Roy Ladurie, *Les Paysans de Languedoc* (Paris, 1966); a more general discussion of agriculture in Europe is T.H. Aston and C.H.E. Philpin, *The Brenner Debate. Agrarian Class Structure and Economic Development in Pre-Industrial Europe* (Cambridge, 1985); see also D. Hickey, 'Innovation and Obstacles to Growth in the Agriculture of Early Modern France: The Example of Dauphiné', in *French Historical Studies*, xv, no. 2 (1987), 208–40. The Labrousse model is examined in L.M. Cullen, 'History, Economic Crises, and Revolution: Understanding Eighteenth-Century France', in *Economic History Review*, xlvi, no. 4 (1993), 635–57.
28. Meuvret's views are available in his collection of articles published as *Etudes d'Histoire Economique* (Paris, 1971).
29. For a discussion of Meuvret's ideas, see G. Grantham, 'Jean Meuvret and the Subsistence Problem in Early Modern France', in *Journal of Economic History*, xlix, no. 1 (1989), 184–200.
30. See, for example, J. Dewald, *Pont-St-Pierre, 1398–1789: Lordship, Community, and Capitalism in Early Modern France* (Berkeley, 1987), and Root, *Peasants and King in Burgundy*.
31. Quoted by Grantham, 'Jean Meuvret', 193.
32. Classic histories are C.W. Cole, *Colbert and Century of French Mercantilism* (2 vols, New York, 1939); C.W. Cole, *French Mercantilism, 1683–1700* (New York, 1943) and E. Heckscher, *Mercantilism* (2 vols, London, 1955).
33. R. Davis, *The Rise of the Atlantic Economies* (London, 1973) does not use it.
34. The full text is in Clément (ed.), *Lettres, Mémoires et Instructions de Colbert*, vii, 233–56.
35. On Colbert and his policies see I. Murat, *Colbert* (Paris, 1980) and J. Meyer, *Colbert* (Paris, 1981); also Bluche, *Louis XIV*, 145–52, Mettam, *Government and Society*, section 7, J. Meuvret, 'La France au Temps de Louis XIV: Les Temps Difficiles' in his *Etudes d'Histoire Economique* (Paris, 1971), 17–37, and D. Parker, *Class and State in Ancien Régime France: The Road to Modernity?* (London, 1996), Chapter 2.
36. Davis, *Rise of the Atlantic Economies*, 220–4.
37. Pillorget, *France Baroque, France Classique*, i, *Récit*, 775.
38. On the numbers of French ships involved in commerce, see J. Delumeau,

'Le Commerce Extérieur Français au XVIIe Siècle', in *XVIIe Siècle*, nos. 70–1 (1966), 81–104.

39. See L. Rothkrug, *Opposition to Louis XIV: The Political and Social Origins of the French Enlightenment* (Princeton, 1965).
40. See T.J. Schaeper, *The French Council of Commerce, 1700–1715: A Study of Mercantilism after Colbert* (Columbus, 1983); also his essay, 'The Economic History of the Reign', in Sonnino (ed.), *The Reign of Louis XIV*, 27–43.
41. Rothkrug, *Opposition to Louis XIV*, 242–9.
42. Ibid., 249–86.
43. Ibid., 357–64.
44. Mettam, *Government and Society*, 132.
45. Act 5, Scene 1, line 1,492.
46. Bluche, *Louis XIV*, 112–13.
47. Mettam, *Government and Society*, 129–68.
48. See C. Chêne, *L'Enseignement du Droit Français en Pays de Droit Ecrit (1679–1793)* (Geneva, 1982).
49. See above p. 6–7.
50. See J.M. Hayden, 'Rural Resistance to Central Authority in Seventeenth-Century France', in *Canadian Journal of History*, xxvi, no. 1 (1991), 7–20.
51. Grantham, 'Jean Meuvret', 187.
52. See next chapter.
53. See Chapter 1.
54. Those of his works relevant to this discussion are available in English translations as *The Court Society* (Oxford, 1983), and *The Civilizing Process* (2 vols, Oxford, 1978–82).
55. *The Court Society*, Chapter 7.
56. S. Kettering, 'The Decline of Great Noble Clientage During the Reign of Louis XIV', in *Canadian Journal of History*, xxiv, no. 2 (1989), 157–77.
57. Ibid., 165.
58. F. Dubost, 'Absolutisme et Centralisation en Languedoc au XVIIe Siècle', in *Revue d'Histoire Moderne et Contemporaine*, xxxvii (juillet–septembre, 1990), 384.
59. Ibid., 393.
60. 'Dr. Edward Browne's Miscellaneous Observations and Journal of a Journey in France, 1663–1664' (British Library, Sloane MS 1906, f.80).
61. R.F.E. and J.A.H. Ferrier, *The Journal of Major Richard Ferrier, M.P., while Travelling in France in the Year 1687* (Camden Miscellany, London, 1895, vol. 9), 26.
62. J. Lough (ed.), *Locke's Travels in France, 1675–9* (Cambridge, 1953), 252.
63. 'Eloge de Winslow', *Histoire et Mémoires de l'Académie Royale des Sciences* (1760), 167.

4   LOUIS XIV AND THE CHURCHES

1. Bluche, *Louis XIV*, 382–6.
2. Ibid., 397.
3. Blunt, *Art and Architecture*, 223–4, 238–9.
4. General surveys are in J. le Goff and R. Rémond (eds), *Histoire de la France Religieuse* (3 vols, Paris, 1988–91), ii, *XIVe – XVIIIe Siècle*; Mousnier, *Insti-*

tutions, i, Chapter 7; see also, H. Phillips, *Church and Culture in Seventeenth-Century France* (Cambridge, 1997).

5. On this subject see the essays in R. Briggs, *Communities of Belief: Cultural and Social Tensions in Early Modern France* (Oxford, 1989).

6. For a summary see A.G. Dickens, *The Counter Reformation* (London, 1968), 172–81; and Le Goff and Rémond (eds), *Histoire de la France Religieuse*, ii, Chapter 3.

7. The final chapter of J. Bergin, *The Making of the French Episcopate, 1589–1661* (London, 1996) indicates the situation at the beginning of Louis's personal reign.

8. R. Briggs, 'The Catholic Puritans: Jansenists and Rigorists in France', in *Communities of Belief*, 339–63; F. Hildersheimer, *Le Jansénisme en France aux XVIIe et XVIIIe Siècles* (Paris, 1992); J. Plainemaison, 'Qu'est-ce que le Jansénisme?', in *Revue Historique*, 553 (1985), 117–30; A. Sedgwick, *Jansenism in Seventeenth-Century France* (Charlottesville, 1977); R. Taveneaux, *La Vie Quotidienne des Jansénistes aux XVIIe et XVIIIe Siècles* (Paris, 1985).

9. The Five Propositions were: (1) some of God's commandments are impossible to observe because He withholds the grace required to fulfil them, (2) in a state of fallen nature no person can resist interior grace, (3) for an act to be meritorious or unrighteous, it must be free from constraint, although not from internal necessity, (4) it is heretical to claim that there is an interior grace which the human will can choose either to resist or obey, (5) it is an error to claim that Christ died for all men.

10. On Quietism see J-R. Armogathe, *Le Quiétisme* (Paris, 1973) and L. Cognet, *Crépuscule des Mystiques* (Paris, 1991).

11. On the Huguenots, E.G. Léonard, *Histoire Générale du Protestantisme* (3 vols, Paris, 1955–64) remains a classic; also D. Ligou, *Le Protestantisme en France de 1598 à 1715* (Paris, 1968) and M. Prestwich (ed.), *International Calvinism* (1541–1715) (Oxford, 1985). The *Bulletin de la Société de l'Histoire du Protestantisme Français* for 1985 dedicated its issues to the Revocation of the Edict of Nantes; see also J. Garrisson, *L'Edit de Nantes et sa Révocation. Histoire d'une Intolérance* (Paris, 1985); E. Labrousse, *La Révocation de l'Edit de Nantes* (Paris, 1985).

12. These figures are from P. Benedict, *The Huguenot Population of France, 1600–1685: The Demographic Fate and Customs of a Religious Minority* (*Transactions of the American Philosophical Society*, vol. 81, pt. 5, 1991), 1–163; see also his 'La Population Réformée Française de 1600 à 1685', in *Annales ESC*, 42e année, no. 6 (1987), 1433–65.

13. Summaries of these demographic changes are in Benedict, *Huguenot Population*, 75–8.

14. Pillorget, *France Baroque, France Classique*, i, 935.

15. The classic work on this subject is W.C. Scoville, *The Persecution of Huguenots and French Economic Development, 1680–1720* (Berkeley, 1960).

16. See L.M. Cullen, 'The Huguenots from the Perspective of the Merchant Networks of Western Europe (1680–1790): the Example of the Brandy Trade', in C.E.J. Caldicott, H. Gough and J-P. Pittion (eds), *The Huguenots and Ireland: Anatomy of an Emigration* (Dun Laoghaire, 1987), 129–49.

17. This is a theme developed in A. Goldgar, *Impolite Learning: Conduct and Community in the Republic of Letters, 1680–1750* (New Haven, Conn., 1995).

5   LOUIS XIV AND THE DIRECTION OF IDEAS IN FRANCE

1. A survey is available in D. Maland, *Culture and Society in Seventeenth-Century France* (London, 1970).
2. See R. Maber, 'Colbert and the Scholars: Ménage, Huet, and the Royal Pensions of 1663', in *Seventeenth-Century French Studies*, vii (1985), 106–14.
3. Clement, *Lettres... de Colbert*, vol. 5, Appendix, lists the grants by year.
4. D.S. Lux, 'Colbert's Plan for the Grande Académie: Royal Policy towards Science, 1663–67', in *Seventeenth-Century French Studies*, xii (1990), 177–88.
5. Blunt, *Art and Architecture in France*, 194–6, 209–13.
6. On literature see A. Adam, *Grandeur and Illusion: French Literature and Society, 1600–1715* (London, 1972).
7. On the Académie des Sciences see R. Hahn, *The Anatomy of a Scientific Institution: The Paris Academy of Sciences, 1666–1803* (Berkeley, 1971), A. Stroup, *A Company of Scientists: Botany, Patronage, and Community at the Seventeenth-Century Parisian Royal Academy of Sciences* (Berkeley, 1990); D.J. Sturdy, *Science and Social Status: The Members of the Académie des Sciences, 1666–1750* (Woodbridge, 1995).
8. T. Hedin, *The Sculpture of Gaspard and Balthazar Marsy* (London, 1984) develops the theme of individualism.
9. See H.C. Barnard, *The French Tradition in Education* (Cambridge, 1922; rep.1970), L.W.B. Brockliss, *French Higher Education in the Seventeenth and Eighteenth Centuries* (Oxford, 1987), J. de Viguerie, *L'Institution des Enfants: L'Education en France, 16e–18e Siècle* (Paris, 1978).
10. De Viguerie, *L'Institution des Enfants*, 109–10.
11. The college had 60 students: 15 from Pignerol, 15 from Alsace, 20 from Flanders, Artois and Hainault and 10 from Roussillon and Cerdagne.
12. The arts comprised two sets of studies: the *trivium* (grammar, rhetoric and dialectics [philosophy]) and the *quadrivium* (arithmetic, geometry, music and astronomy).
13. 'Le XVIIe Siècle Epoque de Crise Universitaire', in J. Mesnard, *La Culture du XVIIe Siècle* (Paris, 1992), 100.
14. See H-J. Martin, *Livre, Pouvoirs et Société à Paris au XVIIe Siècle (1598–1701)* (2 vols, Paris, 1969) and H. Phillips, 'Culture and Control: Censorship under Louis XIV', in *Newsletter of the Society for Seventeenth-Century French Studies*, v (1983), 61–9.
15. Burke, *The Fabrication of Louis XIV*, Chapter 10.
16. Ibid., 148–9.
17. See for example, Rothkrug, *Opposition to Louis XIV*, and A. Tilley, *The Decline of the Age of Louis XIV, or French Literature 1687–1715* (New York, 1929 [1969]).
18. See Chapter 4.
19. Adam, *Grandeur and Illusion*, 158–64.
20. See P.K. Leffler, 'French Historians and the Challenge to Louis XIV's Absolutism', in *French Historical Studies*, 14, no. 1 (1986), 1–21.
21. See J-P. Brancourt, *Le Duc de Saint-Simon et la Monarchie* (Paris, 1971).
22. Created in December 1715 they were: ecclesiastical affairs, war, the navy, domestic affairs, finance, commerce.

6   LOUIS XIV AND EUROPE

1. See R. Hatton (ed.), *Louis XIV and Europe* (London, 1976).
2. J. Meyer, 'Louis XIV et les Puissances Maritimes', in *XVIIe Siècle*, no. 123, 31e année, no. 2 (1979), 155–72.
3. The Secretaries of State for Foreign Affairs were: Henri-Auguste de Loménie de Brienne, 1643–63; Hugues de Lionne, 1663–71; Simon Arnauld de Pomponne, 1672–79; Charles Colbert, Marquis de Croissy, 1679–96; Jean-Baptiste Colbert, Marquis de Torcy, 1696–1715. The Secretaries of State for War were: Michel le Tellier, 1643–77; François-Michel le Tellier, Marquis de Louvois, 1677–91; Louis-François-Marie le Tellier de Barbezieux, 1691–1701; Michel Chamillart, 1701–09; Daniel-François Voysin, 1709–15.
4. For a general discussion of the mechanisms of diplomacy see W.J. Roosen, *The Age of Louis XIV: The Rise of Modern Diplomacy* (Cambridge, Mass, 1976); L. Bély, *Espions et Ambassadeurs au Temps de Louis XIV* (Paris, 1990) is a monumental study of the subject which concentrates on the period leading up to the Treaty of Utrecht (1713); an analysis of this book and other works relating to the subject is by J.C. Rule, 'Gathering Intelligence in the Reign of Louis XIV', in *The International History Review*, xiv, no. 4 (1992), 732–52.
5. A. Corvisier, *La France de Louis XIV, 1643–1715: Ordre Intérieur et Place en Europe* (Paris, 1979), 294–5.
6. See A. Corvisier, 'Guerre et Mentalités au XVIIe Siècle' in *XVIIe Siècle*, 148, 37e année, no. 3 (1985), 219–32.
7. Ibid., 224.
8. See A. Corvisier, *Louvois* (Paris, 1983); also C. Jones, 'The Military Revolution and the Professionalisation of the French Army under the Ancien Régime', in M. Duffy (ed.), *The Military Revolution and the State, 1500–1800* (Exeter, 1980), 29–48; G. Parker, *The Military Revolution: Military Innovation and the Rise of the West, 1500–1800* (Cambridge, 1988); R. Martin, 'The Army of Louis XIV', in Sonnino (ed.), *The Reign of Louis XIV*, 111–26; J.A. Lynn, *Giant of the Grand Siècle: The French Army, 1610–1715* (Cambridge, 1997).
9. Jones, 'The Military Revolution', 30; P. Kennedy, *The Rise and Fall of the Great Powers: Economic Change and Military Conflict from 1500 to 2000* (London, 1988), 128.
10. J.E. King, *Science and Rationalism in the Government of Louis XIV, 1661–1683* (reprinted New York, 1972), 246, n.10.
11. King, *Science and Rationalism*, 277; Sturdy, *Science and Social Status*, 130.
12. In descending order the main ranks were: marshal, lieutenant-general, *maréchal de camp*, brigadier, master of infantry or dragoons, lieutenant-colonel, captain, lieutenant, sub-lieutenant (or *cornette* in the cavalry) and ensign (King, *Science and Rationalism*, 248, n. 17).
13. D.C. Baxter, *Servants of the Sword: French Intendants of the Army, 1630–70* (Urbana, 1976).
14. See G.W. Symcox, 'The Navy of Louis XIV', in Sonnino (ed.), *The Reign of Louis XIV*, 127–42.
15. Kennedy, *Rise and Fall*, 129.
16. E. Asher, *Resistance to the Maritime Classes* (Berkeley, 1960).

17. Sonnino (ed.), *Mémoires... of Louis XIV*, 26–8.
18. J. Black, 'Louis XIV's Foreign Policy Reassessed', in *Seventeenth-Century French Studies*, x (1988), 199–212.
19. J. Black, 'Aggressive but Unsuccessful: Louis XIV and the European Struggle', in *The Historian*, no. 32 (1991), 4.
20. Bibliothèque Nationale de France, MS Français 4240, f.394.
21. H. Weber, 'Une Bonne Paix: Richelieu's Foreign Policy and the Peace of Christendom', in J. Bergin and L.W.B. Brockliss (eds), *Richelieu and his Age* (Oxford, 1992), 45–75.
22. See above, p. 33–4.
23. A modern account is C. Dulong, *Le Mariage du Roi-Soleil* (Paris, 1986).
24. The legal and constitutional implications of the marriage can be traced in M. Valtat, *Les Contrats de Mariage dans la Famille Royale en France au XVIIe Siècle* (Paris, 1952).
25. P. Sonnino, *Louis XIV and the Origins of the Dutch War* (Cambridge, 1989); on the outcome of the war: C.J. Ekburg, *The Failure of Louis XIV's Dutch War* (Chapel Hill, 1979).
26. The Polish crown was elective; John Casimir had abdicated in 1668, and in the event the Polish Diet chose neither the French nor the Austrian candidate, but a Polish aristocrat as King Michael.
27. See *The Peace of Nijmegen, 1676–1678/79: International Congress of the Tricentennial* (Amsterdam, 1980).
28. These manœuvres and the progress of the war can be traced in A. Lossky, *Louis XIV and the French Monarchy* (New Brunswick, 1994), Chapter 10.
29. J.H. Elliott, *Imperial Spain, 1469–1716* (London, 1969), 368–70 discusses the main factions; see also Lossky, *Louis XIV*, Chapter 11.
30. Petitfils, *Louis XIV*, 579–83.
31. An important article still is M.A. Thomson, 'Louis XIV and the Origins of the War of the Spanish Succession', first published in the *Transactions of the Royal Historical Society*, series 5, no. 4 (London, 1954), and reprinted in R. Hatton and J.S. Bromley (eds), *Louis XIV and William III* (Liverpool, 1968), 140–61; a more recent assessment is W. Roosen, 'The Origins of the War of the Spanish Succession', in J. Black (ed.), *The Origins of War in Early Modern Europe* (Edinburgh, 1987), 151–75; see also Corvisier, *La France de Louis XIV*, 327–30.
32. J. Meyer, *L'Europe des Lumières* (Paris, 1989), 21, 95–9.

7 CONCLUDING DISCUSSION

1.   There exists an extensive bibliography on absolutism; two good general studies which also include wider bibliographical guides are J. Miller (ed.), *Absolutism in Seventeenth-Century Europe* (London, 1990), and N. Henshall, *The Myth of Absolutism* (London, 1992); Bonney, *The Limits of Absolutism* concentrates on France, but also ranges further afield; on France, see J.B. Collins, *The State in Early Modern France* (Cambridge, 1995), Mettam, *Power and Faction*, and Parker, *Class and State* (Chapter 1 of this book discusses 'Approaches to French Absolutism').
2.   See J.H. Franklin, *Jean Bodin and the Rise of Absolutist Theory* (Cambridge, 1973); also, 'Bodin and the Development of French Monarchy', in Bonney,

The Limits of Absolutism.

3. For a discussion of the movement of ideas on absolute monarchy in France from medieval times to the nineteenth century, see H.H. Rowen, *The King's State: Proprietary Dynasticism in Early Modern France* (New Brunswick, 1980).
4. J. Bodin, *Six Books of the Commonwealth*, abridged and translated by M.J. Tooley (Oxford, 1967), 1.
5. Ibid., 6.
6. Ibid., 36.
7. Ibid., 21.
8. Ibid., 31.
9. M.P. Holt, *The Duke of Anjou and the Politique Struggle during the Wars of Religion* (Cambridge, 1986), 76–87.
10. See D. Parker, 'Sovereignty, Absolutism and the Function of Law in Seventeenth-Century France', in *Past & Present*, 122 (1989), 36–74.
11. For example Beik, *Languedoc*.
12. S. Clark, *State and Status: The Rise of the State and Aristocratic Power in Western Europe* (Cardiff, 1995).
13. For example Mettam, Parker.
14. Parker, *Class and State*, Chapter 2; the chief exponents of causative links between 'absolutism' and 'capitalism' whose views Parker challenges are P. Anderson, *Lineages of the Absolutist State* (London, 1974), R. Brenner whose ideas are discussed in T.H. Aston and C.H.E. Philpin (eds), *The Brenner Debate* (Cambridge, 1977), and I. Wallerstein, *The Modern World System* (2 vols, London, 1974–80).
15. For the development and application of the theory of *raison d'état* to French foreign policy, see E. Thuau, *Raison d'Etat et Pensée Politique à l'Epoque de Richelieu* (Paris, 1966).
16. The essays in Miller (ed.), *Absolutism in Seventeenth-Century Europe* cover the international dimension to absolute monarchy.
17. This is argued by Miller in his essay on 'Britain', ibid., 195–224; also by the same author in his *Bourbon and Stuart: Kings and Kingship in France and England in the Seventeenth Century* (London, 1987).
18. The question of the varying positions of the crown in England, Scotland and Ireland may be followed in R.G. Asch (ed.), *Three Nations – A Common History?* (Bochum, 1993).

BIBLIOGRAPHICAL GUIDE

It is not the aim of this exercise to present a comprehensive bibliography on Louis XIV and his reign. The reader who seeks further information should consult bibliographies printed in recent books listed below. Each year there is published in France the *Bibliographie Annuelle de l'Histoire de France*, which is the most wide-ranging of all guides to French history. The journal *French Historical Studies* prints lists of recent books and dissertations on French history. The major historical journals in the English language include review sections which likewise provide the student with critical assessments of recent work. Inevitably, the text of this book includes references to people, institutions and other facets of seventeenth-century French government and society on which the reader might like more detailed information. Four extremely useful historical dictionaries which can be consulted are L. Bély (ed.), *Dictionnaire de l'Ancien Régime* (Paris, 1996), F. Bluche (ed.), *Dictionnaire du Grand Siècle* (Paris, 1990), G. Cabourdin and G. Viard, *Lexique Historique de la France d'Ancien Régime* (Paris, 1978) and R. and S. Pillorget, *France Baroque, France Classique, 1589–1715* (2 vols, Paris, 1995); these last two titles are available in paperback.

1. GENERAL STUDIES OF THE REIGN

The reader who is new to the subject of Louis XIV and would like a short introduction can consult J.H. Shennan, *Louis XIV* (Lancaster Pamphlets; London, 1986). P.R. Campbell, *Louis XIV 1661–1715* (London, 1993) provides a concise study of aspects of the personal reign, and illustrates his themes with a selection of documents. R. Mettam, *Government and Society in Louis XIV's France* (London, 1977) contains a broad selection of documents, each group of which is introduced by judicious comment. P. Sonnino (ed.), *The Reign of Louis XIV: Essays in Celebration of Andrew Lossky* (London, 1990) contains essays on different aspects of the reign; the authors provide a summary of current thinking on each subject. A. Lossky, in whose honour the Sonnino collection is composed, presents his own general assessment of Louis XIV in *Louis XIV and the French Monarchy* (New Brunswick, 1994). Louis XIV's reign is placed in longer perspective by R. Briggs, *Early Modern France, 1560–1715* (Oxford, 1977) and J. Cornette, *Absolutisme et Lumières, 1652–1783* (Paris, 1993). R. Hatton, *Louis XIV and his World* (London, 1972) is a balanced account which still commands attention.

How have French historians depicted Louis XIV? The interpretation which dominated the first half of the twentieth century was that of Ernest Lavisse, who saw Louis XIV as the modernising forerunner of modern France. His work on Louis has been reissued as E. Lavisse, *Louis XIV* (Paris, 1989), with an introduction by R. and S. Pillorget. The Pillorgets outline Lavisse's life, career and political commitments which found expression in his analysis of *le roi soleil*. One of the leaders of the French reaction against the classic interpretation was P. Goubert, whose *Louis XIV and Twenty Million Frenchmen* (London, 1970) cast a critical eye on the reign; Goubert restates some of his views but revises others in *Le Siècle de Louis XIV* (Paris, 1996), a collection of his essays and articles (divided into sections with introductory commentaries) ranging from the 1950s to the 1990s. Two more recent French interpretations are F. Bluche, *Louis XIV* (Oxford, 1990) and J-C. Petitfils, *Louis XIV* (Paris, 1995); the former is in English translation, the latter is available only in French. They make an interesting comparison. Most commentators are struck by the minimal attention apparently paid by Bluche to the work of non-French historians, and to the extent to which he defends Louis against criticism. Petitfils has cast his bibliographical net much wider, and has written an excellent study which achieves a high level of objectivity. Somewhat older, but good on military affairs is A. Corvisier, *La France de Louis XIV, 1643–1715: Ordre Intérieur et Place en Europe* (Paris, 1979). Also good on the military aspects of the reign is the American historian J.B. Wolf, whose *Louis XIV* (London, 1968) is still to be read with profit. R. Mettam, *Power and Faction in Louis XIV's France* (Oxford, 1988) has the air of a polemic: it resolutely rejects many aspects of the 'classic' interpretation of Louis XIV, and emphasises instead the weaknesses of Louis XIV and the limitations within which he operated.

2. LOUIS AND REPRESENTATIONS OF KINGSHIP

Although J.C. Rule (ed.), *Louis XIV and the Craft of Kingship* (Columbus, 1969) in some respects is dated, it is still a valuable collection of essays exploring the complexities of kingship and the conscientiousness with which Louis approached the task. His own thoughts on kingship are expressed in his *Mémoires*, which are available in an English translation by P. Sonnino entitled Mémoires *for the Instruction of the Dauphin by Louis XIV* (New York, 1970). Sonnino has also discussed 'The Dating and Authorship of Louis XIV's Mémoires', in *French Historical Studies*, iii, no. 3 (1964), 303–37. The nature and consistency of Louis's political ideas are discussed by J-L. Thireau, *Les Idées Politiques de Louis XIV* (Paris, 1973). Early modern monarchy expressed many of its ideals through ritual as much as the written word, and this is a subject which has attracted sociologists and anthropologists as well as historians. E. Kantorowicz, *The King's Two Bodies: A Study in Mediaeval Political Theology* (Princeton, 1957) is an essential work which establishes many of the themes pursued by later scholars; equally venerable and essential is M. Bloch, *The Royal Touch: Sacred Monarchy and Scrofula in England and France* (London, reissued 1973). These two authors placed monarchy in a mystical tradition which expressed itself through elaborate ritual and miraculous powers.

S. Wilentz (ed.), *Rites of Power: Symbolism, Ritual and Politics since the Middle Ages* (Philadelphia, 1985) and D. Kertzer, *Ritual, Politics and Power* (London, 1988) explore these and other themes concerning the importance of ritual in early modern monarchy. The significance of various types of French monarchic ritual is discussed by M. Fogel, *Les Cérémonies de l'Information dans la France du XVIe au Milieu du XVIIIe Siècle* (Paris, 1989) and A. Boureau, 'Les Cérémonies Royales Françaises entre Performance Juridique et Compétence Liturgique', in *Annales ESC*, 46e année, no. 6 (1991), 1253–64. The most important ceremony in which the king was involved was the coronation. R. Jackson, *Vive le Roi! A History of the French Coronation from Charles V to Charles X* (Chapel Hill, 1984) presents an analytical survey of the evolution of royal inauguration procedures. Jackson brings to his subject a sensitivity towards the tenacity of medieval concepts of monarchy well into the early modern period. Other forms of monarchic ritual are discussed by L.M. Bryant, *The French Royal Entry Ceremony* (Geneva, 1985) which explores the symbols of reception erected in the towns and cities into which French kings made formal entry, and S. Hanley, *The* Lit de Justice *of the Kings of France: Constitutional Ideology in Legend, Ritual, and Discourse* (Princeton, 1983). Some of Hanley's contentions – notably that the *lit de justice* (a ceremony in which the king personally attended the Parlement of Paris to impose the royal will) emerged in the sixteenth century – have been challenged by E.A.R. Brown and R.C. Famiglietti in *The* Lit de Justice*: Semantics, Ceremonial and the Parlement of Paris 1300–1600* (Sigmaringen, 1994). They maintain that the *lit de justice* went back to at least the 1300s, and was usually an instrument of cooperation between crown and *parlement*; it was the Wars of Religion and the crises of the seventeenth century which changed the ceremony into an occasion for the exertion of royal authority.

Louis XIV and his advisers paid close attention to visual and ritualistic representations of the king. They are outlined in P. Burke, *The Fabrication of Louis XIV* (London, 1992), which uses copious illustrations to good effect. J.M. Apostolides, *Le Roi-Machine: Spectacle et Politique au Temps de Louis XIV* (Paris, 1982), L. Marin, *Portrait of the King* (London, 1988), and M. Martin, *Les Monuments Equestres de Louis XIV: Une Grande Entreprise de Propagande Monarchique* (Paris, 1986) deal with different aspects of the means whereby images of the king were conceived and displayed. Versailles, more than any other single location, was the setting wherein a varied iconography was devoted to *le roi soleil*. G. Walton, *Louis XIV's Versailles* (London, 1986), is to be recommended, but there are lavishly illustrated books aplenty on the palace and its grounds. The life of the court has attracted the attention of sociologists, notably N. Elias, whose *The Court Society* (London, 1983) – which should be read in conjunction with his *The Civilizing Process* (2 vols, Oxford, 1978–82) – investigates the social and political dynamics of a setting which may be envisaged as the kingdom in miniature. The significance of Elias's views is assessed by J. Duindam, *Myths of Power: Norbert Elias and the Early Modern European Court* (Amsterdam, 1996). Another excellent study of the French court is J-F. Solnon, *La Cour de France* (Paris, 1987). Among contemporary observers and commentators, the Duc de Saint-Simon has pride of place. Numerous editions of selections from his *Mémoires* are in print; J-P. Brancourt, *Le Duc de Saint-Simon et la Monarchie* (Paris, 1971) discusses the political philosophy underlying Saint-Simon's diaries.

3. LOUIS'S MINISTERS

From about the 1950s, if not before, many historians in France regarded biography as unworthy of serious scholarship. The historian, so it was widely held in France, aimed to identify and analyse those profound forces which determined the broad movement of history. History, in this view, aimed to explain massive, long-term movements, not the careers of individual people; no matter how famous they were. In the last two decades, however, historical biography has recovered its prestige in France, where leading historians are prepared to return to a historical genre which the English-speaking world never abandoned. Louis XIV's mother, Anne of Austria, is the subject of R. Kleinmann, *Anne of Austria, Queen of France* (Ohio UP, 1987), while the careers of some of his ministers likewise have been systematically examined. On Louis's chief cardinal-minister there is P. Goubert, *Mazarin* (Paris, 1990); Mazarin is also assessed in G.R.R. Treasure, *Mazarin: The Crisis of Absolutism in France* (London, 1995). Other biographies from French scholars include A. Corvisier, *Louvois* (Paris, 1983), D. Dessert, *Fouquet* (Paris, 1987), I. Murat, *Colbert* (Paris, 1980) and J. Meyer, *Colbert* (Paris, 1981). The last minister is assessed in a collection of essays presented at a conference on the tercentenary of Colbert's death (1983), and edited by R. Mousnier, *Un Nouveau Colbert* (Paris, 1985).

4. THE FRONDES AND THEIR AFTERMATH

Around the Frondes has gathered a massive bibliography which cannot be reproduced here. O. Ranum, *The Fronde: A French Revolution, 1648–1652* (New York, 1993) is the most recent general assessment of the risings, but students aiming to familiarise themselves with issues raised by the Frondes should also consult A.L. Moote, *The Revolt of the Judges. The Parlement of Paris and the Fronde, 1643–1652* (Princeton, 1971), R.J. Knecht, *The Fronde* (Historical Association. Appreciations in History, v, 1975), and the relevant essays in R. Bonney, *The Limits of Absolutism in* Ancien Régime *France* (Aldershot, 1995). As its title suggests, A.N. Hamscher, *The Parlement of Paris after the Fronde, 1653–1673* (Pittsburgh, 1976) deals with the extent to which crown and *parlement* accommodated themselves to post-Fronde realities. He takes the story further in *The Conseil Privé and the Parlements in the Age of Louis XIV: A Study in French Absolutism* (Philadelphia, 1987). J.H. Shennan, *The Parlement of Paris* (London, 1968) provides a general discussion of the evolution of the *parlement*, its adaptation to the political problems of the seventeenth century, and its development in the eighteenth century.

5. GOVERNMENT AND SOCIETY

Many problems of central government are treated in the books listed in Section 1 above. The great printed documentary compilations published in the nineteenth century remain an important source. They include P. Clément, *Lettres, Instructions et Mémoires de Jean-Baptiste Colbert* (8 vols, Paris, 1861–82), and

G-B. Depping, *Correspondance Administrative sous Louis XIV* (4 vols, Paris, 1850–70). R. Mousnier, *Les Institutions de la France sous la Monarchie Absolue* (2 vols, Paris, 1974–80) – available in English translation as *The Institutions of France under the Absolute Monarchy, 1598–1789* (2 vols, London, 1979–84) – contains, among other things, much information on the instruments and procedures of government. The question of the significance of 1661 and Louis XIV's decision to rule personally is discussed by D. Dessert, *Louis XIV prend le Pouvoir: Naissance d'un Mythe?* (Paris, 1989) and P. Goubert, *L'Avènement du Roi-Soleil* (Paris, 1967). The problems of finance are discussed by R. Bonney, who has clarified many of the issues attaching to this difficult subject. In addition to articles reproduced in *The Limits of Absolutism*, the reader should consult his *The King's Debts: Finance and Politics in France, 1589–1661* (Oxford, 1981) and R. Bonney (ed.), *Economic Systems and State Finance* (Oxford, 1995). A survey of the century as a whole is in J. Dent, *Crisis in Finance: Crown, Financiers and Society in Seventeenth-Century France* (London, 1973). On the question of the mechanisms and personnel involved in the government's borrowing from financiers, and of the social implications of this dependency, two works are extremely informative: D. Dessert, *Argent, Pouvoir et Société au Grand Siècle* (Paris, 1984) and F. Bayard, *Le Monde des Financiers au XVII Siècle* (Paris, 1988). The attempt by the government to broaden the tax base by the introduction of the *capitation* is discussed by A. Guéry, 'Etat, Classification Sociale et Compromis sous Louis XIV: la Capitation de 1695', in *Annales ESC*, no. 5 (1986), 1041–60. Justice – which with finance occupied much of the attention of the king and his advisers – is treated in many of the books in Sections 1 and 10, but A. Lebigre, *La Justice du Roi* (Paris, 1988) provides a general survey.

R. Bonney has written on the intendants, and although his *Political Change in France under Richelieu and Mazarin, 1624–1661* (Oxford, 1978) ends with the death of Mazarin, much of what it has to say is of relevance to the later period. For the personal reign of Louis XIV the key works on the intendants are by A. Smedley-Weill: *Correspondance des Intendants avec le Contrôleur Général des Finances, 1677–1689. Naissance d'une Administration* (3 vols, Paris, 1989–91), and *Les Intendants sous Louis XIV* (Paris, 1995). Colbert and the development of economic policy have long interested historians. The biographical studies by Meyer and Murat have been noted in Section 3 above. Two classic works which are still helpful are by C.W. Cole: *Colbert and Century of French Mercantilism* (2 vols, New York, 1939), and *French Mercantilism, 1683–1700* (New York, 1943); E. Heckscher, *Mercantilism* (2 vols, London, 1955) also has the status of a dated classic. T.J. Schaeper, *The Economy of France in the Second Half of the Reign of Louis XIV* (Montreal, 1980) and *The French Council of Commerce, 1700–1715: A Study of Mercantilism after Colbert* (Columbus, 1983), deal with the period when the French economy was languishing and attempts were being made to revive it. At the turn of the seventeenth century there was much debate in France over the most advantageous future course for the economy. The arguments are followed in L. Rothkrug, *Opposition to Louis XIV: The Political and Social Origins of the French Enlightenment* (Princeton, 1965).

The complexities of relations between central government and the provinces have generated considerable historical interest. E.L. Asher, *Resistance to the Maritime Classes* (Berkeley, 1960) showed with what effect the intentions of Colbert could be frustrated if they ran counter to local vested interest; likewise J.M. Hayden, 'Rural Resistance to Central Authority in Seventeenth-Century France', in *Canadian Journal of History*, xxvi, no. 1 (1991), 7–20 investigated this phenomenon. On the other hand, W. Beik, *Absolutism and Society in Seventeenth-Century France: State Power and Provincial Aristocracy in Languedoc* (Cambridge, 1985), F. Dubost, 'Absolutisme et Centralisation en Languedoc au XVIIe Siècle', in *Revue d'Histoire Moderne et Contemporaine*, xxxvii (juillet–septembre, 1990), 369–97, J.B. Collins, *Classes, Estates, and Order in Early Modern Brittany* (Cambridge, 1994) and J. Dewald, *Pont-St-Pierre, 1398–1789: Lordship, Community, and Capitalism in Early Modern France* (Berkeley, 1987), show that collaboration between centre and province could be effective. Elaborating on this theme, S. Kettering has published several studies around the theme of patronage and clientage; they include *Judicial Politics and Urban Revolt in Seventeenth-Century France: The Parlement of Aix, 1629–1659* (Princeton, 1978), *Patrons, Brokers, and Clients in Seventeenth-Century France* (Oxford, 1986), 'The Decline of Great Noble Clientage during the Reign of Louis XIV', in *Canadian Journal of History*, 24, no. 2 (1989), 157–77 and 'Patronage and Kinship in Early Modern France', in *French Historical Studies*, 19 (1989), 408–35. At every level of French society, patronage and clientage were essential to the functioning of political, economic and other forms of relationships. R. Harding, *Anatomy of a Power Elite: The Provincial Governors of Early Modern France* (London, 1978) and J.M. Smith, '"Our Sovereign's Gaze": Kings, Nobles, and State Formation in Seventeenth-Century France', in *French Historical Studies*, 18, no. 2 (1993), 396–415 develop some of these points on a kingdom-wide scale.

6. SOCIAL AND ECONOMIC PROBLEMS

On a somewhat different basis, works such as P. Goubert, *Beauvais et le Beauvaisis, 1600–1730* (Paris, 1960), R. Pillorget, *Les Mouvements Insurrectionnels de Provence entre 1596 et 1715* (Paris, 1975), and H.L. Root, *Peasants and King in Burgundy: Agrarian Foundations of French Absolutism* (London, 1987) investigate provincial life under Louis XIV, and demonstrate again how complex were relations between the central government and the provinces, and between the various elements which comprised provincial society. The largest section of French society was, of course, the peasants, whose condition defies easy generalisation. E. Le Roy Ladurie, *Les Paysans de Languedoc* (Paris, 1966) advanced many of the hypotheses which later scholars have taken up; especially the proposition that rural life and economy to all intents and purposes were stagnant in the early modern period. A debate on the validity of this thesis was occasioned by Robert Brenner; it can be followed in T.H. Aston and C.H.E. Philpin, *The Brenner Debate. Agrarian Class Structure and Economic Development in Pre-Industrial Europe* (Cambridge, 1985). Also on the peasantry and their condition are P. Goubert, *The French Peasantry in the Seventeenth Century* (Cambridge, 1986) and D. Hickey, 'Innovation and Obstacles to Growth in the Agriculture of Early Modern France: the Example of Dauphiné', in *French Historical Studies*, xv, no. 2 (1987), 208–40.

The towns and cities of France may have been small by present-day standards, but they exerted a political and economic influence out of proportion
to their size. Paris, of course, dominated urban life. H. Bannon, *The Paris of
Henri IV: Architecture and Urbanism* (New York, 1991) is pre-Louis XIV, but
explains the emergence of a tradition which Louis followed. O. Ranum, *Paris
in the Age of Absolutism* (London, 1968), and L. Bernard, *The Emerging City:
Paris in the Age of Louis XIV* (Durham, NC, 1970) trace the developing relationship between city and Bourbon monarchy, while the lavishly produced
series *Nouvelle Histoire de Paris* has two volumes covering the seventeenth
century: R. Pillorget, *Paris sous les Premiers Bourbons, 1594–1661* (Paris, 1988)
and G. Dethan, *Paris au Temps de Louis XIV* (Paris, 1990). P. Benedict (ed.),
Cities and Social Change in Early Modern France (London, 1989) looks more
widely at the phenomenon of French urbanisation. The evolution of a town
over a long period is traced by R.A. Schneider, *Public Life in Toulouse,
1463–1789: From Municipal Republic to Cosmopolitan City* (Ithaca, 1989). Histories of most of the great cities of France are available in the series *Histoire des
Villes* directed by P. Wolff.

Research into the wider context of French socio-economic life in the seventeenth century continues to stimulate important questions. What were the
dynamics behind demographic growth or decline? What was the relative
economic importance of local, 'national' and long-distance commerce? Indeed,
to what extent had a 'national' economy emerged by the end of the seventeenth century? These and other issues are discussed in works such as
J. Dupâquier (ed.), *Histoire de la Population Française* (4 vols, Paris, 1988),
R. Davis, *The Rise of the Atlantic Economies* (London, 1973), J. Delumeau, 'Le
Commerce Extérieur Français au XVIIe Siècle', in *XVIIe Siècle*, nos 70–1
(1966), 81–104, E. Labrousse *et al.* (eds), *Histoire Economique et Sociale de la
France*, ii, *Des Derniers Temps de l'Age Seigneurial aux Préludes de l'Age Industriel
(1660–1789)* (Paris, 1970), E. Labrousse, *Esquisse du Mouvement des Prix et des
Revenus en France au XVIIIe Siècle* (2 vols, Paris, 1984), and J. Meuvret, *Etudes
d'Histoire Economique* (Paris, 1971). Meuvret's ideas are examined in
G. Grantham, 'Jean Meuvret and the Subsistence Problem in Early Modern
France', in *Journal of Economic History*, xlix, no. 1 (1989), 184–200.

7. RELIGION AND THE CHURCHES

French society, as elsewhere throughout Europe, was sustained by bodies of
religious belief and practice, and by ecclesiastical institutions, which integrated
all but a few deviants and outcasts into the body of the Catholic Church or
the Huguenot Church. R. Briggs, *Communities of Belief: Cultural and Social
Tensions in Early Modern France* (Oxford, 1989) is a collection of essays which
look in particular at the Catholic Church and the measures which it adopted
to exert its control over society. A good general survey of the role of the
churches in French life from the medieval to modern times is J. Le Goff and
R. Rémond (eds), *Histoire de la France Religieuse* (3 vols, Paris, 1988–91); also
R. Taveneaux, *Le Catholicisme dans la France Classique, 1610–1715* (2 vols, Paris,
1980) presents a comprehensive account of the seventeenth century. The

bishops are the subject of a prosopographical analysis by J. Bergin, *The Making of the French Episcopate, 1589–1661* (London, 1996); although this book ends as Louis's personal reign was beginning, it has much of importance to say on the 1640s and 1650s. P. Blet has written extensively on the clergy: *Le Clergé de France et la Monarchie. Etude sur les Assemblées du Clergé de 1615 à 1666* (2 vols, Rome, 1959); *Les Assemblées du Clergé et Louis XIV de 1670 à 1693* (Rome, 1972); and *Le Clergé de France, Louis XIV et le Saint Siège de 1695 à 1715* (Rome, 1989).

French Catholicism had to come to terms with a variety of heterodox movements. They included Jansenism, which has been studied by A. Antoine, *Du Mysticisme à la Révolte: les Jansénistes au XVIIe Siècle* (Paris, 1968), L. Cognet, *Le Jansénisme* (Paris, 1991), F. Hildersheimer, *Le Jansénisme en France aux XVIIe et XVIIIe Siècles* (Paris, 1992), J. Plainemaison, 'Qu'est-ce que le Jansénisme?', in *Revue Historique*, 553 (1985), 117–30, A. Sedgwick, *Jansenism in Seventeenth-Century France* (Charlottesville, 1977), and R. Taveneaux, *La Vie Quotidienne des Jansénistes aux XVIIe et XVIIIe Siècles* (Paris, 1985). J-R. Armogathe has written on *Le Quiétisme* (Paris, 1973), A. Talon has investigated *La Compagnie du Saint-Sacrement, Spiritualité et Société (1629–1667)* (Paris, 1990), and L. Cognet, *Crépuscule des Mystiques* (Paris, 1991) examines the mystical tradition.

Protestantism in France likewise has attracted much scholarly attention. E.G. Léonard, *Histoire Générale du Protestantisme* (3 vols, Paris, 1955–64) is somewhat encyclopaedic and covers the whole Protestant movement, not just that in France; and his notion of a period of expansion of French Protestantism in the sixteenth century followed by stagnation in the seventeenth, now commands little support. Nevertheless, these volumes are a valuable work of reference. Calvinism, the French form of Protestantism, in its wider setting is the subject of M. Prestwich (ed.), *International Calvinism (1541–1715)* (Oxford, 1985). D. Ligou, on the other hand, limits himself to France in *Le Protestantisme en France de 1598 à 1715* (Paris, 1968). The question of Huguenot demography is taken up by P. Benedict, 'La Population Réformée Française de 1600 à 1685', in *Annales ESC*, 42e année, no. 6 (1987), 1433–65, and again in *The Huguenot Population of France, 1600–1685: The Demographic Fate and Customs of a Religious Minority (Transactions of the American Philosophical Society*, vol. 81, pt. 5, 1991), 1–163. The policies and events leading up to the Revocation of the Edict of Nantes can be followed in J. Garrisson, *L'Edit de Nantes et sa Révocation. Histoire d'une Intolérance* (Paris, 1985), E. Labrousse, *La Révocation de l'Edit de Nantes* (Paris, 1985) and J. Orcibal, 'Louis XIV and the Edict of Nantes', in R. Hatton (ed.), *Louis XIV and Absolutism* (London, 1976), 154–76. The economic consequences of the Revocation were assessed by W.C. Scoville, *The Persecution of Huguenots and French Economic Development, 1680–1720* (Berkeley, 1960); most present-day scholars argue that he exaggerated the damage which Revocation did to the French economy. C.E.J. Caldicott, H. Gough and J-P. Pittion (eds), *The Huguenots and Ireland: Anatomy of an Emigration* (Dun Laoghaire, 1987), and I. Scouloudi (ed.), *Huguenots in Britain and their French Background, 1550–1800* (London, 1987), look at aspects of the Huguenot diaspora.

8. CONTROL OF CULTURAL AND EDUCATIONAL LIFE

Artists, architects, writers, scientists and others do not work in a social or political vacuum. D. Maland, *Culture and Society in Seventeenth-Century France* (London, 1970) provides a broad survey of the subject, while H. Phillips, *Church and Culture in Seventeenth-Century France* (Cambridge, 1997) examines the sometimes difficult relations between the demands of Catholic orthodoxy and cultural innovation. A recent collection of stimulating essays ranging far and wide over the connections between culture and politics is K. Cameron and E. Woodrough (eds), *Ethics and Politics in Seventeenth-Century France: Essays in Honour of Derek A. Watts* (Exeter, 1996).

A. Blunt, *Art and Architecture in France, 1500–1700* (London, 1953) is still the standard guide to the visual arts, while V-L. Tapié, *The Age of Grandeur: Baroque and Classicism in Europe* (London, 1960) contains an entire section devoted to the reception of baroque in France. Excellent short guides to the entire range of visual arts are available in the series entitled *La Grammaire des Styles* published by Flammarion: J-F. Barrielle has written both *Le Style Louis XIII* and *Le Style Louis XIV* (both 1982).

A. Adam, *Grandeur and Illusion: French Literature and Society, 1600–1715* (London, 1972) looks more specifically at the literary arts in their social context. There exists a vast bibliography on French literature during the reign of Louis XIV, but on the question of the regime's ambivalent attitude to writers and their craft, H. Phillips, 'Culture and Control: Censorship under Louis XIV', in *Newsletter of the Society for Seventeenth-Century French Studies*, v (1983), 61–9 deals with the mechanisms whereby the government sought to control what was published; relevant sections of the classic work by H-J. Martin, *Livre, Pouvoirs et Société à Paris au XVIIe Siècle (1598–1701)* (2 vols, Paris, 1969) also develop this and other aspects of publishing industry in Paris.

Like its predecessors, the regime of Louis XIV employed writers to produce histories explaining the purposes and achievements of the king. O. Ranum, *Artisans of Glory: Writers and Historical Thought in Seventeenth-Century France* (Chapel Hill, 1980) and M. Tyvaert, 'L'Image du Roi: Légitimité et Moralité Royales dans les Histoires de France au XVIIe Siècle', in *Revue d'Histoire Moderne et Contemporaine*, xxi (1974), 521–47 investigate the methods by which historians were selected by the crown, and the principles according to which they then wrote their histories. Colbert was prominent in the exercise of these and other forms of royal patronage; R. Maber, 'Colbert and the Scholars: Ménage, Huet, and the Royal Pensions of 1663', in *Seventeenth-Century French Studies*, vii (1985), 106–14 explains some of the procedures adopted by Colbert. The minister had ambitious plans for a multi-disciplinary academy which would bring together many cultural spheres, and would provide the regime with a convenient institutional framework for its patronage: the scope and possibilities of the plan are discussed by D.S. Lux, 'Colbert's Plan for the Grande Académie: Royal Policy towards Science, 1663–67', in *Seventeenth-Century French Studies*, xii (1990), 177–88.

The association between the regime and the sciences was especially strong, and was channelled principally through the French Academy of Sciences. Two recent works which contain extensive bibliographies are A. Stroup, *A Company of Scientists: Botany, Patronage, and Community at the Seventeenth-Century Parisian Royal Academy of Sciences* (Berkeley, 1990), and D.J. Sturdy, *Science and Social Status: The Members of the Académie des Sciences, 1666–1750* (Woodbridge, 1995). R. Hahn, *The Anatomy of a Scientific Institution: The Paris Academy of Sciences, 1666–1803* (Berkeley, 1971) devotes most of its attention to the eighteenth rather than the seventeenth century. J.E. King, *Science and Rationalism in the Government of Louis XIV, 1661–1683* (Baltimore, 1949; reprinted New York, 1972) is a fascinating account of the extent to which the regime of Louis XIV sought to apply scientific principles to problems of government. Education provided the underpinning for much French cultural activity. L.W.B. Brockliss, *French Higher Education in the Seventeenth and Eighteenth Centuries* (Oxford, 1987) is an essential work, whose bibliography also provides wider guidance on the subject. H.C. Barnard, *The French Tradition in Education* (Cambridge, 1922; rep. 1970) remains helpful, while J. de Viguerie, *L'Institution des Enfants: L'Education en France, 16e–18e Siècle* (Paris, 1978) is a fine, concise study of the evolution of education at every level.

9. THE ARMED FORCES AND FOREIGN POLICY

The biography of Louis XIV by J.B. Wolf and Corvisier's history of France under Louis XIV [see Section 1] and Corvisier's study of Louvois [Section 3] are all relevant here. The wider context within which the evolution of the French army and navy was set can be traced in G. Parker, *The Military Revolution: Military Innovation and the Rise of the West, 1500–1800* (Cambridge, 1988) and C. Jones, 'The Military Revolution and the Professionalisation of the French Army under the Ancien Régime', in M. Duffy (ed.), *The Military Revolution and the State, 1500–1800* (Exeter, 1980), 29–48. Since this text was written there has been published the comprehensive study of the French army: J.A. Lynn, *Giant of the Grand Siècle: The French Army, 1610–1715* (Cambridge, 1977). A. Corvisier, 'Guerre et Mentalités au XVIIe Siècle' in *XVIIe Siècle*, 148, 37e année, no. 3 (1985), 219–32 reflects on the social values surrounding warfare in the seventeenth century. R. Martin, 'The Army of Louis XIV', in P. Sonnino (ed.), *The Reign of Louis XIV*, 111–26 [Section 1], presents a short assessment of the chief developments within the land forces, while G.W. Symcox, 'The Navy of Louis XIV', ibid., 127–42, does the same for the navy. Some of Symcox's ideas can be read at greater length in his *The Crisis of French Sea Power, 1688–1697: From the 'Guerre d'Escadre' to the 'Guerre de Course'* (The Hague, 1954). D.C. Baxter, *Servants of the Sword: French Intendants of the Army: 1630–70* (Urbana, 1976) examines an important aspect of military administration,

As regards foreign policy, two articles by J. Black assess Louis's policy as a whole: 'Louis XIV's Foreign Policy Reassessed', in *Seventeenth-Century French Studies*, x (1988), 199–212, and 'Aggressive but Unsuccessful: Louis XIV and the European Struggle', in *The Historian*, no. 32 (1991), 3–8. The essays in R. Hatton (ed.), *Louis XIV and Europe* (London, 1976) are a mixture of general essays and case studies on aspects of Louis's foreign policy. The relevant passages of P. Kennedy, *The Rise and Fall of the Great Powers: Economic Change and Military Conflict from 1500 to 2000* (London, 1988) place Louis's foreign policy in a long chronological framework. The works of L. Bély mark a renewed interest by French scholars in international relations in the early modern period. In *Les Relations Internationales en Europe (XVIIe et XVIIIe Siècles)* (Paris, 1992), and *Guerre et Paix dans l'Europe du XVIIe Siècle (1618–1721)* (3 vols, Paris, 1991–92) which he has edited with Y-M. Bercé and others, Bély has placed the subject back in the forefront of French historical interest. French methods of diplomacy in the seventeenth century are discussed in W.J. Roosen, *The Age of Louis XIV: The Rise of Modern Diplomacy* (Cambridge, Mass., 1976), and are assessed, especially during the later part of the reign of Louis XIV, in L. Bély, *Espions et Ambassadeurs au Temps de Louis XIV* (Paris, 1990). The diplomacy preceding the war against the Dutch Republic (1672–78), and the consequences of the war are discussed in P. Sonnino, *Louis XIV and the Origins of the Dutch War* (Cambridge, 1989), C.J. Ekburg, *The Failure of Louis XIV's Dutch War* (Chapel Hill, 1979), and *The Peace of Nijmegen, 1676–1678/79: International Congress of the Tricentennial* (Amsterdam, 1980), a collection of excellent articles which range far beyond the particular circumstances of 1678. J. Black (ed.), *The Origins of War in Early Modern Europe* (Edinburgh, 1987 contains two essays on Louis XIV's wars (one a general review of the wars, and the other a discussion of the War of the Spanish Succession). Of course, Spain figured prominently in Louis's calculations over Europe. C. Dulong, *Le Mariage du Roi-Soleil* (Paris, 1986) assesses the hopes for international peace which were vested in Louis's marriage to Maria Teresa, and the conditions which the Spanish attached to the match. In the long term Louis had to fight to retain the Spanish Succession; the intricate details of the immediate pre-war situation between 1700 and 1702 are unravelled in M.A. Thomson, 'Louis XIV and the Origins of the War of the Spanish Succession', first published in the *Transactions of the Royal Historical Society*, series 5, no. 4 (London, 1954), and reprinted in R. Hatton and J.S. Bromley (eds), *Louis XIV and William III* (Liverpool, 1968), 140–61. A survey of Louis's relations with England and the Dutch Republic – as crucial as those with Spain – are discussed in J. Meyer, 'Louis XIV et les Puissances Maritimes', in *XVIIe Siècle*, no. 123, 31e année, no. 2 (1979), 155–72. The two major peace settlements near the beginning and end of Louis's reign – Westphalia and Utrecht – are analysed in A. Osiander, *The States System of Europe, 1640–1990: Peacemaking and the Conditions of International Stability* (Oxford, 1994), Chapters 2 and 3.

10. ABSOLUTISM

The literature on absolutism is considerable. P. Anderson, *Lineages of the Absolutist State* (London, 1974) is an erudite exposition of a Marxist understanding of absolutism; a more recent exposition from a Marxist viewpoint (and one which is critical of Anderson on several points) is D. Parker, *Class and State in Ancien Régime France: The Road to Modernity?* (London, 1996). The development of Parker's ideas over the years can be traced in some of his other publications: *The Making of French Absolutism* (London, 1983), 'Class, Clientage and Personal Rule in Absolutist France', in *Seventeenth-Century French Studies*, ix (1987), 192–213, and 'Sovereignty, Absolutism and the Function of Law in

Seventeenth-century France', in *Past and Present*, 122 (1989), 36–74. I. Waller-stein, *The Modern World System* (2 vols, London, 1974–80) is a wide-ranging study which places the emergence of 'absolute' forms of government in the context of the emergence of an international economy.

Critical assessments of the validity of the term 'absolutism' are available in R. Bonney, *The Limits of Absolutism in* Ancien Régime *France* (Aldershot, 1995), R. Hatton (ed.), *Louis XIV and Absolutism* (London, 1976), N. Henshall, *The Myth of Absolutism: Change and Continuity in Early Modern European Monarchy* (London, 1992), A. Lossky, 'The Absolutism of Louis XIV: Reality or Myth?', in *Canadian Journal of History*, xix, no. 1 (1984), 1–15 and J. Miller (ed.), *Absolutism in Seventeenth-Century Europe* (London, 1990). P.K. Leffler, 'French Historians and the Challenge to Louis XIV's Absolutism', in *French Historical Studies*, 14, no. 1 (1986), 1–21, sets Louis in the context of French historiography. Comparisons between absolute monarchy in France and England are made by J. Miller, *Bourbon and Stuart: Kings and Kingship in France and England in the Seventeenth Century* (London, 1987); the British dimension to the debate (that is, the differing experiences of England, Scotland and Ireland) is discussed in a collection of stimulating essays in R. G. Asch (ed.), *Three Nations – A Common History?* (Bochum, 1993).

A central problem in interpreting absolutism is that of 'the state' and the extent to which it had adopted 'modern' features by the late seventeenth century. S. Clark, *State and Status: The Rise of the State and Aristocratic Power in Western Europe* (Cardiff, 1995) looks at the implications for the social elites of the emergence of the European state, while J.B. Collins, *The State in Early Modern France* (Cambridge, 1995) concentrates on that country alone. J. Russell Major, *Representative Government in Early Modern France* (London, 1980) is an important work which goes back beyond the seventeenth century, while his *From Renaissance Monarchy to Absolute Monarchy: French Kings, Nobles and Estates* (London, 1994), surveys the sixteenth and seventeenth centuries and devotes its last main chapter to Louis XIV. J.H. Franklin, *Jean Bodin and the Rise of Absolutist Theory* (Cambridge, 1973) analyses the thought one of the founders of the theory of the modern state. H.H. Rowen, *The King's State: Proprietary Dynasticism in Early Modern France* (New Brunswick, 1980) argues the case that under Louis XIV the French state became not a disembodied, almost spiritual, entity to which all (including the king himself) were subject, but a form of property belonging to the king.

INDEX